James Edwin Thorold Rogers

**Paul of Tarsus, an Inquiry Into The Times**

and The Gospel of the Apostle of the Gentiles

James Edwin Thorold Rogers

**Paul of Tarsus, an Inquiry Into The Times**
*and The Gospel of the Apostle of the Gentiles*

ISBN/EAN: 9783743349117

Manufactured in Europe, USA, Canada, Australia, Japa

Cover: Foto ©Lupo / pixelio.de

Manufactured and distributed by brebook publishing software (www.brebook.com)

James Edwin Thorold Rogers

**Paul of Tarsus, an Inquiry Into The Times**

*AN INQUIRY INTO THE TIMES AND
THE GOSPEL OF THE APOSTLE
OF THE GENTILES.*

By A GRADUATE.

BOSTON:
ROBERTS BROTHERS.
1872.

# PREFACE.

THE author of the following pages has for some time past attempted, out of the materials which were at his disposal, to construct for himself a sketch of the times in which St. Paul lived, of the religious systems with which he was brought in contact, of the doctrine which he taught, and of the work which he ultimately achieved. It seemed that some interest might be felt by others in these researches, and they have therefore been published.

The influence which St. Paul has exercised over the Christianity which completely leavens modern civilization is wider and more lasting than that which has been wielded by any other man. One other person, St. Augustine of Hippo, has had a similar, but a far less energetic authority. If the contents of this book enable the reader to realize more adequately what was the social and religious condition of the world in which St. Paul lived, and what it was that he sought to teach, the immediate purpose of the publication will be satisfied.

The writer has taken for granted that the writings

ascribed to St. Paul are genuine. The evidence which has been alleged against the authenticity of the Pastoral Epistles, and of some among the other letters, does not seem strong enough to render these writings suspicious. On the other hand, the Epistle to the Hebrews could not have come from St. Paul. These epistles are the principal, almost indeed the only, source from which to construct the Pauline theology.

Among the Scriptures of the New Testament is a work which gives an account of the doings of some among the Apostles, and particularly of Peter and John, Barnabas and Paul. It seems that this book is either a collection of extracts from some very copious archives, or that it contains the fragments of a comprehensive work. Such a compilation may have been made because only portions of the original survived, or the book may be an ancient Eirenicon, intended to prove a substantive harmony between the tenets of the Jewish Christians, and those of the Gentiles to whom Paul imparted his gospel. The latter opinion seems to be confirmed by the manifest parallelism between the recorded doings and sayings of Peter and of Paul. It does not indeed follow, because the facts are selected, that the narrative is not to be depended on. But if any one wishes to get an insight into the causes of that strife which was waged between the Apostle of the Gentiles and the heads of Jewish Christianity, he will examine the Epistles to the Galatians and to the Romans, rather than the history of the controversy in the Acts of the Apostles.

It has been found necessary, in giving quotations from the Pauline epistles, to deviate from the words of the authorized version. It is well known that the translation of this part of the New Testament is frequently unsatisfactory, and is sometimes unintelligible. It is hoped that these deviations from the words of a version which is justly regarded as one of the noblest exemplars of the English language will be justified by the assistance which they give the reader in comprehending the scope of St. Paul's words.

It will be found that the writings of St. Paul are treated as human compositions only. It may be the case, as popular Christianity avers, that the religious sentiments of the writers whose works are contained in the Scriptures are too exalted for the unassisted powers of man, and that the manifestation of this peculiar genius was confined to a few favored individuals. Such an opinion, partly dictated by the reverence which is naturally felt towards the founders of a religion, partly due to the energy with which controversy has hallowed the authorities from which it draws its arguments, is not countenanced by the language of the New Testament. However transcendent may be the value of these writings, it must at least be admitted, that neither the Jewish nor the Christian Scriptures speak with the egotism of the Koran.

Whatever may be the power which guided the writers of the New Testament, the student of Primitive Christianity must needs, unless he merely intends to declaim on a foregone conclusion, free himself from preconceived opinions and traditions, and strive to look on the teaching of such an Apostle as Paul from the stand-point of a listener at Thessalonica, Athens, or Corinth, and to whom the message of the new religion has come for the first time. He must not merely take a layman's view of Christianity, or, in other words, consider his subject as one does who has no professional sympathies, and no professional antipathies; but he must, if possible, divest himself of those habits and associations which pervert a critical judgment. It is not too much to say, that the defence of popular Christianity is constantly irrational and inconsistent, while the attack on it is as frequently peevish and angry. If the contents of this volume are written in a different spirit, the author hopes to have given some assistance towards the solution of that far larger question, — By what means, and under what pressure, have the dogmas of later Christianity been developed from the Pauline original?

# PAUL OF TARSUS.

## CHAPTER I.

JUDAISM was the cradle of Christianity, and Judaism very nearly became its grave. The first teachers of Christianity were all Jews, and were deeply imbued by the traditions and observances with which the restored Israelites had overlaid the generous teaching of the great prophets. These refinements were partly glosses on the Law, partly additions to those tenets which constituted the Judaism of the monarchy. From such traditions and observances many of the Jewish converts tore themselves with infinite difficulty and pain, while not a few of them were willing to sacrifice the last command of Christ to the urgent claims of the Mosaic ritual. From so serious a peril one man saved Christianity; and this at a time when the words and acts of Christ had been recorded in no written gospel. The career of no man has ever produced such lasting effects on the world's history as that of St. Paul. But, in attempting to estimate the work which he did, it is essential that we should know what was the material with which he had to deal, and what were the agencies which assisted and thwarted him. And, first, for his countrymen.

About a century before that memorable day on which Paul of Tarsus was making a journey to Damascus, and was just in sight of the city whose antiquity was such that even the great ancestor of the Hebrews had visited it, a trial was going on at Rome. The person inculpated was a member of that distinguished family which appears in the earliest recorded memories of the Republic, and which is said to have been continued to within a century of the present time. A proconsul of the Roman province of Asia had been accused of extortion. He had been prætor of the city during Cicero's consulship and the maturity of Catiline's conspiracy, and had given great assistance towards detecting and frustrating the plot. He had obtained his province in order to recruit his fortunes, for Rome rewarded her officials by lucrative provincial appointments. The power of these governors was almost absolute. In order, however, to provide a check against the wrongs which power commits when a ruler is hard and greedy, the central government at Rome made these officials liable to a trial for extortion, and, on conviction, inflicted the severest penalties which the Roman law had enacted against the misdemeanors of its aristocracy.

Lucius Valerius Flaccus was acquitted, as we are informed, through the eloquence and interest of Cicero. The charge of extortion was seldom brought home to the accused, even when the guilt of the governor was notorious. The luxury and waste of the Roman nobles were sustained by the spoils of the provinces. In course of time these nobles employed their ill-gotten gains in civil war, and were divided into hostile camps. At last, and of necessity, "the settled world," as men called it, came under the despotism of a single ruler, who was garrisoned by an imperial guard. The settled world found that its material interests were, benefited by the change, for the rule of a single despot is more tolerable than that of a legion of despots. But the moral interests of the world suffered utter havoc, while the two remedies of moral evil, resistance and patience, were seeking for their opportunities. Resistance was hopeless, and patience at length created a new society on the ruins of the old. But this reconstruction was effected four centuries after the trial of Flaccus.

Among the charges brought against the proconsul, was that of his having forbidden the exportation of certain moneys which had been collected by the Asiatic Jews on behalf of their metropolis, — Jerusalem. Those among the Jews who had settled outside the Land of Promise, held themselves bound to regularly transmit their first-fruits to the Temple, as well as to obey the ceremonial law of Moses. This voluntary tribute, paid by many votaries, was the source of these sacred treasures which Pompey spared, and Crassus pillaged. There is no doubt that the wealth of the Jewish hierarchy was great. It is probable that much of that opulence for which Herod the Great was conspicuous, and which he employed in conciliating leading men at

Rome, and in constructing fortifications throughout Judea, was derived from the spontaneous revenue which was paid by the expatriated Jews.

As proconsul of Asia, Flaccus had impounded this gold of the Jews, had probably appropriated it. The act had given great offence to the Jewish race, especially to those at Rome; for Cicero even accuses the prosecutor of having designedly selected the court for holding the trial. It was erected, he says, in a quarter of the city where the compatriots of these Asiatic Jews could make themselves felt by their clamor, and baffle the defenders of the inculpated satrap. This region, we are told by Philo, was on the left bank of the Tiber, and near those gardens of Cæsar which were bestowed by the great dictator on the Roman people. It was reckoned to contain a colony of 8,000 Jews in the time of Augustus. But Cicero appeals to what was deemed policy in those days, and for many a century after. "The conduct of Flaccus," he says, "in prohibiting the exportation of the precious metals is patriotic, is admirable. It is a policy which I have often recommended to the senate, and which the senate has adopted at my recommendation. These Jews collect treasure from all parts of the empire, from Italy itself, and pour it into Jerusalem." The notion that money is wealth was a maxim with Roman statesmen.

The trivial and ordinary parts of human society, at any epoch of its history, attract no attention, find no record. The annalist merely narrates that which strikes his imagination, rouses his curiosity, is unlike his ordinary experience. To us, however, that which a Roman of Cicero's day found commonplace would be, if we could recall it, profoundly interesting: that which he thought worthy of record is only that which history is eternally repeating, — the ambition of great men, and the means and acts by which that ambition is satisfied or disappointed. What if we could reproduce precisely the social condition of that Rome in which Cicero was speaking, and the Asia which Flaccus had pillaged and provoked! The fancy of Eastern nations is always dreaming of some city which has been suddenly crystallized into a perpetual sleep, and in which the traveller, if he could only reach it, would see what were the doings of those primeval races whose empire has long since passed away. And yet the East changes slowly. The Damascus of to-day does not perhaps differ much from the Damascus which Abraham visited, differs hardly at all, except in its magnitude and prosperity, from the city where Paul lodged in the street which is called Straight, which was in the principal boulevard of the town. We in the Western world, who exult in change, and progress, and growth, are very far removed from those facts, the knowledge of which would allow us to reconstruct the social state which constituted the cradle of our faith. The East is the best school in which to study the outline of that civilization which is still an antiquarian puzzle, but the interest in which is perennial, the historical reconstruction of which is a necessary condition to the comprehension of the Christian Origines.

The Ghetto of Republican Rome helped to swell the noisy crowd at the Aurelian ascent, where, the orator tells us, the clamor was such that the accused person was placed at a great disadvantage. On this occasion the Roman Jews collected in great numbers, in order to support the charge against the rapacious proconsul who had forbidden them to send their pious offerings to the temple at Jerusalem; and they exhibited a formidable organization.

The Roman nobles treated native religions with toleration, — even with favor. This attitude was partly due to the contempt with which a conquering race viewed the faith of the vanquished, whose superstition was beneath the notice of an irresistible power, whose gods had become the subjects of the Capitoline Jove, when the nation had submitted to the senate and people of Rome. It was partly due to that habit which the Romans had of identifying the theocracy of foreign nations with their own, and by which, for example, they acknowledged Jehovah Sabaoth, under the name of Jupiter Sabazius. But it was still more due to policy. Rome wished to make subjects, not to collect converts. Occupied with the business of constructing an empire, the Roman statesman would have considered it a mere waste of force to combat the religious opinions of the dependencies, when his primary business was to ensure their political subjection. If, indeed, religious fanaticism was enlisted on the side of the combatant, the Roman showed no more mercy to the religious than he did to the political sentiment. But, during the growth of that empire, Rome only once had to fight with fanatics, and then she found the struggle fierce enough to task her greatest energies. It was only a fragment of the Jewish race which fought against Vespasian and Titus. Even this portion was split up into bitter factions, and was disorganized by furious enmities. The effect, however, of the last Jewish war was prodigious, and the conquerors marked their sense of the impulses which gave force to the struggle, by razing the site of the Holy City, by proscribing the sacred Name, and by rigorously banishing the Jews from Palestine.

The slight sketch of Jewish nationality which Cicero gives us is reproduced several generations later by Tacitus, and hinted at by Juvenal. The historian explains the extraordinary vitality and growth of the race by the intense home sentiment of the Jews. To be childless was a reproach in Israel, and few Jews were unmarried. As is the manner of Roman writers, when they comment on races whom they despise or dislike, Tacitus speaks coarsely of the Jewish temperament and creed, while he admits the loyalty of the race to the metropolis of its nation, notes its abhorrence of any anthropomorphic religion, and refers to the sedulous care with which the Jew fenced off his domestic life from any intercourse with the people among which he sojourned.

The Jews of antiquity, like their modern descendants, always dwelt in cities, forming a separate community in some well-defined locality or ghetto. This was and is inevitable. It was only in Palestine that they were agriculturists. Their law forbade the use of certain kinds of animal food. Even that flesh which was permitted them had to be carefully prepared, and had to be legally healthy. Under certain restrictions and limitations, their great Lawgiver permitted mixed marriages, and the practice of the ancient Jews was even less rigid than the rule of the Mosaic code. The tenderest narrative in the Old Testament, after the story of Joseph and his brethren, is the Eastern idyl of Ruth. This pastoral tells us how a daughter of the accursed Moab — of a race which was to be perpetually excluded from the congregation — married into the first family of the tribe of Judah, after having claimed the right of a widow against her husband's next of kin. The great King of Israel married the daughters of Canaanite chieftains. The harem of his magnificent son was filled with women who worshipped strange gods. The Song of Songs is reputed to be, in its primary meaning, an epithalamium on the marriage of Solomon with an Egyptian princess. In the story of Esther, a Jewish maiden is taken into the seraglio of the Persian monarch, and advanced to the post of principal wife, without any demur on the part of her nearest male relative and guardian. But after the captivity a more rigorous rule prevailed. In the days of Ezra and Nehemiah — the Puritans of Jewish history — we read that all mixed marriages were proscribed, that those who contracted them were excommunicated, and that the offspring of these marriages were deprived of civil rights. At the beginning of our era, the Jew would marry no woman who was not of his own race. It seems that Jewish women did occasionally contract marriage with Gentiles. Paul vouches for the piety of Eunice and Lois,— the mother and grandmother of Timothy; but the father of this disciple was a Greek; and it is plain that these pious women did not think the ceremonial law, represented by its most obligatory and universal rite, binding on the child whom they so carefully instructed in the Jewish scriptures.

The most important colony of Jews was that of Alexandria. It dates from the commencement of the voluntary dispersion, and is coeval with the foundation of the city. We are told that, after the destruction of Tyre, the Macedonian conqueror marched on Jerusalem, that he was welcomed by the high priest, and informed of the success which the prophet Daniel had predicted for Greek valor and discipline. It is added that Alexander treated high priest and temple with scrupulous respect. There were Jews who accompanied his army, who refused to pollute their hands with the work of rebuilding the temple of Belus, who were instruments in the vengeance which the captive Psalmist imprecated on the daughters of Babylon. So Jews were enrolled among the colonists of Alexandria.

The successors of Alexander continued the favor which he showed to the Jews. Seleucus gave them the freedom of citizens in Antioch and Seleucia, and favored those banking establishments which they set up in the principal towns of Asia Minor. But the Lagid dynasty established in Egypt treated them with the greatest confidence. The corn trade of Alexandria fell almost entirely into their hands at a very early period. Two Jews were the captains of the household troops under Philadelphus, and another Jew farmed its revenues under Evergetes. The armies of Philometor were led by Jewish generals. The settlers were wealthy, and, as was to be expected from the callings which they followed, unpopular. Hence the later monarchs of the dynasty occasionally sacrificed them to the anger or alarm of the Alexandrian mob.

These Jews followed and were faithful to the fortunes of Cæsar, who rewarded them by confirming them in all their rights and privileges, and by allowing them to elect a ruler or chief magistrate over themselves, under the title of Alabarch. In the same way, according to Benjamin of Tudela, the Abassid Caliphs of Bagdad permitted the Jews of Central Asia, in the twelfth century, to elect a chief of their own race, under the title of the Prince of the Captivity. The nation throve, and in the days of Tiberius it was reckoned, according to Philo, that Alexandria contained 200,000 out of the million Jewish settlers in Egypt. The same authority informs us that two out of the five wards into which the city was divided were entirely occupied by Jews.

Many troubles fell on the Alexandrian Jewry during the reign of Tiberius, and under the administration of Sejanus, the father of the notorious minister whom Tiberius trusted, detected and destroyed. This Sejanus was succeeded by Flaccus Avillius, who followed the policy of his predecessor, and encouraged the Alexandrian mob in acts of violence on the Jewish quarters. For a time, the seclusion, the sufferance, the patience, the profound humility of this people, enabled them to avoid the hostility which they could not disarm. "The race," says Cicero, "is slavish to the core." There was, however, a limit to this submission — there was an act of tyranny which could rouse this people to enthusiastic resistance. They might be insulted, plundered, tortured, and they would fawn on the wrong-doer. But they were stung to frenzy if any insult was offered to their God, and to His temple.

Caligula resolved to be worshipped as a god. The empire was prostrate before the majesty of the Cæsar. It began by worshipping his fortunes, and it at last reached the inconceivable meanness of adoring the man. This baseness was not unknown in the days of Augustus; it grew during the reign of Tiberius. But the degradation was voluntary, was confined to places and individuals. Caligula strove to make it compulsory, and to extend it over the whole empire.

The promulgation of this new religion gave an opportunity of which the enemies of the Alexandrian Jews availed themselves, in order to satisfy the malignity of their perpetual feud. Flaccus secretly encouraged every excess against Israelites, every outrage which could be committed. The Jewish quarters suffered all the horrors of a sacked city. At last Flaccus was recalled, — it was a satisfaction to the pious Jew to know that the enemy of his nation was ruined, disgraced, and finally banished to an island in the Egean.

Here, as he bemoaned his fate, Caligula remembered him. This emperor suffered from one of the common symptoms of madness, continual want of sleep. In an hour of this watchfulness, he bethought himself of the numerous exiles who were confined in their insular prisons, and among them of Flaccus, and despatched his executioners after him. Philo again exults over the horrible circumstances which attended the legate's slaughter.

Still the troubles of the Jews were not ended. Petronius was charged in Judea with the duty of setting up the statue of the emperor in the temple, and the Alexandrian Jews were harassed because they did not worship Cæsar. So they resolved to send an embassy to Caligula, with the view of deprecating his wrath, and of pleading their inability to fulfil his command. The leader of this forlorn hope was Philo. This eminent person has given an account of his interview with the madman who was ruling the world, and of the danger which the deputation ran in the attempt to conciliate him. Fortunately for the embassy, Caligula was not in one of his savage moods, and merely amused himself with his trembling petitioners. He was occupied in decorating a palace, and had no present appetite for blood. So he dismissed Philo and his companions for a time, observing that they were rather to be pitied than blamed for their unwillingness to worship him.

The Jews of Alexandria were distinguished for their culture as well as for their wealth. They founded a school of philosophy, or at least amalgamated the speculations of the great Greek thinkers with their own theosophy. Many of them were thoroughly versed in the literature of Greece, and Philo in particular quotes largely from the most famous poets. The system which they constructed was eclectic. They adopted the mystic theory of numbers which characterized the tenets of the Pythagoreans, incorporated the Platonic ideas, and accepted the Aristotelian logic, as the vehicle of their formularies, and as a support to their allegories.

The doctors of the Jews recognized under the name of Memra, a Word or Reason of God, whom they called the son of God, the mediator between God and man. The same conception is traceable in the Apocryphal book of wisdom, which is supposed to have been the work of an Alexandrian Jew. But in Philo, the Word is the true High Priest, the legate of the Most High, the archetypal exemplar, the creative power, the perpetual Mediator. This conception, enlarged, exalted, and identified with Christ, is the central figure in the fourth gospel, the form under which Jesus the Prophet, the Teacher, the Redeemer, the King, the Mediator, the Judge of humanity, is exhibited as the eternal Son, the Sharer in the creative power of the Almighty.

To our modern habit of thought, the allegories of Philo would seem childish and forced. With this author, for example, the story of the Patriarchs was not only a narrative of Israel's childhood, but a mine from which the treasures of Divine truth might be extracted, the profound verities of religion might be illustrated or demonstrated. St. Paul himself has not disdained to use this method of exposition in his parallel between the Law and the Gospel, the son of Hagar and the son of Sarah; and again in his contrast between the heavenly bread and miraculous water which followed the wandering Israelites, and the spiritual sustenance which Christ affords those who are within His covenant of grace.

But though sometimes the Alexandrian theologian of the Jewish school was apt to make the Almighty rather a Power than a Person, to represent Him as Universal as well as One, and so to almost adopt a Pantheistic conception of the Divine nature,—the idea which he entertained as to the action of God is lofty, just and consolatory. His most marked attribute is that of a protector to suffering humanity, an avenger of highhanded insolence, of mercilessness, of wickedness, and of wrong-doing. As a servant of such a God, the Jew of Alexandria could hold no man in slavery. The essence of the Divine nature is His Providence, His universal, unsleeping sight, His absolute knowledge of each man, in act, in word, in thought, in heart. And if sometimes His hand is slow to strike the wrong-doer, and His ear seems closed to the wail of misery,—the prayer of the poor destitute,—He is sure to perform at last what His long-suffering tenderness delays. It was this firm confidence which made the Jew patient in adversity, trustful in the direst need. It is this trust which has given unity and unchangeableness to a race now exiled for eighteen centuries from its fatherland. He could endure all things, if he held fast to the cardinal tenet of God's eternal being, if he was jealous of God's honor, if he clung to the crowning consolation of an ultimate deliverance, to be worked by the power of Him who is mighty to save. It need hardly be said that this calm, confident hope is the thought which penetrates the devotional books of the Old Testament, which has made the Psalter a perpetual solace to Jew and Christian, which gave the great prophets of old so mighty a power of interpreting the letter by the spirit, as to make them, instead of being the Ulemas of a scanty Syrian tribe, the teachers of the whole human race. Even now the revelation which these fathers make of the Divine nature is inferior to the luminous exposition which the Gospel gives of the Almighty counsels, in degree only, not in kind, as the dawn of a summer's day differs in brilliancy only from the sun-light in its strength.

Among the practical rules of Judaism, none was insisted on with greater emphasis than the duty of succoring the poor, the fatherless, the widow. The reaping of the harvest, the gathering of the vintage, the shaking of the olive-trees, must not be too complete, that this rule of kindly care for the helpless may not be lost sight of, even in the urgent business of life. The servitude of Jew to Jew was permitted, but only for a brief space, since the Sabbath-year must see the Hebrew bondman free. The pledge must not be mercilessly enacted, in some cases must be restored. Nor could a Jew perpetually alienate the inheritance of his fathers. Between Jew and Jew those money-dealings which, more than aught else, make men harsh and unfeeling, must not be stimulated by the condition of usury or increase. Nay, similar rules attend the usage of the brute creation. The laboring ox must be unmuzzled when he treads out the corn, in order that he, too, may share in the bounty of Him who gives both seed-time and harvest. It is a cruelty which the Law forbids, to take the mother bird and her young; it is unnaturally harsh even to seethe the kid in his mother's milk. Is it not also likely that the horror of eating blood — the life of living beings — which is treated as the oldest command of the Law, may not have had the same humanizing object of inculcating gentleness and tenderness, and the avoidance of that familiarity with violence and slaughter which always brutalizes man?

Commands like these, energetically interpreted, — extended so as to include the spirit of the Law, as well as its letter, — educated the Jew in the habit of generous dealing towards those of his own nation who needed the aid which he could give. Until he was maddened beyond endurance by the insults which despotism heaped on his faith, and the dishonor which was done his God, the patriotism of the Jew did not consist so much in the glorious memories which belonged to his race, as in the active exercise of benevolence towards his fellow-countrymen, — in the readiness with which he listened to the cry of distress. It is by this, as well as by his pure monotheism, that the Jew stands out so markedly in the civilization of the ancient world. And it was this spirit which Christianity incorporated into its ethical code, the best inheritance which it gained from the older creed. Judaism, it is true, confined, in theory at least, its kindliness to the race of Abraham, though it is impossible that a carefully trained gentleness of nature should be wholly bounded by the ties of blood — should be deaf to any cry for pity which may rise from those of an alien race. But Christianity, in the hands of its great missionary, accepted as its cardinal truth, that all the generations of mankind should be blessed by the great Son of Abraham and David, and so enforced the beneficent maxims of the Jewish code on behalf of all those who are gathered within the church of Christ. Here was the contrast between the hard, selfish, haughty pride of the Roman, and the boundless charity of the Christian convert. Here was the origin of that marvellous conversion, which, leaving St. Paul in possession of his ancient courage and indomitable will, made him able to endure all things, and yet acknowledge the duty of universal charity.

As God was the Maker of all, the Judge of all, the Saviour of all, so He is in this Alexandrian Judaism the Author of all grace. St. Paul himself did not plead more vehemently against self-righteousness and self-sufficiency than Philo does when he says, that the man who recognizes the work of his own mind only, and does not see God in what he can do, is a brigand who robs another of his due.

That the philosophy of Alexandria had a wide influence is known. It is clearly traceable in the writings of Seneca, who was the pupil of a Jewish doctor. But its influences on Christianity were abiding. It contributed largely to that speculative spirit which early busied itself with abstract dogma, from the days of Origen to those of Athanasius and Cyril. The chief city of Egypt was the cradle of dogmatic theology, the workshop from which issued these definitions and distinctions which tore Christianity into sectarianism. And, unhappily, it was also the earliest home of bitter intolerance. The birthplace of turbulent theological factions, of persecuting ferocity, of insane asceticism, of frivolous ceremony, of arrogant sacerdotalism, it canonized these passions in the person of Cyril, who, Christian bishop as he was, rivalled Flaccus in his outrages on the Jews, and gloried in being the murderer of Hypatia.

It was inevitable that the Greek conquest of Asia should have powerfully affected Semitic habits of thought. Alexander and his successors gave their subjects an army and a discipline. Army and discipline, it is true, rapidly deteriorated. He gave them also an administration, which must have remained Greek to a large extent, though it was accommodated to Eastern habits. Those Greek customs, also, the gymnasium and the sophist's lecture, took root in the Asiatic and Egyptian cities. Schools of philosophy, the basis of whose training was laid in the formularies of the great Athenian thinkers, flourished among these outlandish towns which the Greeks generalized as barbarian. The most famous Jewish doctors accepted and employed some of these philosophic forms. The Pauline epistles contain many illustrations of the exactitude with which the nomenclature of the Peripatetic system was known to the Apostle, however little the Aristotelian syllogism may appear in his writings. The young Pharisee who sat at the foot of Gamaliel learned from him technical terms which were much more nearly like the method of the Academy and the Porch, than akin to the discipline of these schools of the prophets which Samuel seems to have founded, and whose influence, moral and political, was so great during the epoch of the kings. Some of the dispersed Jews, whose allegiance to the Mosaic code was loose, even frequented the gymnasium, and took part in the games. It is not at all inconsistent with human nature that this laxity of conduct and discipline coexisted with a ferocious patriotism and a fanatical spirit towards those who appeared to secede from Jewish unity. The dispersed Jews were always the bitterest enemies of the Apostle, both in Jerusalem and elsewhere.

It seems, moreover, that the chief civil and ecclesiastical magistrates of Judea exercised a precarious criminal jurisdiction over their dispersed compatriots. They may have obtained this authority by the consent of the Roman senators, who were always well disposed towards an established religion, the dignitaries of which might be useful instruments for the maintenance of order. The controversial essay of Hippolytus, bishop of Ostia, in which the tenets of the more prominent heretics in the early part of the third century are expounded, shows that the exercise of the Jewish religion was protected in Rome at this epoch. The empire may have connived at this *imperium in imperio,* feeling with Gallio, that it was not the part of a dignified Roman to adjudicate on the squabbles which broke out among the devotees of a despicable superstition, and that it was quite out of the question to expect that a Roman judge should attempt to understand the by-laws of a ghetto. This contemptuous toleration was of infinite value to the infant churches. It was only when the political and social system of the Roman empire seemed to be imperilled by the growth of Christianity, that systematic persecution began.

The Roman law favored all voluntary associations. It conferred a legal status on such parties as united themselves into a corporation, and enacted by-laws for their own order and guidance. Perhaps the most valuable inheritance of Roman civilization is the spontaneous municipality, the collegium of the jurists, the voluntary corporation, on which law bestowed some of the personality of the social unit. The peculiarities of the Jewish creed, the marked servility, and the equally marked pride of its devotees, — qualities which have made them at once the most pliant and the most conservative of races, — led them to eagerly adopt those provisions of the law which gave their associations a legal color and standing.

The rigid monotheism of the restored Jew, and his hatred to all anthropomorphic conceptions of God, markedly distinguish the Israelite whom Ezra led back from Persia, and the Macchabees marshalled against the gross nature-worship of Syria, from the Israelite of the Davidic kingdom, who perpetually fell into Canaanite idolatry. The Scriptures of the Old Testament prove how easily the ancestors of the later Jews were seduced into adopting the gods of the heathen, Baal and Ashtaroth, Moloch and Chemosh. It is not unlikely that intercourse with their Persian conquerors may have aided the children of the captivity in forming those strict conceptions of monotheism, which insulated the Jew of the Roman Empire. It assuredly developed that dualism, the perpetual conflict between a good and an evil power, which constituted the basis of Aryan theology, which, almost absent from the system of the Old Testament, is allowed in the New, which has at length been taken by many sects to constitute the essence of the Christian creed, and which is the most poetical as well as the most stirring form in which men can put before themselves the ends and the means of the religious life, though it is far from being the noblest conception of divine love and gentleness.

It is easy to see, then, how this Jew, forced or induced to quit his native land, secluded from the society in which he lived by ceremonial obligations, by an ineffaceable rite, by a persistent patriotism, whose nationality was fed by a host of magnificent memories, and sustained by an energetic organization, should have eagerly adopted those means of association which the Roman law permitted. The dispersed Jews levied a voluntary tax on themselves, and transmitted the proceeds to the hierarchy at Jerusalem. The economy of ancient society supplied a ready means for this transmission, for the mechanism by which foreign exchanges were effected was well known to the old world. The Parable of the Talents is proof that so much of the system of banking, as is contained in the practice of giving interest on deposit accounts, was so familiarly used in Palestine as to become an obvious and popular illustration in a religious apologue. It is plain that if a Syrian banker was ready to encourage depositors with an offer of interest, he must have used these deposits either as advances on loan, or as the means for effecting exchanges with distant countries, and that the latter object is much more likely than the former. The Jew has traded in money from the days of the Macchabees.

Sometimes these *collegia*, as the Roman law called them, were declared unlawful. Occasions frequently arose, on which the haughty conservatism of the Roman noble was led to proscribe that which it always despised, on the plea uttered at Philippi, — that the practice was not lawful to a Roman, that the public morality was debased by the presence of foreign superstition, or that the gods of the Republic were insulted by rivals. The religion of Rome was essentially domestic. The great gods of the city were to the state what the Penates were to the household. Generally it was thought politic to conciliate a foreign deity. But it was another thing to introduce his unlicensed *culte* into Rome, or into a colony which was constitutionally a part of Rome. And much more frequently, as it is conceived, the wealth of these Jewish collegia roused the avarice of those Roman nobles, whose rapacity was even more devouring than their pride. Verres and Flaccus were the types of a class.

The Old Testament sanctions no particular form of government, prescribes no single system of secular authority, enforces no uniform organization of society or administration. The eternal purpose of the Almighty does not condescend to define a form of polity for man. The house of Aaron is gifted with the priesthood, the fierce tribe of Levi is dedicated to Jehovah. But neither priest nor Levite is invested with magisterial functions. The only office which the priest of the old covenant exercised was that of a judicial decision on the condition of a person suspected of leprosy, with the duty of pronouncing the social excommunication of one convicted of this disease. The taint of leprosy, incurable by any remedy which lay in the power of man, became, by an obvious metaphor, the representative of the moral taint of sin, of which man cannot rid his fellow-man, which must be cleared away by some act of divine beneficence, and which, being inheritable, designates the inherent depravity of the human race, a moral as consequent upon a physical death. But the priest of the Pentateuch and the early historical books of the Old Testament is not a ruler, not even a magistrate. Before the monarchy, there was no central government in Israel, except during the occasional supremacy of some eminent judge.

In Palestine itself, after the rise of the Asmonean dynasty, the offices of high priest and monarch were for a time united. Later on, they were divided, the high priest becoming the centre of that ecclesiastical system to which the scattered Jewish communities owed allegiance and tribute. This Israelite pope was assisted by a council, or conclave, or sanhedrim, or presbytery, as St. Paul himself calls it. It was before this assembly that Stephen, the first martyr, was brought, and by it that he was condemned. It was in imitation of this central organization that the Christian Church of Jerusalem established the sacred College over whom James was set, and by whose authority it was intended that all the converts of the gospel should be governed. It was this assumption which St. Paul resisted with so much energy and with such success at Antioch. It is doubtful, however, whether the College at Jerusalem would not have ultimately succeeded in establishing its pretensions, had not the capture and total destruction of the city dispersed the organization of the Christian Jews in Palestine.

It is possible that the form which the permanent council of the high priest assumed was borrowed from the usage of Greek and Roman politics. In the view of Aristotle, the senate was essentially a popular institution, and was characteristic of that political civilization which the Greeks achieved. The Roman municipality had officers and senate, as in Rome,—duumviri, who represented the consuls; curiales, who were the councillors of the provincial towns. So, where the dispersed Jews were in numbers sufficient for a synagogue, they had a chief of their community, and a council of advice. Such synagogues, for example, existed at Thessalonica, Athens, Corinth, and Ephesus, and were, naturally, the first theatre for the Apostle's preaching, as they were constantly the source from which mischief threatened him. The captivity of St. Paul, with which the direct narrative of the Apostle's life ceases, was primarily the work of those Asiatic Jews whom he had often confronted in their synagogues, and from whom he had finally separated his converts during the time of his last visit to Ephesus. In its beginnings, Christianity, like the Judaism of the Christian era, was the religion of towns-folk. The heathenism of the villages was not assailed till long after the apostolic age. But we shall see the effects of this hereafter, in considering what was the organization of the Church in its early stages of existence.

It does not appear that the Jews of the apostolic age were profoundly conversant with all the books of the Old Testament. A general acquaintance with the Pentateuch, a more thorough knowledge of the Psalms, and with some of the leading Messianic prophecies, seem to constitute the Biblical learning possessed by a carefully taught Jew. The New Testament contains few allusions to the history of the chosen people during the years which intervened between the settlement of Canaan and the reign of David, or during the rival monarchies. And yet it would have been expected — had the writers of the New Testament been well acquainted with the historical books of the Old — that allusions would have been frequent, that types and allegories would have been discovered abundantly, and that the spirit of the prophetic books would have been invoked constantly and successfully against a blind obedience to much of the ceremonial law which the Israelite followed. The story of the chosen people is full of passages which might have been used freely for the purpose of spiritual analogy. What, for example, is more obvious than the long doom of that kingdom whose rulers persistently made Israel to sin; and the religious significance of the lesson? What story is more fitted for typical illustration than the exquisite narrative of Joseph? What indicates more forcibly the single-heartedness of the Christian than the career of Joshua, his zeal than that of Elijah? One would like to know what scriptures those were in which Apollos was mighty. Moses, we know, was read on the Sabbath. Christ commented on the prophecy of Isaiah in the synagogue of Nazareth. St. Paul, however, quotes the Old Testament scriptures frequently, especially in the Epistle to the Romans.

Some even of these scanty quotations are inaccurate. Jeremiah is credited with a passage from Zechariah. The author of the Epistle of St. James ascribes the drought in the days of Ahab to the efficacy of Elijah's prayers, but the narrative in the Book of Kings designates the prediction of this visitation as a revelation from Jehovah, and the return of the customary showers as a similar announcement, the prophet being a perfectly passive instrument. Again, the Epistle of Jude quotes as genuine, and without the slightest suspicion, the Book of Enoch, and refers to the legend of a dispute between Michael and the Devil over the body of Moses, as though it were part of the sacred history.

It is almost superfluous to say that the critical faculty which investigates facts judicially, and which considers their reality as relative to their probability, is of recent growth. Nothing, indeed, is or can be told with perfect accuracy, — no description, for example, gives all the circumstances which have come before the sight. Still less is it possible to assign all the causes and motives of an action. The utmost that can be done is to narrate as much of the event as is needed to give a clear and distinct impression of its leading features, to tell the story as it invited the attention or affected the imagination of the narrator. Even under these circumstances, two independent witnesses, both of whom endeavor to give a genuine account of their impressions, may traverse, or even contradict each other in particulars, as one sees every day in judicial proceedings. The habit of criticising events, as though they were marshalled before a court of law and in view of the verdict of a jury or the sentence of a judge, and with such strictness as to make it requisite that dates, places, and persons should be precisely identified, is modern. And it may very possibly happen that what is gained in precision by such an analytical process, is more than lost in the weakened vivacity of the tale and even in its substantive veracity. To treat that only as a fact which is a likelihood, reduces history to a dull drama of mechanical puppets, which has far less reality than a confessedly poetical narrative.

The authors of those books which have come down to us under the collective name of the New Testament, lived in a thoroughly matter-of-fact world, with which their affections and their hopes were very little in harmony. They were the helpless subjects of a devouring and remorseless despotism. Before the empire was inaugurated, these subjects from time to time strove to free themselves from the yoke. After this epoch, the Jewish struggle in the later days of Nero was the last effort which a nationality made to vindicate its autonomy. It is impossible for us to realize the deadening effects of such a despotism. From it there was no escape, even no exile. Outside its barriers were surging up those hordes, which in the end poured over it like a flood. But in the early days of the Roman empire these marauders were kept effectually at bay, along a vast range of frontier, flight over which was rarely open to the discontented. The civilized world was literally bound in fetters. Cæsar and his legions were everywhere, crushing down every thing with the iron heel of power, enslaving every one. Speech was watched, for the empire swarmed with spies and informers. Thought was hardly free, for the tremendous interpretations given to the law of treason, made every man suspicious and suspected. The reputation of eminent virtue and of daring vice was equally dangerous. The best hope of safety lay in insignificance and obscurity. The saddest lot was to be of Cæsar's kinsfolk, the luckiest was to be his favorite slave. "It is a rare happiness," says Tacitus, writing in the better days of Trajan, "to think as you will, and to speak as you think." It is amazing that in such an age, Christianity laid its foundations so deeply and so broadly.

The long indulgence of every sensual passion makes Eastern sovereigns, we are told, feel a languid pleasure in cruelty for its own sake. It becomes an excitement to inflict pain. But these Eastern despots must be roused from a more delicious apathy in order to entertain this pleasure. The worst of the Roman emperors had a horrible activity in the pursuit of this gratification. Caligula and Nero, the former from a ferocious insanity, the latter from very wantonness, were pre-eminently cruel. The former demanded divine honors to be paid him; the latter, beyond his unnumbered outrages upon the people whom he ruled, worked special havoc on the imperial house. Mother, wife, cousin, were his victims. And these monsters of despotism — so totally crushed was the people — fell by their affronted soldiers, not by the daggers of those whom they had outraged or wronged. The Roman emperor had no one to fear but his prætorians, and the bodyguard of the emperor was generally faithful to its paymaster. The mission of St. Paul was cast in the darkest era of the world's history. It was a long day of despair.

From such overwhelming misery there are two kinds

of refuge. Men may forget their degradation in profligacy, or escape into the haven of religion. Cæsar may claim their life, their goods, their corporeal liberty, but he cannot quench their passions, or he cannot coerce their souls. They may drown their moral consciousness in debauchery, or they may take the wings of a dove, and fly to the rest of the people of God, — may possess their souls in patience.

The fragments of a romance, professedly written in the days of Nero — and which may well have been composed at that time — still exist under the title of the Satyricon of Petronius Arbiter. The name of the book means no more than that the composition is partly prose, partly verse. It contains a few passages of great beauty, and one of genuine humor, the tale of the Ephesian matron. But the greater part of the fragments is the narrative of a licentious revel. It is the mere delirium of debauchery. And yet it is probably a picture of the expedients by which a Roman noble strove to forget the despotism under which he lived. Much which the Cæsarism of that age could not crush, it utterly debased. Aristophanes, Lucian, Rabelais are coarse and licentious enough, but Petronius is transcendently impure.

Another novel has come down to us entire. It is of a later date than the fragments of Petronius, but it is tainted in the same way, though in an inferior degree. The Golden Ass of Apuleius has been said to be a romance inculcating the worship of the good goddess — the deified power of nature. As a picture of social life, it justifies the indignant condemnation of the Apostle, when he reckons up, with characteristic vehemence, the accumulated misdeeds of those who are given up by their own vices to a reprobate mind, who know how great is their own depravity, but indulge it, and encourage others to the like.

The other refuge from the slavery of Cæsarism, from the subjection of the physical man and his material possessions to despotism, was religion. And this religion was of two kinds. One had been long in existence, partly as a protest against the gross superstitions of the popular theology, partly as an inquiry into the conditions of mind and being. It had now become the defiant avowal of the superiority of moral right over brute force, even though it was constrained to occupy the attitude of passive resistance. This was philosophy, especially that of the later Stoics. The other alternative was new, obscure, despised, — a foolish refinement, as was thought, upon a Syrian superstition. This was Christianity, as taught by Paul and his associates. The last struggle between the ancient religion of the heathen world, and the new force which was to leaven civilization, came in the form of a controversy between philosophy and Christianity, — a struggle which continued vigorously in Athens and Alexandria long after the Empire professed the Faith, and which was at last concluded by the compulsory silence of the philosophers. And if Christianity converted the Constantines, philosophy numbered the Antonines among its disciples and devotees.

The philosophers of the Empire did not aim at providing a system which should leaven society at large. They merely purposed to instruct those who had capacity and leisure. They did not demand that their disciples should be rich, well-born, influential. It was the pride of philosophy that it totally ignored rank and wealth, or treated them as superficial and unimportant circumstances. The fact that the satirist sometimes depicts the philosopher as hanging on to the skirts of the rich, of being a parasite, is negative testimony that such practices were a dishonor to the profession which the philosopher made, and that the majority of these savants were free from the imputation of such aims. When a churchman is described as rapacious, luxurious, or licentious, and emphasis is laid on characteristics of this kind, the satirist of the individual intends to imply that such a person is an exception and a scandal. When Boccaccio depicts the clergy of his day, he expresses no indignation against their profligacy, gluttony, and mendacity. These were, at that epoch, the general vices of the order.

The philosophies of antiquity could not address themselves to the general mass of the community. They did not appeal to sympathy, which is a universal bond, but to intelligence or reason, which is a limited faculty, an exceptional endowment. Still, the philosopher intended to influence society at large. But this was to be effected by attracting and instructing such minds as could rule or guide mankind. The greatest victory of this discipline was to be achieved when the philosopher should rule, or the ruler become a true and competent philosopher. "Under existing habits of thought," says Plato, "this is a tremendous paradox, the advocates of which will be saved from active hostility only by a torrent of ridicule. But," the speaker continues, "it is only in this way that society can be saved." Nor can it be doubted that the object which the Stoic and Platonist of the empire had before him, was an attempt to supplant, by his better way, a brutal military system, and that any success in this direction was a prodigious gain to mankind. Few monarchs have reached the simplicity, piety, truthfulness, and zeal for the public good, which characterized Antoninus and Aurelius. The age of these great princes is the one oasis in the desert of the Roman Empire. They were the ripest and the best examples of what philosophy could do for man. But theirs was not a lasting example. The general vices of despotism ruin society, and its occasional virtues are incompetent to restore it.

That Christianity has affected the mass of mankind is primarily due to the fundamental propositions which it affirms. It says, that mankind has been saved or restored by the life and death of Christ, however differently the profession of Christianity has understood both life and death, however limited or however wide may be its interpretation of the benefit which mankind has gained by that Great Fact in the history of the world. The more wretched, forlorn, depraved, has been the condition of those who have been introduced to this gospel and who have received it, the clearer has the benefit been. Hence, however much the teaching of Christianity may appeal to the reason, it appeals still more urgently to the feelings, reaching to their lowest depths, and stirring them profoundly and completely. It demands faith, but it demands action as a proof of faith. It addresses the individual, and, therefore, from its very beginnings it markedly repudiated that most preposterous outcome of Nihilism, under which the Buddhist longs for annihilation and absorption. It is true, that after a time this gross superstition attacked the Eastern Church, and produced those swarms of hermits and monks who travestied Christianity in the third century. Even now, the descendants of these Buddhist devotees, the Lamas of Central Asia, closely resemble, as MM. Huc and Gabet affirm, the monkish orders of the Greek and Roman churches. Had such an absurdity been developed during the life of Paul, and in the churches which he founded, his indignation would have vented itself in language like that in which he denounces the Judaizing bigots of Jerusalem, when he writes to the Galatians.

But though the Christianity of the apostolic age addresses the individual, it supposes him to be at one with other believers in Christ. Man is not saved for himself only, any more than he is saved by his own efforts. He is not, and cannot be, the isolated object of the Divine mercy and grace. Christ came to save the world. The arrogance and self-complacency which induce men to think themselves the particular object of God's favor, that affected thankfulness which is real contempt for others, is the temper of the Pharisee, not of the Christian. The Christian must teach his fellow-man, by word it may be, by deeds of necessity. The individual is converted, to be enrolled into a church, with an organization, a government, a corporate power, a corporate grace.

The apostles preached in towns. The intinerary of St. Paul is from Philippi to Thessalonica, Berœa, Athens, Corinth. Nothing is said about halting at intermediate places, and preaching the gospel in the villages or small towns which were interspersed throughout this route. The social arrangements of cities were more available for the message of the gospel than the population of the pagi and demes was. It is not, indeed, to be supposed that the country folk of Greece and Italy, of Asia Minor or Palestine, were planted in scattered households. They dwelt together for purposes of mutual defence, and generally had their stronghold to which they might convey their possessions when marauders were about. So, in all probability, the form of the English village, where the houses are clustered together near the church, is derived from the time in which the country was liable to the incursions of Danes and other Norsemen, and when the church was a common hall in times of quiet, a storehouse, an arsenal, and a castle in times of danger.

It was easier to gather a church together in these

cities. There was the synagogue, or the place of prayer; there were the dispersed Jews, sometimes friendly, often hostile; there were the devout Greeks, who had been attracted from nature worship and its coarse superstitions to the pure monotheism of the Jews, though they did not accept its ceremonial obligations. Sometimes they had even learned so much as to comprehend that interpretation of the letter by the spirit, which was known as John's baptism, and which was the restoration of that generous and living zeal which characterized the Hebrew prophet of the kingdom. This was ground prepared for the seed. But once within the believing church, the Apostle taught that there was an absolute oneness and equality in Christ. The distinction between Jew and Greek was to disappear; the ancient rite which sealed the covenant of Abraham, and was renewed under the captaincy of Joshua, was now obsolete; the foreigner was a citizen of the new Church, the Jerusalem which was from above. The Scythian savage might become the docile disciple, or the active preacher; the slave was the Lord's freeman, the freeman was bought with the price of Christ's death. The nature of the convert was changed, the old man was put off—there was no further fellowship with bygone habits, practices, and beliefs, which were now for ever abandoned; for in their place was a new being, ever growing, ever developing, ever renewing itself, and gradually by its spiritual introspect, as it knows more and more, reaching that likeness of the Creator, for which it once ignorantly yearned, into which it is now being transformed.

To those who lived within this mystic union, the outer world seemed lifeless or corrupt, — an unreal thing, which was passing away. The religion of the heathen was a sacrifice to devils, its political system a mystery of iniquity, — a revelation of Antichrist, — of the Man of Sin. For a time, many of the converts had lived in and for this system, — had been enslaved to its grossness, or overpowered by its prestige. They had now been enlightened; and to go back, even in thought, to that from which they had escaped, was as impossible as it would be for a child to again accept the errors which have been utterly dispelled by a sudden and large experience. They enjoyed the full light of a clear and perfect faith, the intensity of which corresponded to the freshness of its growth, and contrasted with the black debasement from which the man had effected his escape. With men in this state of happy, joyous trust, who lived in an age when charity had not been throttled by dogmas and definitions, there was no doubt to torment the mind, no gloss on the law of liberty, which should seek to make it an intolerable bondage.

It is in this absolute seclusion from past interests that we must account for the indifference to public questions which formed an early reproach on the Christian community, and that timidity, or, at least, acquiescence in the established order of things, which characterized the Apostolic age. The casuistry of a later age perverted the tenets which justified this policy into a permanent political creed, and attempted to make that a rule for the conduct of a Christian community which was intended to secure to these new converts complete isolation from a social system which could not be touched without impurity. The early Christians dared not exercise the rights of citizens without forfeiting or imperilling the most precious privileges of their faith. It was even doubtful whether they might hold social intercourse with unbelievers. Life was short, and immortality lay beyond it.

Besides, it is manifest that all — apostles and people — looked forward to the immediate consummation of the world. St. Paul was possessed by this impression. The times were in God's own power — the day and the hour were not revealed to the Christ in the days of His flesh, but hid in the counsels of the Father. But the time was assuredly short — there were those living who would be caught up in the air, to be for ever with Him. They were near Him now in spirit, they would be speedily near Him in the body. In the view of that faith which bridged over the interval of the Divine counsels, and already gave the assurance of the immediate presence of God, the world, its cares, its purposes, its pomp, its power, its threatenings, became most remote, most insignificant, a mere speck in the dawning Infinity.

## CHAPTER II.

THE principles of morality are not peculiar to one epoch of civilization nor to one religion. They are as permanent and as universal as other laws of nature are. It is true, that like all those general positions which are relative to the social condition of man, they are often imperfectly understood, often ignored, often violated to the detriment of society, to the injury of those who do not know them, or knowing break them. In just the same way, communities and individuals understand the laws of health or of political economy imperfectly, defy them or break them. The perfection of moral science consists in the accurate knowledge of all moral obligations; the theory of civilization presumes a general acquiescence in these moral obligations, while its completeness is effected by prompt and general obedience to the precise rules of conduct and duty.

It would not be difficult to construct several systems of pure morality which should be almost perfect, and therefore alike, from a host of independent sources. The duties of individuals to society at large, and to the forces which compose society, are to be found in the Vedas, in the Zendavesta, in the works of the Athenian philosophers, in the Kabbala and Talmud, in the Koran, as well as in the New Testament. The author of the Epistle to the Romans bears witness to the universality of the moral law, and to its sufficiency as an exposition of moral duty. It is an error to arrogate the affirmation of this moral law to one system of religion, and no less an error to argue that such parts of different systems as coincide must have been derived from some common source, or to see in some agreement that the one is a plagiary of the other.

It is easy to discover a close resemblance between the morality of the Talmud and that of the New Testament, easy for a partisan to exalt the gloss of the Jewish doctors over the rules of the Christian life as promulgated by the Evangelists and Apostles, or to ignore the teaching of the Rabbis in estimating the service which Christianity has done to the moral purification of the world. It is not inconsistent with what we read of Christ in the gospels that He should have been, as Jewish writers have alleged, the pupil of that Rabbi Simeon who was noted as the chief of the Ascetics, the great teacher of the Essenes. It may be true that a close resemblance may be found between the comparison of the lily of the field with the glory of Solomon, and a recorded saying of this famous doctor; that the eagerness with which a lost sheep is sought, and the tenderness with which it is welcomed back — one of the most touching of Christ's parables — may have its counterpart in a parable of the same sage. He is reported to have said that a certain man had a flock of sheep which were daily led to pasture. Here they were joined by a gazelle, who regularly fed with them, and returned with them to the fold. The owner of the flock bade his shepherds take the greatest care of this stranger; and when he was asked why he showed it such favor, answered, This creature has left the wilderness, and, in spite of its own untamed and timid nature, has joined the flock. It is well that I should welcome it more affectionately than I do those who have been fed by me, and tended by my care. For that which is customary with them, is strange to the gazelle. And thus, continues the Rabbi, God will welcome the stranger who joins himself to the chosen people, more than He will those who have always had the blessing of His covenant, because they are born to Israel.

Does the Christian law bid man love his neighbor, and assert that they who, serving God, do this, are near to the kingdom of God? The great Doctor Hillel says, that not to do to your neighbor that which is distasteful to yourself is the whole law; while another teacher infers the universal obligation of charity and beneficence from the fact that man is created in the image of the Almighty.

Again, the grace which is given to the humble, when expressed by the Jewish doctors, is stated under the form that in the humble dwells permanently the Shekinah of the Almighty. The Divine Master bids those who would be first among men to be their servants; the Rabbi gives a conversation between the chief among the Jews and Alexander the Great,—

"What should a man do who wishes to gain the love of his fellow-men? Avoid all rule and authority over them." Are the disciples informed that he who exalteth himself shall be abased, and he that humbleth himself shall be exalted? — we are reminded of the maxim of Hillel, "My humiliation will be my exaltation, my exaltation my humiliation." "The knowledge of God is not in heaven," says Moses; and the gloss of the Rabbi is, "Do not look to find it among those who raise their pride to heaven. He who makes himself little in this world for the sake of the Law will be great in the world to come." The Gospel bids the forgiveness of injuries, and the Talmud advises as follows: — "They who undergo injury without retaliation, who suffer themselves to be traduced and do not retort, and who accept the ills of life cheerfully, for them is that which was written in the prophets, 'The friends of God shall shine as the sun in his strength.'" And again, "God ranges Himself on the side of the persecuted, whether the persecutor and persecuted are equally just or equally wicked. Nay, as He assists the just man who is persecuted by the unjust, so He even aids the unjust when he is persecuted by the just." Are the disciples to be wise as serpents and harmless as doves? — the Talmud says that "Israel is as brave as a lion, wise as a serpent, but that he has also the simplicity of a dove." It would be possible to extend these examples indefinitely. It would be possible to exhibit similar parallelisms from the teaching of the older Platonists and the later Stoics. The canons of morality are universal and immutable, for they are the highest laws of social life.

And here should be noticed one marked peculiarity in the ethics of ancient Judaism, which is precisely continued in the modern development of this primeval faith. No moral code has ever rested so profoundly on home duties and home ties — on the love of parent and child — as the Jewish has. The birth of a son is the highest reward for Abraham's faith. Paternal love almost makes a hero of Jacob, and gives dignity to a character which is otherwise furtive and mean. What is more tragic than the sorrow of Jephthah, what is brighter than the filial duty of Jonathan, what more touching than the grief of David over that rebellious son who inflicted on his father the most atrocious insults that could have been perpetrated? The Psalmist's picture of a pious and happy family, cf the laborious and contented husbandman, whose wife is as the fruitful vine, whose children are like the comely olive trees, full of assured promise, is a sketch, the nature of which is perpetually bright and fresh. The sorrows of Jeremiah are over wasted homes; his deepest grief is felt at the "children and sucklings swooning in the streets of the city, who faint like the wounded in battle, and pour out their soul into their mother's bosom." The home was the centre of Jewish life, the type of that archaic epoch when every man did that which was right in his own eyes, when Israel dwelt securely under his vine and fig-tree, of the golden age of the nation. Even now the Jew, with no little color of truth, complains that Christianity has exalted the monastic spirit, and disparaged home, and asks for the gain which social life has effected by this contempt of the natural affections.

The sanctions of morality, apart from such evidence as can be gained from the experience of obedience and the blessings which such obedience entails, are found in religion. To yearn after the supernatural, and thereby to satisfy the longings of the soul — to address one's self to God, so that the weakness of humanity may be aided in achieving the great destiny which lies before it — to trust in God, that He can and will redress the evil and wrong-doing which blot His creation, — are the earliest and the most lasting religious instincts, and belong to every creed except those which exhibit the Deity as a remorseless and inevitable fate, or a capricious despot. Even ruined and debased religions may often be traced to a pure original.

The Jewish creed recognized the long-suffering, the beneficence, the providence of God. He was the avenger of the helpless, the judge of the wicked, the protector of His people, the defence of His servants. He was surrounded by majesty, by light unapproachable, by every symbol of awful power. But He deigned to visit men, to serve and save them. High as His dwelling is, He humbles Himself to a watchful providence over man. He is King, Teacher, Father. This last title is, as we all know, His universal name in the New Testament. But it is not unknown or unfamiliar in the Old. "Doubtless," says that prophet, whose writing has been incorporated with the sayings of an elder Isaiah, "Thou art our Father; though Abraham be ignorant of us, and Israel acknowledge us not, Thou, O God, art our Father, our Redeemer." The Paternity of God extends beyond the narrow range of human kindred or human patriotism. There was a bitter feud between Ephraim and Judah. It has even continued to our day, — is a feud of twenty-four centuries, — for the Samaritan is the wasted representative of the Israelite kingdom, as he was in the days of Christ, as he was to Benjamin of Tudela. But there was one Father to both, — to the worshipper at Jacob's well, and to the Pharisee of David's city. Nay, the outcasts of Abraham and Isaac, the men whom Ezra and Nehemiah scornfully rejected from the company of those who were restored after their captivity, could claim Him as their Father and Redeemer, exiled and maligned as they were.

The really Jewish scriptures contain no affirmative statement as to the immortality of man's soul. They are similarly silent as to that final judgment which forms so marked a characteristic in the religion of Christianity. We know that even when some of the later doctors of the Law taught the doctrine of man's immortality, other doctors were hostile to the tenet. Nay, even those who accepted the doctrine often qualified it by a wild metempsychosis. There are, they hold, a certain number of created souls, which pass from body to body, and when their transmigrations are completed the Messiah shall come. This appears to have been the opinion of Josephus. There are traces of this compromise between the doctrine of man's immortality, and the absence of recorded authority on the subject, in the language of the gospels. The antenatal sin, which the blind man in the Gospel of St. John may have committed, is an illustration. Nor does the language of the New Testament contravene the more refined conception which was included in the theory of transmigration, that, namely, of a purifying process. There is a final day of judgment, but there is almost complete silence as to the intermediate condition of the departed. Once only Christ lifts the veil, and displays the rich man suffering, repentant, but not despairing. The spiritual Abraham, the father of all, does not address the lost as his sons.

It is well known that the Jews were divided on this subject, — that the Pharisees accepted, under various forms, the doctrine of the soul's immortality, of the enduring personality of the dead, and that the Sadducees rejected the doctrine, or at least held that the soul was absorbed into some general Intelligence or Power. It would seem that the former doctrine, which Christianity affirmed with peculiar emphasis, was adopted after the captivity, and that it formed a characteristic tenet of the stricter spirituality which the ascetic Pharisees taught. This tenet is an inevitable consequence of the spiritual life. If men are once persuaded that the enjoyment of life is not its end, if they understand that man does not merely live to receive his just portion in those good things of material existence which a beneficent Providence bestows, and a wise economy distributes and secures, they necessarily conclude that man's being is not bounded by his visible personality. It is, indeed, plain that the moral and intellectual progress of society is due to the efforts of those who deliberately daff the lawful pleasures of life, in order that they may effect the general good of humanity. But neither the stimulus to this prodigious service nor its reward can be found in the satisfaction with which a limited existence could survey the unlimited good which it has effected. "If," says the apostle Paul, in that remarkable passage, where deep conviction struggles for eloquence, "our hopes in Christ are bounded by this life only, we are the most pitiable of mankind." It is not impossible to suffer patiently on behalf of a creed which offers no prospect but annihilation; it is impossible to do bravely, to labor with unceasing and untired energy, to go about doing active good, and withal to believe that all this power and force, this concentrated influence which rouses and elevates the soul of a generation, and leaves permanent effects on the whole nature of man, is abruptly terminated in an eternal negation. And as the doctrine of the soul's immortality begins with the development of the spiritual life, so it is intensified and confirmed by the determination to serve man for God's sake. The doctors who compassed sea and land to make one proselyte, could not but affirm that the soul which had enlightened his fellow-man in the knowledge of God partakes of the eternity which belongs to the Most High. The fruit of their labor may have been worthless, a mere growth of malignity and pride, a mere slavery to the letter, but the activity which is patient in winning souls, no matter to what creed, cannot but believe in its own immortality.

The leading tenet of Jewish teaching was the dignity of man. It is a tradition of the Rabbans that God said to Jacob, "I am the God of those on high, thou art the god of those below," — a legend derived from or confirmed by these words of the Psalmist which are quoted by Christ, as a patent justification of His claim to the Divine Sonship. The Kabbalists taught that the true habitation of God, of which tabernacle and temple were but types, was the body of man; and they compared each member of man's body to some one or the other among the divisions of the building, placing the Holy of Holies in the heart. They extracted from this symbolism at once the duty of religious purity, and the obligation of charity, since the wound of one part in the mystical as well as the natural body is the suffering of all parts. And in the same strain, as if by way of comment on the declaration that man is created in the image of God, the Jewish doctors affirmed that "the soul of man is higher than the nature of angels; that man is the counsellor of God in creation, His associate in the work of heaven and earth; that he is the stay and foundation of the universe; and that the angels desire to hold converse with the just, that they may learn of them the mysteries of the eternal God." And as the last favor which the Almighty grants His favored servants, He deigns to let them know His incommunicable name. It is in accordance with this highest mark of divine condescension and indwelling, that, according to the Talmudists, the wonders which Christ did were due to the power which He possessed from the full revelation of what constituted that mysterious title. The same idea is current in Mohammedan legends. It is by the possession of that name that the great Solomon gained his empire over all creation, over men, and angels, over birds and beasts, over genii and devils. So, says Benjamin of Tudela, David el Roy, who claimed about the middle of the twelfth century to be the Messiah, and who thereupon stirred up the Jewish nation in the caliphat of Bagdad, exercised magical powers by virtue of the same rare knowledge.

According to the teachers of the Talmud, the regeneration of man was due to the Eternal Word. This was expounded to be, "God incarnate in the Law, and continuing itself from age to age." Man is degraded by the sin of Adam, but restored by this Divine Essence, which permeates his heart and life, which through him purifies and restores the world and all creation. It makes man, by his own soul and will, by his own conscience, the first and chief, nay, almost the solitary instrument of his own regeneration. How man may best facilitate the process is matter of teaching, and the details of the teaching are to be found in the works of the Jewish schoolmen. "The doctrine," says one of the latest expositors of Hebrew theology, "which most nearly represents the Jewish machinery of regeneration, is that which is known in Ecclesiastical history as Semi-Pelagianism — which admits the infirmity, the sinfulness, of human nature, but which also conceives it possible that man may work out his own salvation." The redemption which the Word effects, according to this author (Ben-amozegh), is wholly internal. "The passion, the condemnation, the death, the garden of olives, the Prætorium, and Golgotha, are all internal, subjective facts, having for their theatre the spirit and heart of the man, where the Word sacrifices itself perpetually for the benefit of humanity, and on the altar which the man raises for himself." Man, in short, is self-made — the architect of his spiritual, as well as of his temporal fortunes — the sufficient master of his own eternal destiny. This seems like the teaching of Hegel; it is not far from the teaching of the Gemara.

The Jew was encouraged in being profoundly national. It is needless to adduce proofs of this fact, or of the endurance of the sentiment. That the national feeling was hardened by centuries of persecution is certain; that it has been weakened by the development of toleration first, and of civil equality afterwards, is no less manifest. That a few generations of justice will almost efface the characteristics of Judaism, may be safely predicted from the conditions of human nature. The effort, which is now made to prove that the peculiar tenets of Christianity had their origin in the teaching of those Rabbis who flourished in the Asmonean epoch, reveals a different spirit from that contemptuous hatred which retorted scorn on the savage persecutors of the Jewish creed. The comparative gentleness with which the Jewish theologian of the nineteenth century treats the mission and teaching of Christ is of another temper to that which induced the Spanish Jew in the twelfth century to speak of Jesus, in the phrase of the Talmud, as "that man"—as the disobedient prophet whom the lion slew. The Israelite of our day finds abundant authority in the writings of the Hebrew schoolmen to warrant his assertion, that these sages taught the equality and fraternity of mankind. But it should be remembered that the reasonings of the teacher are no evidence of the temper which inflamed the pupil, still less of the passions and fears which occupied rulers and people. The Rabban may be calm and tolerant, while the chief priests and elders are rousing the fury of an excitable populace.

As the religious life of the earlier Israelite was complete without the tenet of the soul's immortality, so it was satisfied with such felicity as can be obtained by obedience to a moral law. The later apologist of the Jewish creed, as contained in the traditions and glosses of the Jewish schoolmen, may speak of human life as the vestibule — as the eve of the Divine Sabbath — as the time of labor — as the now, while eternity is designated as the time of retribution — as to-morrow. "One whole hour," say the same authorities, " of virtue and repentance are worth more than all eternity — for eternity can give no more than the man brings to it, — and thus it is not without reason that Solomon said, 'a living dog is better than a dead lion.'" But the eternity is itself a gloss on the text. It takes its substance from the life of the man, not its color only. It is a Paradise — an Elysium — a garden of divine delights — an eternity of the land of promise. There have been ascetic Jews, as there have been proselytizing Jews. But the tendency of the Jew is to be intensely active in the material occupations of life — to be cosmopolitan in his treatment of secular business — to know no country, no patriotism, no allegiance — nothing but obedience to the political institutions under which he lives, and the value of which he thoroughly comprehends. "Throw no stone," says the Jewish proverb, "into the well from which thou hast drawn water" — implying that men should be respectful to the society which shelters them. Israel, if it be any thing, is an *imperium in imperio*. When it ceases to be an institution, it ceases to be a special creed — is dissolved into some one or the other of those creeds which are either rigidly monotheistic and iconoclast, or which are developments of the monotheistic tenet. If the time had been favorable to it — had any terms of compromise been found — Judaism might have been merged in some religion of antiquity, as it is likely that it was deeply colored by the monotheism of the Persian conquerors of Babylon, for the prophet speaks of Cyrus as the Lord's shepherd — as His anointed, and Daniel, the hero of Ezekiel's prophecy, is the chief of the magicians at Babylon.

The Jews of the first century held that a pagan who confessed God, and kept the moral law, might be saved; that Socrates and Plato would be in Paradise with Abraham, Isaac and Moses. Abraham, they said, was the first-born of the promise, only because he was the first proselyte. "I call heaven and earth to witness," says a doctor of the Law, "both man and woman, slave and free, Jew and Pagan, it is only by the works of man, that the Spirit descends on him." "Why," says another, "is there only one race of man? It is that no man may say, My father and mother are greater than thine." And, to prove that these words were not without the confirmation of facts, we are informed, that the teachers of Hillel and Schemaiah were proselytes, that one of the great and venerated doctors was descended from Haman the Amalekite, another from Sennacherib, and others from Sisera; the legend typifying that Israel would not shut its doors to those who were the offspring of the most hateful names in Jewish history. Nor was this welcome limited to strangers of illustrious learning and virtue. The prophetic authority of Zephaniah was cited as a proof that the final unity of mankind was part of the counsels of God.

The Jew averred that the revelation of God in the Law was complete. "'The Law,' indeed, was not comprised in the Pentateuch only. This is the code of the Jews, their civil, political, ritual code — a monument of vigorous and manly genius, a system of which the exemplar is a characteristic, indestructible nationality. This code is ennobled and exalted by inspiration; it breathes with a moral, spiritual, dogmatic vitality, which gives an intense energy to all its details, but it is only a code." It needs an interpreter. For a series of ages this interpretation was found in the teaching of the prophets, those sages whom God raised up in order to declare His will, or to announce His judgments. Sometimes these men, like Samuel, were brought up within the very precincts of the tabernacle, and lived daily within sight of the Shekinah. At another time, the interpreter of the age, like a Marabout or Dervish, appears suddenly from the desert or the mountain, clad in the rough dress of the Ishmaelite, and denounces the apostate king, or faithless people scorching them with the wrath of God, and zealous even to slaying. Another is the wise counsellor, the polished courtier, but one who never forgets his mission from the Almighty; who ejects a perfidious, idolatrous, murderous dynasty, substitutes a more obedient family in its room, and then counsels, warns, strengthens the monarch as Elisha does. Later on, the prophet is a still more important personage. He is called by no succession or ordination, but by the voice of God, by the Word of the Lord, by some inward warning, or in some ecstatic vision. He is a scion of the royal house, as Isaiah; or a herdsman, as Amos; or a priest, as Jeremiah — whose statesmanship was unavailing to save the falling throne of David against the headstrong king, and his more headstrong nobles; or another priest, as Ezekiel, the captive in the land of the Chaldeans; or the comforter of a ruined nation, who assures them of God's sure though tardy vengeance on the enemies of Israel. He is sent indifferently to the revolted house of Joseph, or to the faithful tribe of Judah. His mission is to awaken the conscience, to purify the heart, to call back the people to the God of their fathers, whom they have forsaken in word and thought.

The nearest parallel to the Jewish prophet is to be found in those reformers who have set themselves to the task of turning, in some age of spiritual deadness, the hearts of erring children to the purer religion of their fathers. Such were Basil and Benedict, Francis and Dominic, Wiklif, Luther, Loyola, Wesley — men whom their own generation has intensely loved, and intensely hated, but who have assuredly stirred humanity from its very depths, who have effected permanent revivals. In one particular, however, these men differed notably from the Jewish prophets. They were ecclesiastics, not statesmen. They founded sects. They reformed the religion of their day, but they created an organization by which they fondly hoped that their spirit would live, their work be continued. But in the prophetic age, there was no place for a sect. The Jewish creed had few dogmas: it may be said to have had only one, — I am the Lord your God. The discipline of Jewish society was the perpetual interpretation of the letter by the spirit, in case the Law was perverted to unrighteous ends; or more frequently the warning of the Almighty Word, the chastisement of the Almighty judgment on public and private sins. But it is impossible to found a sect except by dogmas, impossible to maintain one without a permanently organized discipline.

The open vision passed away. The Jews of the restoration entrenched themselves in sacerdotalism. They exacted evidence of pure descent from all those who were to partake of the privilege of Israel. We are informed that this strictness led to the extensive forgery of pedigrees. They refused alliance with the Samaritans, and created a perpetual schism between themselves and their own kindred. They read that the Ammonite and Moabite should not come within the congregation for ever, and the Jews of Nehemiah's age expelled the children of mixed marriages from the nation. This rigorous nationalist forgot the permission which the great lawgiver gave that the settlers in the Promised Land might marry the women of the country, and that the prince of the house of Judah was wedded to Rahab of Jericho. Nay, was there not one woman, whose gentleness and love have made her for generations the type of perfect womanhood, and was not she a daughter of the accursed Moab, of the race which hired Balaam, and which made Israel to sin? And yet was not this woman also married to the chief of the house of Judah, and did she not become the ancestress of David?

The Rabbi became the successor of the prophet. It is probable that the school of this teacher was formed on the model of those academies in which the sages of Greece instructed their pupils. It was in such a school that the youthful Jesus was found, engaged in questioning the master, and answering those queries which the master put to his disciples. Such questions and answers, such sayings of the teacher, were handed down orally, and gathered at last into those commentaries which are known as Talmud, or Gemara, or Kabbala. They formed that vast body of tradition out of which the Scribe and the Pharisee obtained their skill in casuistry, sometimes indeed using their knowledge to fortify the true interpretation of the Law, often as a power by which they might rule and oppress their fellows.

There was, therefore, a continual commentary on the Law, which professed to be a revelation of its meaning. The Jew declared that this revelation was complete. The Christian declared that it was imperfect, or at best could only be interpreted by the commentary of the Gospel. The gist of the Epistle to the Hebrews is that the Son of God has revealed that which was unknown, has interpreted that which was obscure, has fulfilled that which was inchoate. The founder of Christianity asserts the high prophetic gifts of the Baptist, but puts him below the least in the kingdom of Heaven. "The Law," says the great Apostle, "was our schoolmaster, to bring us to Christ." It dealt with the age of childhood: the Christian has come to the stature of a full-grown man.

While the Christian claimed a full revelation, compared with which the light of Sinai was dim, and the utterance of the prophet faltering, the wild theogony of the Gnostics accepted the earlier revelation as complete, but asserted the development of the Divine Nature itself. They held, we are told, that the God of the Jews was an imperfect essence, both in his moral and spiritual nature, and that, his function over, he was succeeded by a greater, holier, and more powerful Being. It seems that this dreamy succession of supernatural existences was developed from the bosom of Judaism, if, as is commonly reported, Gnosticism has Simon of Samaria for its founder. It is supposed by most persons that it is to these transcendental genealogies of the Gnostics that St. Paul refers in his First Epistle to Timothy, and it is alleged that such an allusion casts a doubt on the authenticity of the epistle. The objection does not, for many reasons, seem valid. M. Asher, the editor and commentator on Benjamin of Tudela, understands these genealogies to be the pedigrees which were forged after the captivity, which are, he adds, to be found in the book of Chronicles, and which were as apocryphal and silly as their modern equivalents. If this interpretation be correct, the Apostle is urging his disciple to discourage the vanity of the Jewish converts at Ephesus, and thus is reaffirming the necessity for repudiating every tendency towards distinctive Judaism in a Christian church.

The Christianity of the Apostolic age ran a double danger from Judaism. It had to withstand the furious animosity of those who regarded Christ as a deceiver, and His apostles as the emissaries of a pernicious and unpatriotic sect. It had also to resist the still more dangerous intrigues of those who insisted on conformity to the Jewish ritual as a condition of membership in the new Church, who would have made the Jerusalem which is above, and which is the mother of all Christian men, a mere cramped and narrow faubourg in the metropolis of Judaism. The bitterness of the former could find no stronger language of hatred than the words which the Jews addressed to Christ: "Say we not well that thou art a Samaritan and hast a devil?" — combining in the charge the intensest feelings of political and polemical rancor. The pedantry of the latter is the first example of that spirit which has perpetually vexed Christianity, in its attempts to coerce conscience by a rigid and implacable dogmatism. "Except ye be circumcised and keep the law of Moses, ye cannot be saved." This is the first of these anathemas by which men have tried to fetter Christianity. Perhaps our own age has said the last.

It has been said that in the administration of secular business, the majority should rule, the minority should influence. But they who are concerned with such business, are much more ready to affirm the former position than they are to allow the latter. In our own country, people very often attempt to coerce the minority by calumniating its objects, and one of the commonest words used for this purpose is the term unenglish. Now, the nationalist party among the Jews might have called the converts unjewish. Heated by a narrow patriotism, they were ready to join the cry of the depraved rabble in the heathen cities, and stigmatize the Christian as the enemy of the human race, because his sympathies were comprehensive. Now, we need not be told that religious animosities are inconceivably more bitter than political differences are. Men who will tolerate one whom they call a partisan are implacable towards another whom they are pleased to name a schismatic or a heretic. The modern Jew denies that he ever entertains, or that his race has ever entertained, religious enmities. The history of Paul's travels is abundant proof to the contrary. And yet Paul always abstains from that topic which invariably irritated the Jews to frenzy,—the charge, namely, that they had repudiated the teaching, and murdered the person of Christ. They hear him till he speaks of his mission to the Gentiles. He has only to avow this as the business of his life, and they strive to tear him in pieces, conspire to assassinate him.

It cannot be denied that the teaching of Christianity ignores patriotism. It ignores it, however, only because patriotism is transient, is inferior to the large purposes which can be obtained by evangelizing a federal humanity. The State is superior to the family, and asserts its claim to break up all domestic ties in view of the public good, for it sacrifices the father in the citizen. But it does not, except under this constraint, disparage the family; on the contrary, it cherishes and encourages the love of home. And, similarly, the claims of a federal humanity are stronger than those of patriotism, and, as civilization advances, the latter will be sacrificed if it clashes with the former. Patriotism is encouraged only as the school of a higher life. And, it should be remembered, that if patriotism has given magnificent examples of self-sacrifice, of heroic devotion, of ardent courage, of noble enterprise, these very qualities have been called out because a spurious loyalty has armed the oppressor with a power which a true patriotism has sometimes successfully defied. But where, alas, could the preacher of the apostolic age find the material for patriotic impulse in the hopeless slavery of the Roman Empire? He is turned, perforce, to the *civitas Dei*. He does not, indeed, forget to prescribe the conduct of a pure and happy home. Between that and the spiritual kingdom there was a desert. If the Lord had not shortened those days, no flesh should be saved.

The sacrifice of life, of home, of father and mother, of husband, of wife, of child, is demanded only as an alternative to the desertion of God. The State claims all these possessions; if its own being is imperilled, often if its own pride is wounded, its ambition is unsated. And can God, whom all religion recognizes as the Author of all benefits, claim less than the exigencies of human society demand from its citizens? Is loyalty due to king, race, country; is political unity a boon for which no sacrifice is too costly; and is no hearty allegiance due to the Father of heaven and earth; is the maintenance of a universal gospel worth no sacrifice from those who profess to be the city of the Great King? The closer, the tenderer, the more affectionate are the relations which religion affirms to exist between man and his Maker, the more earnest must needs be the devotion of the former to the latter. It is the

Paternity of God which is foreshadowed in the Old Testament, but which thoroughly permeates the New. The hostility which the Jews of the apostolic age entertained towards the Church was akin to that which the Jew of Palestine bore to the Samaritan. The enmity which men are apt to feel towards those who swerve from some particulars of the faith, is far bitterer than that which they cherish against unbelievers. We have daily experience of such a temper among sectaries. And it is clear, notwithstanding the general affirmation of Jewish doctors, that there is not, and must not be, an eternity of punishment; that the Christian reformation is glanced at in the statement, that "he who profanes holy things, who despises solemnities, who annuls our alliance with Abraham our father, who gives to the law a sense contrary to the true, who puts his neighbor to the blush in public — will have no place in the world to come." The zeal of Saul was shared by other zealots. High Priest and Council, Sadducee and Pharisee, were of one accord in the cry, — "Away with such a fellow from the earth."

Still more dangerous, however, was the narrow conscience of the converted Jew. To him the ritual and discipline of Moses were the unalterable will of the Almighty. Departure from the covenant involved the terrible doom of anathema from his people, obedience to it was the peremptory condition of the Divine blessing and favor. Was it not written, that Moses, speaking by the power of God, warned Israel to obedience; and did he not utter, on those who disobeyed the statutes and commandments of the Law, those terrible curses which are found in the last revelations of the Pentateuch? Had it not been by disobedience that Israel was scattered, impoverished, humiliated, enslaved? Had he not preserved his national existence by the righteousness of some, by the remnant which saved the race from becoming as Sodom and as Gomorrah? Do not Law, chronicle, prophet, confirm this obligation; is not Jewish history a continual consolation to the faithful, a fearful warning to those who forget God? Christ came to fulfil the Law: He expressly stated that He was not here to destroy it. Can you, who were with Him from the beginning, — who were witnesses of His life, His death, His resurrection, — who had been appointed to this office by the Wisdom of God, by Him who knew whom He had chosen — can you recall any saying of His in which he revoked the law of Moses? For ages that law has made us a peculiar people, by it we have resisted an idolatrous world, through it we have known and worshipped the God of our fathers — can we abandon it now? How can we be one fold, under one shepherd, except by one obedience? How can the Gentiles be raised up as children to Abraham, except they keep the covenant which was once delivered to the father of them who are faithful? In something like this fashion, they who came down from Jerusalem must have argued at Antioch and Ephesus, in Galatia and in Crete, even after Peter had given his healing counsel, Paul had narrated the success of his mission, and James had uttered the terms of the compromise which the apostolic college proposed and authorized.

Even if the ancient Law had not been revealed with so much solemnity, supported by such sanctions, confirmed by such examples, enforced by such warnings,— had it not made a nation illustrious, a page in the world's history luminous and real,— had it not twined itself so closely round the heart and brain of the Jew, — the mere habit of obedience to its precepts would have given it sanctity and majesty in the eyes of those who had followed it. To us, at this distance of time, it may seem strange that the Jewish ritual should have had such an overwhelming influence over the Jewish Christian; that he should not have eagerly embraced relief from observances which his forefathers could not bear, and which he had found oppressively onerous. But a little reflection will remind us of the tenacity with which men cling to forms, guarantees, rites, obligations, the origin and continuance of which are far less suggestive and intelligible than the unexpanded ritual of Moses, — which are as oppressive and unsatisfying as the grievous burdens with which the Pharisees loaded men's shoulders, and which they made necessary to the Jewish salvation.

But whatever may have been the attachment which the converted Jew felt towards the code of Moses, it was imperatively necessary that the Gentile convert should be freed from them. Even had he not resented the interference with his own mission, — had he not been indignant at an attempt to reconstruct the foundation of his gospel, — had he not been stirred to denounce those, as he does over and over again, who were designedly creating schisms in the Christian community, — Paul was too acute and far-sighted a man not to discern that the mission of Christ would be annulled, that Christ would profit the convert nothing, that He would be of no effect to mankind, if men suffered themselves to submit to the bondage of Judaism. There was an immediate advantage in the conversion. This was the avoidance of persecution. If the Jewish Christian could induce the Gentile proselyte to submit to the covenant, the hostility of the unconverted Jew would be disarmed. This, as we know, was the opinion of the apostolic college at Jerusalem, who persuaded Paul to go through certain marked observances on the occasion of his last visit to Jerusalem. In the eyes of the great missionary they were of no importance. It was his habit to gain men's hearts, or to disabuse their suspicions. If his concession involved no sacrifice of principle, he was ready to conciliate Jew and Greek in non-essentials.

Had the Christian converts allowed themselves to submit, it is not difficult to see the consequences. The Jews would have had, could have had, no permanent difficulty in allowing the prophetic mission of Christ, and in permitting the formation of a sect which should see in Him the greatest of the prophets, the Son of God. Could they only have secured the perpetual supremacy of the Mosaic ordinances, they would have willingly acquiesced in the formation of a school which should accept, affirm, propagate the tenets of the Nazarene prophet. They would not have been greatly offended had this school anathematized its rivals, or extinguished them, any more than the head of Roman unity was alarmed at the feud between the Dominicans and Franciscans, or at that between the Minorite friars and the endowed orders. Unanimity was not, is not, to be expected in the spiritual any more than in the material life, but uniformity may be demanded and must be insisted on. The question was: Shall Christianity be lost in Judaism, or shall it assert its supremacy over the older covenant, by boldly claiming to be the successor of a defunct organization?

Familiarity with Jewish observances endeared them to the Jewish converts. But the acceptance of a peculiar and ineffaceable sign, the fact of which became especially notorious to the habits of ancient civilization, the obedience to a number of exact precautions against ceremonial defilement, which compelled the Jews to live apart from the nations with whom they sojourned, were conditions of church membership which were intolerably distasteful to the Gentiles. They were told that Christianity was a law of liberty, — a religion, the acceptance of which, forthwith, worked an instant purification from any taint which adhered to human nature, was a salvation by Grace; and they were invited, nay, constrained by the threat of perdition, to submit to these strange rites. There were portions of the Jewish law which they could willingly adopt. "The habit," says Josephus, in his Apology for his nation against the malignant calumnies of Apion, " of imitating many among the rites of Jewish worship is general. There is no city of Greeks or barbarians — no race of mankind — which is unfamiliar with the custom of keeping the Sabbath, of resting on that sacred day. There is none where certain of our rites are not observed — as fastings, the burning of lamps, and the avoidance of much that our law forbids. They affect," he adds, "to imitate our concord and liberality, our industry in the arts, our heroic resolution to die rather than abandon our law." The Jews did not establish an active propaganda, at least in the capital. They knew the danger of attracting noble converts. In the nineteenth year of our era, the conversion of Fulvia, wife of Saturninus, to Judaism, — by the endeavors of some enthusiast, who persuaded his neophyte to send a great present to Jerusalem under the name of first-fruits, and who was charged with the intention of appropriating the offering to his own use, — provoked a dangerous reaction from the toleration, and even favor with which Augustus had treated the nation. Four thousand of these Jews, say Josephus and Tacitus, were transported to Sardinia. The latter adds, that if the unwholesomeness of the island was fatal to them, it would be a cheap loss. Adherence to the tenets of Judaism, therefore, on the part of such converts as were of Gentile origin, though it might check the hostility of the synagogue and the Sanhedrim, would provoke the animosity of the prætorium and the senate. The yoke was intolerable, the obligation superfluous, the maintenance of the ritual obstructive and dangerous.

The most superficial study of the Acts of the Apostles teaches us that this controversy was the earliest and the latest of which that narrative takes cognizance. The struggle commences with the mission of Peter to Cornelius, and the suspicion with which the chief apostle is treated — a suspicion which is disarmed only by the authority of a special revelation, and of a miracle, and by the testimony of the brethren who accompanied Peter in his journey from Joppa to Cæsarea. How it harassed the life of Paul is well known. It was the subject of long and anxious debate before the apostolic college. It led to the arrest and imprisonment of Paul. Even when he came a prisoner to Rome, he instantly anticipates that this unsettled question will follow him thither. He finds the Jewish residents ignorant of any specific charge against him, — perhaps because the bitterness with which he was assailed had been assuaged by his captivity. The men of Judea send no complaint. But elsewhere, everywhere, his preaching is spoken against. Almost the last fact in this historic book of the New Testament is the declaration that the salvation of God is sent to the Gentiles, and that they are to hear it.

The attitude which Paul took in this question is, at first sight, ambiguous. It appears, though the language used is not perfectly clear, that the Apostle gave way in the case of Titus, not from compulsion, but for the sake of peace. It is known that he spontaneously put this discipline on Timothy. It may be that when he sought, in the case of any among his disciples whom he wished to employ as missionaries, the authority or license of the apostolic synod, he conceded the point. It was his avowed principle to conciliate men by a concession in non-essentials. Christianity was a new creation — the ceremonial characteristics, the observances of Judaism, were nugatory, antiquated, superfluous. Only, if some of the brethren still cherished them, he could not fight for trifles. To resist would stir up bitterness, and might prolong the existence of a sentiment which time would weaken, and finally extinguish.

But the case was very different when an attempt was made to exalt this sentiment into a rule of Christian life, as a condition precedent to salvation. The emissaries of the narrower school had intruded on his special province, had raised the cry of Jesus, not Paul, in the place where Paul had labored, had taught another gospel, had questioned the authority of the Apostle's mission, had insinuated doubts of his orthodoxy. Nor had this attempt been unsuccessful. It had produced dissensions in Corinth. It had thoroughly disorganized the Galatians, a people of European origin, but who had been settled in the interior of Asia Minor for three centuries. This nation had once been the scourge of Asia, but had latterly become peaceful. Up to the fifth century after Christ, the country folk of Galatia still spoke with the Celtic tongue of their forefathers. The people in the towns knew Greek, but were probably bilingual.

These Asiatic Celts possessed the peculiarities of their race. They had strong religious feelings, and high conceptions of moral purity, great quickness of apprehension, keen affections, loyal natures. The higher qualities of the Galatian race are illustrated by the story of Chiomara, with whom Polybius had conversed. She had been taken captive by a Roman, and had been made to endure the last insult by her captor. She was ransomed, but contrived, like Judith, to bring back to her husband the head of her ravisher, in proof of her conjugal fidelity and courage, of her unpolluted and heroic chastity.

But, as these Galatians readily gave in to one set of religious impressions, so they as readily permitted their first impressions to be supplanted by others. They accepted the Apostle's teaching with warmth, as he preached to them during his intervals of sickness. And now, with the fickleness of tender and religious natures, they were terrified by the denunciations of these teachers of the narrow school, and were almost disposed to submit themselves to the despotism of the Law. They had given way in some points, had already consented to observe the ceremonial seasons of the Jewish calendar, were on the brink of sacrificing themselves irrevocably to the claims of the Jewish covenant.

To this emergency the Apostle addresses himself without hesitation. It is the occasion for a supreme effort. Unless he succeeds in crushing this apostasy, his mission is annihilated, his labors are vain, his gospel is repudiated. So he wrote to the Galatians a letter which has had a more powerful effect on the religious history of mankind than any other composition which was ever penned, any other words which were ever spoken. It severed, conclusively, though not at once, Christianity from Judaism; it declared the old revelation imperfect and transitory. It even pointed to a covenant older than that of Moses, older than any rite by which God had distinguished the objects of His promise. This manifesto was a final and deliberate schism, an act as defiant as the Confession of Augsburg, and vastly more complete. At this distance of time, when the din of the first theological fight has long since been hushed, it is not easy to estimate the extraordinary boldness of this sally. Though written to the Galatians, it was probably published and disseminated with great rapidity through the various Christian communities. St. Peter, or whoever else was the author of the second epistle which goes under his name, might well say that there were things hard to be understood in his fellow-apostle's writings. The hardest thing of all, however, was to find an answer to the question which was put over and over again by the contemporaries of the Apostle,—How can a man who is a Jew, who is trained in the Law, who has profited much, as he says, in the religion of his fathers, utterly reject the authority of Moses, repudiate the code in which every Israelite glories, believe in Jesus, live for Him and be ready to suffer and die for Him, and escape from the fatal doctrine that a new religion can supersede or render superfluous the foundation on which that religion is built? It is probable that the persons alluded to in the last chapter of the Epistle to the Romans were carrying on, in the church which Paul had not, indeed, founded, but which apparently owed its origin to Aquila, the same interested hostility to that liberal teaching which characterized the Pauline gospel. The "Romans" must have contained a strong Jewish element, else it is unintelligible that the Apostle should have, in this particular epistle, argued so copiously from the Old Testament Scriptures,— more than half his quotations being found in this single letter. But, it is also plain, from the recital of heathen practice and from the reflections made on heathen morals, that the Church of Rome contained, at the date of this epistle, a strong admixture of Gentile converts; and, it is further plain, that the opinion boldly avowed in the Epistle to the Galatians, to the effect that Mosaism is superseded by Christianity, is strongly before the writer of the letter to the Romans.

"I give you my advice," he says, "to take note of these men who are making divisions and stumbling-blocks, in contravention of the instruction in which you have been trained. Keep out of their way. Those people are no servants to our Lord Jesus Christ, but to their own belly, and it is by their fair speeches and plausibility that they deceive the hearts of the unsuspicious." The teachers of a narrow theology were fomenting differences under the pretext of a spurious uniformity.

It is almost unnecessary to say that the Pauline Ethics are as stern and strict as those of any moral system which has ever been promulgated. The liberty on which he insisted was no cover, no apology, no defence for license, for those wild and profligate excesses which the fanatic's faith has sometimes permitted. The extravagances of the Adamites, of the Cathari, of the Anabaptists, have been quoted as a reproach on the genius of Christianity. In reality they are homage to it. The claim of Christianity on the allegiance of men has been so strong, that they who have repudiated its spirit have affected to call themselves by its name. The Israelites often fell into that idolatry which the Law denounced, chastised, condemned. But there is no reason to think that they forgot their nationality in their offence.

The victory which Paul foreshadowed was not achieved in his life-time. In the latest of his epistles, — if the second to Timothy is from his hand, and no sufficient objection has, it would seem, been alleged against its authenticity, — his mind is still full of Antioch, Iconium, Lystra, and of the perils which he endured in these places. All those who were in Asia were alienated from him, even the converts whom he had made, for whom he had labored, for whose sake he was in prison at Rome. Knaves and charlatans, as he asserts, — the grievous wolves whose mischievous activity he predicted so sadly at Miletus, — were doing their worst on the Christian flock, urging them to quit that liberty to which he had called them, and to adopt those ascetic fancies which would again bind them to Jewish practices.

It has been suggested that the epistles ascribed to

James and Jude are attacks on the Pauline theology; that in the Apocalypse the allusions to the Nicolaitanes, in the message to the churches of Ephesus and Pergamos; the condemnation of those who say they are Jews and are not, in the churches of Ephesus and Philadelphia, and who are branded with the name of the synagogue of Satan, — are reproaches cast on the followers of the Apostle of the Gentiles. The same criticism discovers in the prophetess whom the writer calls Jezebel, and who is expressly said to have seduced Christians to idolatry, and induced them to eat things offered to idols, one of those female teachers who, like Lydia, Priscilla and many others, accepted and furthered the gospel of the Apostle. They who cannot or will not accept this interpretation may yet discern in these vehement denunciations that the writer of the Apocalypse detected laxity of life and doctrine in churches whose characteristic practices had become a monstrous caricature of the freedom which Paul claimed for his converts.

Thus much at least is plain. The influence of the ascetic party was so strong, that although the destruction of Jerusalem loosened the grasp of Judaism on the Church, the tenets of the Egyptian Therapeutæ, and of the Syrian Essenes, offshoots of Judaism, — or more probably of that Buddhism which, as we learn from the Mahawanso, and the inscriptions which Cunningham has interpreted, was preached extensively in Western Asia, and Northern Africa, in the third century before Christ, — encouraged that gloomy austerity which was so characteristic of early Christianity, especially in its Southern and Eastern home. Of this temper Justin Martyr and Tertullian are types. It was in the western world that the genius of Paul was acknowledged and his gospel was adopted, for the western Church detected the polemical value of the Pauline writings when it began its struggle with the Gnostics.

There is an epistle addressed, it is said, to the Hebrews, which popularly goes under the name of Paul. No one, however, who is possessed of the critical faculty in its most rudimentary degree, can fail to recognize that the writing is none of his. The style of this pastoral is that of grave, easy argumentation, and differs totally from the abrupt, involved, and hyperbolic manner which characterizes the Pauline compositions. The language used is almost another dialect from that which the Apostle employed. The matter is an ingenious analogy between the ceremonial of the Jewish law, and the office of Christ as the Great Sacrifice. It might have been written by an Alexandrian Jew, who allegorized in a Christian spirit; by a converted Philo. The weight of tradition assigns its authorship to Apollos. Even in an early and uncritical age, it was seen that it did not proceed from Paul.

The epistle was probably written after the Apostle's death. The writer informs his readers that Timothy is set at liberty, and that they purpose in a short time to visit those to whom the letter was addressed. No name but that of Timothy is found in the letter. The salutation from those of Italy seems to indicate that it was written from some town in that part of the Roman empire. But the writer gives no clew to his personality. It is likely that Timothy had obeyed the summons of Paul, and had shared his imprisonment, but that he had been liberated during the period which followed on the death of Nero, an occurrence which took place about a month after the reputed date of the Apostle's martyrdom. It may be added that the epistle contains fuller indications of a system of church government than any of the Pauline letters do, the teachers being twice bidden in the last chapter to remember and obey those who have the rule over them, an expression which easily squares with the government of the Church at Jerusalem, and of those which were founded on its model. But again, it would seem to be written before the investment and capture of Jerusalem, for it can hardly be conceived that any letter would be composed during that crisis of the nation's agony, and be wholly silent on so terrible a subject.

No better defence could be found for the Jewish ordinal than the successful proof that it was a symbolical and prophetic ceremonial; and with those who held that the substance was given at last in Christ, no better method could be found for concluding that the necessity of the shadow was past. The excuse for a ritual consists in the position that the ceremony or rite presents a distant fact, or a transcendental force under the economy of some visible or sensible sign. Before the mind of the writer of the Epistle to the Hebrews, the priesthood and the sacrifice, the censer and the ark, the cherubim and the sanctuary, were the parts of a grand historical procession, the continuity of which was intended to be a perpetual reminder of some final consummation in which these appointed symbols and shadows would be fulfilled and absorbed. Far away in the dim antiquity, was remembered the majestic figure of the king of Salem, to whom Abraham, the father of the faithful, the conqueror of the four kings of Canaan, did homage and gave tithes, the king of peace, the king of righteousness, who, in those primeval times, united the functions of priest and monarch. This great memory was powerfully impressed on the mind of the Psalmist, who contemplates an eternal priesthood after the similitude of Melchisedek, the mysterious hierarch of whom no father or mother is recorded, no genealogy given, who appears in the midst of an idolatrous and licentious people, and disappears after he has blessed the great patriarch. Who can this be, implies the writer of the Epistle to the Hebrews, unless some heavenly visitant, like them who conversed with Abraham at the door of the tent of Mamre, him who wrestled with Israel, and whose name was sacred, him who appeared with a drawn sword by the wall of Jericho as captain of the Lord's host; who, in short, but the eternal Son of God? Here is the perfect, the perpetual priest, who has not only entered into the holiest place before the vision of God, but has invited those who believe on Him to behold the same glory.

And then, to show that an unchanging purpose shapes the counsel of God throughout, the writer of this epistle enumerates the victories of faith under the older covenants, from the days of Abel to that army of witnesses whose exploits and endurance are told in so fervid a strain of passionate eloquence, as the memory of those ancient heroes passed before the mind of the enraptured allegorist. Nothing is more consummate than the art of this passage; for, while it keeps present the fact that the coming of Christ is the abrogation of the imperfect symbol, it consoles the Jewish believer with the glories of his race, and suggests greater triumphs, under the reign of the King and Priest whose throne endures for ever in heaven.

The law of Christ and the law of Moses are one, only the former is more exact and absorbing than the latter. To do despite to the former is a capital offence; to scorn the latter, and its great sanctions, is to invite an angrier judgment — a speedier wrath. To apostatize from this more perfect law, is to repudiate the place of repentance — to sin like Esau — to fall into the hands of the living God — to draw back unto perdition — to provoke a consuming fire. But to them that believe, Sinai has lost its terrors; and in place of the mountain from which the law proceeded, there is the pleasant prospect of the divine Zion — the city of God — the Jerusalem of heaven, as the prophet Ezekiel foresaw it in vision — the Sabaoth of angels — the Church of the eternal First-born, of the Divine Judge, of the perfected spirits of the just.

# CHAPTER III.

AS races have come to nought, have been ruined or destroyed, — as regions, which were once the gardens of the earth, have become deserts, — so theologies have become extinct. Three of the most notable among these forms, whose antiquity is extremely remote, and which existed when Christianity began its career, still survive. These are the creed of the Jews, that of Brahmanism, and that of Buddhism. The last, which is, nominally at least, the most widely embraced of all faiths, is said to be nearly six centuries older than our era.

Again, some religious systems have utterly perished. No trace survives of the theosophy and ceremonial of Greece, Rome, Egypt, Phœnicia. Zeus, Jupiter, Apollo, Phœbus, Athene, Minerva, — the myriad divinities of the Greek and Roman Olympus, — are as extinct as the most remote geological fauna. So with Isis and Osiris, Anubis and Thoth, and the infinite series of Egyptian gods. The Theogony of Phœnicia, — Dagon, Ashtaroth, Baal, have become mere names, the memorials of which have perished with them.

Some have survived, but are wasted into extreme feebleness. The ancient religion of Zoroaster is said to exist in the Parsee colony of Bombay, among the scanty and expatriated relics of a race which was formerly great and victorious. The Druses and Yesidis are the representatives of some ancient Gnostic religion, once probably as wide-spread as any of the Eastern beliefs. The few Israelite sectaries who still linger at Nablous are the remains of that Samaritan schism which began with the revolt of Jeroboam, was embittered by the rivalry of Tobiah and Sanballat on the one hand, Nehemiah and Ezra on the other, and which was strong enough in the time of Christ to be intensely detested by the Jewish national party. But all these religions are crumbling away, and perhaps in a few generations each will become historical.

It has been stated more than once in these pages that the Christian religion was nearly absorbed by Judaism at the beginning of its career, and that on grounds of human probability it was about to become an obscure Jewish sect, when it was rescued by the vigor and independence of the great missionary-apostle. Paul saved it from this catastrophe, by the peremptory manner in which he insisted on the abrogation of the Jewish code, as far as Gentile converts were concerned; and Paul was ultimately successful in the bold course which he adopted. But the effort was a supreme struggle. It cost the Apostle a life-long martyrdom, and for a time discredited his labors and his success. The attempt to supersede the Jewish ritual excited the warmest hostility. The success of the attempt thrust the Church into a new danger. Paul saved it from being stifled. He lived, it appears, to see it exposed to the attacks of a more ubiquitous and more versatile enemy. In the East, at least, it was nearly supplanted by Gnosticism. It was threatened and even imperilled by the equivalent of Gnosticism in the West.

For a century and a half the Church struggled for existence against the numerous and frequently hostile sectaries who were known under the general name of Gnostics, and who, as will be seen, held certain tenets in common. By far the largest part of that controversial theology which has descended from the earliest Christian times to our own is occupied with the statement and refutation of these Gnostic reveries. The existence of such opinions is alluded to by Justin Martyr. The work of Irenæus consists almost entirely of statements purporting to give an account of the tenets entertained by the various heresiarchs of the Gnostic theogonies. The lately discovered work of Hippolytus, bishop of Ostia, is, for the most part, a treatise on Gnostic opinions. The greater part of Tertullian's works are controversial, and deal with the same tenets. During the days when Christianity was in its infancy, men did not construct creeds, or elaborate definitions on the nature of Christ, and on the work of redemption; but either accepted the simple faith of the apostolic teaching, or exhibited a prodigious theogony, which they collected from all sources, and arranged into the most fantastic systems. Never did the religious imagination run wilder riot. At the same time, it is not impossible to trace those theories to a few simple principles. These principles were recognized in and before the age of St. Paul.

In eastern Iran, and in that part of it which the ancients knew as Bactria, there lived, at a time which it is now impossible to fix with any degree of certainty, a certain Zoroaster. Some facts about the life of this personage, and an exposition of the doctrine which he taught, are contained in the Zendavesta — a scripture written in an ancient Aryan dialect. Zoroaster is the reputed founder of the Magian religion. The characteristic of this creed is dualism — *i. e.*, the existence of two powers, principles, beings, of co-ordinate and nearly equal authority — one of whom is Good, the other Evil; one the author of every blessing which lightens the lot of humanity, the other of all and every misery which depresses and degrades it. These two powers are in constant rivalry; and although the beneficent spirit will and must finally vanquish his enemy, and the enemy of the human race, the struggle is long, arduous, and as yet far from its completion. The name of the Good Being is Ormuzd, that of the evil Ahriman. Lately deciphered inscriptions prove that the system of Zoroaster was the state religion of the Persian people. To Darius, for example, Ormuzd is the author of all prosperity, victory, blessing, and is reverenced accordingly. Both Ormuzd and Ahriman were emanations from Primeval Light. But Ormuzd was the elder, and Ahriman was ambitious, proud, and jealous of the first-born. These faults are an impersonation of the vices and the vindictiveness of those who, in an Eastern dynasty, are near of kin to the ruler, but are subjects to him, and are thereupon suspicious and suspected. Such persons were Smerdis to Cambyses, Cyrus the younger to Artaxerxes.

The principles of the Zoroastrian or Magian religion are to be found in the Scriptures of the Parsees, who are reputed to be the surviving worshippers of the ancient Persian Deity. If we can trust slight hints given in those relics of a faith which was once accepted by the highest civilization of Central Asia, the oldest parts of the Zendavesta point to the existence of pastoral habits among the people to whom Zoroaster was the prophet. The greater part of the Zend scriptures treat of ceremonial defilement and purification, and are even more minute in the rules which they lay down for the atonement of voluntary and involuntary offences than the Mosaic ritual is. It is possible, however, that many of these regulations have been interpolated. That the religion suffered by the conquest of Alexander cannot be doubted. It is said to have declined during the Parthian occupation of Iran, and to have been restored by Ardshir in the third century of our era. This monarch, the first king of the Sassanid dynasty, did for the Scriptures of the Zoroastrians what Peisistratus did for the Homeric poems: he collected them from the memories of those who treasured them into the volume which we know by the name of the Zendavesta. When the Persian empire was overrun by the followers of Mohammed in the seventh century, a few of the adherents of Parsism escaped to India, and obtained permission, under certain conditions, to settle near the mouth of the Indus.

The creed of the Persians was that of a dual monarchy. But the good king was surrounded by a hierarchy of powers whom he had created. Chief among these were six amshaspands, then twenty-eight other powers, one of whom was Mithra, and then an infinite order of pure spirits, all of whom were superior to man. On the other hand, Ahriman, the evil power, created an infinite number of dewas, who are presided over by six evil dynasts. Ormuzd is the creator of the world — a work which he effected in six periods of time. In this new world, Ormuzd placed a man and woman, who are corrupted by the wiles of Ahriman. But, when the earth is most depraved and afflicted, Ormuzd will send his prophets, the chief of whom will regenerate creation and bring it back to its pristine beauty, power and purity. Thereafter will ensue a universal resurrection, and the chief prophet will judge both good and bad. Then those who are found pure will live in eternal felicity. And, on the other hand, Ahriman, his demons, and the wicked will be also purified, but by a torrent of molten metal. In the end, the reign of Ormuzd will commence its uninterrupted course, humanity will be perpetually happy, and all will be engaged in singing the praises of the Supreme Being, the Ancient of Days, the King of Light.

In this life, man is always exposed to the machinations of the dewas and their chief. They who fall into sin become the habitations of evil spirits, and are finally transformed so as to be identical with the demons with whom they have consorted. But the door is never closed to repentance and faith, however great has been the sin, even though its ceremonial lustration is impossible. Furthermore, to know the names of Ormuzd is a power, a talisman, with which to chase away demons, and coerce the wicked. These names, which were revealed to Zoroaster, and are contained in the Zendavesta, are twenty in number, and designate the attributes of the Supreme Being. The name Ormuzd — in the Zend, Ahura-mazda — means the great wise God. His rival's name is Anramainyus, or, as it has been corrupted by Europeans, Ahriman.

One cannot fail to see a close parallel between this Zoroastrian system and the theosophy of the Jews. The angel of God appears frequently in the earlier books of the Jewish canon, though there is hardly any such agency in the Mosaic epoch. But the operation of an evil spirit is scantily hinted at. We first read of such a personage in the story of Saul's madness. We read of him again, in the apologue of Micaiah, when this prophet stood before the misguided Ahab. We read of Satan in the book of Job, the scene of which is not Jewish, but Arabian.

This name Satan — that is, an adversary or an enemy — is used in Hebrew with the article when it denotes the superhuman adversary of man. So Zechariah, one of the later prophets, uses it, after the return from Babylon, and therefore when the conception of a spiritual foe had become familiar to the Jewish exiles. But elsewhere throughout the Old Testament, the evil spirit is only a subordinate instrument of Jehovah, a power whom God permits to deceive the reprobate, to torment the sinner, and to try the good.

In the New Testament, however, but particularly in the Apocalypse, this personage is recognized as an active malevolent being, who seeks to thwart the designs of the Almighty, and to pervert the souls of men. He is permitted to tempt Christ, and his satellites torment the bodies and distract the minds of those whom they inhabit. He is the prince of this world, the power of the air, the father of the disobedient and unfaithful, the enemy of the saints, one who disguises himself as an angel of light, the hinderer of holy purposes, the prompter of impure and unholy thoughts, the devourer, the destroyer, and, hereafter, the inhabitant, with his angels, of everlasting fire. In the Apocalypse he is the leader of a rebel host, who fights against Michael and the angels of God, the dragon, the serpent, the prisoner for a thousand years, who is afterwards set free to harass and vex the faithful, but who will finally be judged and punished. Out of his mouth came those lying prophets who have power to deceive men. He has a mystic name, which is designated by a certain number, and is probably made up of the numerical values of the letters composing it, as those names, Abraxas, Mithras, and Belinus were; the symbolic genii of Gnostic, Persian, and Druidical worship.

The Rabbinical books of the Jews and the writings

of Philo are full of the same facts, for they refer to a hierarchy of angels, evil and good — to the beneficent action of the one, to the malevolence of the other. The Pharisees, we are told, acknowledged angels and spirits, the Sadducees denied the existence of each order. Thus the Gemara even said that the temptation of Abraham was a deed of Satan, the rescue of Isaac an interposition of Jehovah, and a baffling of the enemy. In the romance called the book of Tobit, the machinery of the story is the mission of an angel, who should accompany Tobias on his journey, should defend him and his wife from the machinations of Asmodeus, who had previously slain those husbands to whom Sarah had been wedded, and should bind the evil spirit in the utmost parts of Egypt.

No one can ignore the fact that the Old Testament recognizes, and that its teaching is based on, the perpetual antagonism of good and evil — of the struggles and ultimate victory of the former, of the power and final punishment of the latter. But, while it exhibits infinite goodness under the form of a heavenly Father, it does not impersonate the opposite principle except slightly and imperfectly. Nor, unless we repudiate every rule which would guide us on any other subject when we are discussing the affinities of an opinion or belief, can we doubt that this impersonation of the evil principle in a chief of wicked spirits and in his subordinates, was derived from, or suggested by, the Zoroastrian theology. The Jews had been carried captive into Assyria and Persia, and had been brought in contact with this religion when it was in its full vigor. Daniel, a descendant of the royal house of David, was the chief of the Magi, receiving a name — prince of Bel — by virtue of his eminent position in the priesthood of the Zoroastrian system; while another Jew, a companion of his, was called the servant of Nebo. It was possible for those Jews to retain their worship of the one true God in the midst of Aryan theism, for the Persians were not idolaters. It was possible for a Jewish prophet to recognize a Shepherd in Cyrus, and even to call him the Lord's anointed. But it is impossible to doubt that the Jews who lived in Persia borrowed and transmitted to the returning exiles of Zerubbabel, Nehemiah, and Ezra, some of the dualism with which they were made familiar at Susa and at Babylon. Even when Parsism was depressed by the Parthian dynasty, the Chaldean was known at Rome, and the Babylonian Numbers were consulted by noble ladies at the metropolis of the empire.

When a new religion, however pure and powerful it may be, supplants another, it can hardly help making some compromise with its vanquished enemy. It is no disgrace to Western Christianity, that it conciliated the Paganism which it overthrew, by accommodating its feasts to the cherished memory of ancient rites. Thus we are told, that the Christmas festival was fixed at the winter solstice, because this period was occupied in the Roman calendar by the Saturnalia — a holiday time in which the rigor of slavery was relaxed, and the bondsman was permitted a short liberty. Nor can any one object that the episcopate was founded on the model of those fiscal and military divisions which the empire defined. Church government was found to be a necessity, and men adopted familiar forms for carrying out what was to be done. This kind of compromise accounts for the fetish worship which the Roman church has revived and inculcated in the reverence paid to relics, and for the rationalism which has given the peasantry its local saints, instead of Nymphs and Dryads; which has made the mother of Christ a Juno; and, like her pagan prototype, which has multiplied her by the shrines in which she is worshipped. Not even the stern monotheism of the Mosaic code could extirpate from the Israelite mind all sympathy with the worship of the Hittite. The high places remained; the returning ark, welcomed by the Israelites, found them gathered at Beth-shemesh, the house or temple of the sun; and the house of Jacob constantly associated itself with the gods of the nations round about.

The influence, however, of a religion which guides the life and practice of a great and generous nation, such as the ancient Persians undoubtedly were, cannot fail of being felt in a still greater degree by subject races. Besides, the Zoroastrian creed was not repugnant to the mind of the captive Israelite. The companions of Daniel refuse to honor an image; the chief of the Magians, the eunuch of David's race, declines, on peril of his life, to obey the insidious suggestion of the courtiers of Darius, and still prays to his God, with his windows open in the direction of Jerusalem, three times a day. But the hierarchy of Zoroaster — in which angels were subordinated to the one great Deity — was no way alien to Daniel's orthodoxy. Nothing pleases the imagination more than to people the vast expanse with ministering spirits, to ascribe the sorrows and sufferings of life to the spite of malignant demons. It is the familiar habit of children to conjure up thick coming fancies; and at this epoch — the childhood of civilization and belief — the same energy of imagination delighted in the exuberant growth of these divine and pure emanations, and constructed, as antagonists to them, a host of gloomy and passionate spirits, who strove to drag men down to their own likeness, but who could be resisted, baffled, judged by the wise and pure in heart. To one wrapt in the contemplation of this war in heaven, of which man was the prize, and of which the victory was finally assured, there was no solitude. The lonely hermit was least alone. To one who had in view the pomp and majesty of eastern royalty, there was a far nobler and grander array in the glorious host of heaven, in that angelic band, the power of the lowest of whom was greater than that of the mightiest king, for they are the servants of the Lord of Hosts. The counterpart to this regal splendor is the pomp of faded majesty, the royalty of hell. Just as to the eastern mind, a good and wise king, such as Cyrus, — the father of Persian nationality, who had for his attendants an immortal body guard, — was the highest exemplar of human excellence and beneficence; just as a furious, mad, suspicious tyrant, such as Cambyses, was the impersonation of malevolence and mischief — so the unseen world had its King and His heavenly host, and also its regal fiend, with his attendant demons. The Israelite eagerly engrafted the two systems on his national creed, and, already made familiar with the angels of God, discovered their antagonists in the gods of the heathen, in the devils of the Pauline epistles, in the evil spirits who possessed those unhappy men who fell under their sway. The same dualism has been transmitted to our times, and has become part of the system of popular religion. It is so strongly intertwined with the innermost sentiments of the human heart, that the imagination itself must be extinguished before dualism ceases to be acknowledged.

The creed of the East was a supernaturalism, with an exact ceremonial, typical of personal holiness, and a strict discipline which imposed penances or punishments on those who violated its moral precepts. The creed of the West was the worship of nature, without any permanent ceremonial, and with no higher moral code than was absolutely necessary in order to preserve society from dissolution. The supreme ruler of the Zoroastrian world is a pure spirit to whom sin is loathsome. The ruler of the Greek Olympus is the president of an aristocratical council, a capricious, sensual chieftain, whose providence over human affairs is of the slightest and most uncertain kind. With a strange perversity, men — misled by the dazzling splendor of Greek genius — have tried to discover in the theogony of the Greek creed, and in the social life of which it is the highest exemplar, a lofty and simple morality. They have mistaken poetry for religion. The civilization of Greece, and subsequently that of Rome, were extirpated, because neither was based on religion or morality.

The border-land between the East and the West was occupied by the Jews. It appears that nature worship was nowhere more sensuous than among the Phœnicians of the coast. The God of the Hebrews is absolutely spiritual, absolutely holy, and, as the conception of Him is developed in the prophets, is a Being of perfect justice, who prescribes and enacts obedience to a Law, which is to be interpreted by an intelligent and scrupulous conscience. The creed of the Jew is a single sentence, — I am the Lord your God. Upon this creed the Pharisee induced the dualism of the remote East, while the Sadducee insisted on retaining nothing but the secularism of the Mosaic revelation, in which the immortality of man's soul might be contained by implication, to which it certainly was not repugnant, but by which it was not expressly affirmed. The Sadducee, however, was as monotheistic as the Pharisee, believed as rigorously that the Almighty was a pure Spirit.

The teaching of Christianity was welcome to the religious sense of the western world. Its acceptance enabled the believer to escape from the immeasurable grossness of nature-worship, to take refuge in a pure theology, to apprehend that for which every creation groans and struggles. In those days of conversion, men fulfilled the prophecy of Isaiah, and cast their abominations of silver and gold, which they had made to worship, to the moles and to the bats, to the darkness of that night from which they had emerged. To them Christianity was emphatically a new creation. Old things had passed away, all things had become new. It was an escape from bondage to freedom, to a glorious liberty, and was welcomed with all the freshness of a first enthusiasm.

The case, however, was different with the eastern people. They had already a religious creed, which taught that God was a Spirit, and that they who worship Him must do so in spirit and in truth. They were monotheists, iconoclasts, haters of symbolism, and of nature-worship. They had lived for ages under traditionary customs which no one was prepared to loathe, under rites which had been sanctioned by the same authority which had given them their purer creed. Hence, as has often been said, the Jewish Christians clung tenaciously to the traditions of their forefathers, and nearly wrecked the prospects of Gentile Christianity, by peremptorily insisting on obedience to the Law of Moses. Even when some liberty was given, they insinuated that those who claimed release from Jewish rites were enemies to the spirit of Christianity, and the secret advocates of a compromise with idol-worship and licentiousness. As with other Eastern converts, there was an unwillingness to abandon those gorgeous visions with which the unseen world was peopled, and to accept those simple practical principles by which the Christian life was to be guided. In the West the Magian was an adventurer; in the East he worshipped at the foot of the infant Jesus, was the hierophant of transcendental revelations, the mystic, the gnostic, the man possessed of knowledge, the knowledge which inflated a man with a sense of self-importance, the knowledge which the author of the epistle to Timothy designates as falsely named.

This Gnosticism was born at a time when the human mind was more eager after belief, and more ready to construct systems, than at any epoch in its history. It offered the most energetic and the richest visions to the believer, and it is not marvellous that it had many teachers and a vast following of disciples. It extended itself widely through the eastern world, and affected not a little of the western. Its symbols are still existent in great numbers in the form of gems, engraved with composite emblems and legends. It was a formidable rival of orthodox Christianity up to the sixth century, and unquestionably leavened it with many of its speculative formularies. It did not expire in Europe till just before the Reformation, if indeed its influence may not be traced still later. It constitutes the occult science of Cornelius Agrippa. The description which Mr. Layard gives of the tenets entertained by the Yezidis clearly indicates that the religion of these devotees can be traced to a Gnostic origin. The Gnostics were, in their own language, according to Gesenius, the Elect, and a sect which calls itself elect is apt to have a long vitality.

The fundamental characteristics of Gnosticism are its dualism, its doctrine of emanations, its assertion that the God of the Jews, the God of the visible creation, was an inferior, if not an evil spirit. The schools of Gnosticism differed in many particulars, but they invariably affirmed the three doctrines stated above. A supreme intelligence exists, an eternal, immutable ineffable being, against whose purity and power evil is arrayed, and from whom proceed the various forces by which evil is combated. And as these visionaries thought matter was evil,— a doctrine which may be traced in the philosophy of Greece, — they believed that the creator of the visible world was either unconscious of the mischief which his creation would work on the intelligence which it coerced or restrained, or that he spitefully weighted the pure spirit of man with the gross and polluting burden of matter. Hints of this theosophy are found in the Septuagint, in Philo, in the Kabbala, in the significant words of the first, in the allegorizing theory of the Law, which marks the second, and in the emanations of Adam Cadmon, the typical or perfect man, the macrocosm to whom the individual is the microcosm, of the third. Ten of these emanations, according to the Kabbala, proceeded from the perfect Adam. The same authority, according to M. Matter, affirms that the parts of man's nature, his appetites, his passions, his reason and his spirit, proceed from the four worlds of angels which influence and control him. This fourfold division of man's inner nature is characteristic of Greek philosophy.

Abundant illustrations could be given of the manner in which Gnostic phraseology pervades those writings of the Canon, which are expressly directed against the doctrine which those dreamers inculcated, most of all from the Apocalypse. Here the seven spirits, the twenty-four elders, the Alpha and Omega, the mystic number of the Beast, are all counterparts of that theory of emanations which began with Cerinthus, and was completed by Valentinus and Marcion. But the use of certain Greek words is even more suggestive of the manner in which the language of the apostles was permeated by the phraseology of this wide-spread and versatile school. The reader may find examples of these usages in the elaborate work of M. Matter. The Shepherd of Hermas, once believed to be a canonical book, is framed on a Gnostic model, with its seven women representing the Virtues who wait about the Church. The writers of the New Testament do not, it is true, accept the theory which these words imply, — nay, they are impliedly, or, in express terms, profoundly hostile to the Gnostic hypothesis, — but they could not, in the existing state of theological language, avoid the employment of terms which the speculative temper of the Eastern mind had appropriated and characterized. These words might have been perverted by the wild imagination of the sectaries, but they had the advantage of being definite, and what philosophy has ever disdained to spoil its rivals of their armor?

The narrative of an interview between St. Peter and Simon is contained in the Acts of the Apostles. The latter is described as resident in Samaria, though he was, according to Justin, a native of Gitti, a village near. This man, by his magical arts, had deceived the people of Samaria, who called him the great power of God — which is, by the way, a Gnostic formula. We are further told that Simon enrolled himself among the converts of Philip, and that the apostles came down to Samaria to receive the converts, and, by imposition of hands, to bestow on them the Holy Spirit. Thereupon Simon offered the apostles money, with the request that he might receive the apostolic privilege of conferring this gift of the Spirit. He is sternly rebuked by Peter, who bids him repent and ask for forgiveness; and the narrative, as far as Simon is concerned, is concluded by a request on Simon's part, that the apostles would pray for him, that no misfortune should come on him for his presumption. Henceforth, the Scriptures make no mention of the Samaritan. Another Magian confronts St. Paul in Paphos, is more severely reprimanded, and is visited with a sharper judgment.

The rest of Simon's history is enveloped in a cloud of fable. Justin Martyr says, that he persuaded the Emperor Claudius and the senate to erect a statute to him on the Tiberine Island, the apologist having mistaken a dedication to a Sabine deity for an inscription in honor of the Samaritan. But Simon figures in a host of legends. He is present at the interview between Peter and Paul on the one hand, and Nero on the other, and is represented as perishing in an attempt to fly. He raised himself in the air by the aid of evil spirits, and fell in consequence of the prayer of Peter. In the Clementines, Peter and Simon are represented as arguing together. But, in the whole literature of the early Church, the Samaritan Magian is made the founder of a system which claims to be antagonistic to Christianity. He is not properly an heresiarch, but a rival to Christ, as Apollonius of Tyana was, after the adventures of the Tarsian devotee had been manipulated by his biographer Philostratus.

Simon, according to Irenæus, claimed to be the voice of God. The supreme Being was "He who is fixed," "the root of all things." From this Being emanate three pairs of derived beings, one of which is the mother of all that exists, — spirits, angels, and archangels. This personage is Ennoia or Intelligence, who is perpetually persecuted by evil spirits, and is preserved by the Supreme Being, in order to be manifested to mankind by the agency of Simon. The Jewish God was one of the angels of this Intelligence, and was the author of the visible world. Irenæus adds to his account of Simon, that his followers, a century and a half later, had fallen into gross licentiousness, and excused their vices on the ground that there was neither morality or immorality in external acts. It is only by his dualism that Simon is identified with Gnosticism.

The sect really sprang out of Christianity. The earliest Gnostics came from Egypt, and were familiar with the allegories of Philo. With Cerinthus, Christ was the son of Joseph and Mary, and as a man was superior in justice, foresight, wisdom, and therefore power, to all other men. He received the Divine Nature at His baptism in the Jordan, and was thereupon an emanation from the Supreme Being.

Marcion, the most eminent of the Gnostics, was, we are informed, fond of quoting the saying of Christ, "Put not new wine into old bottles." He meant to imply that those Christians who had been familiarized with the grand complications of the Eastern theogony must needs incorporate their profound and magnificent conceptions with the simple creed of the Apostles. The Gnostic was unwilling, on being admitted within the sanctuary of the new covenant, to strip himself of his gorgeous traditions; he must needs enter clothed in them. They are susceptible of a spiritual interpretation. They are revelations anterior to this last experience of the Divine development, but they can be made to harmonize with Christianity. Some of those persons allegorized the mythology of Greece, and discovered Æons in the Olympian deities, allowing their imagination to run riot in the strangest theories as to the meaning of Greek myths, and the origin of Gentile practices. Some of these interpretations are as grotesque as the latest allegory of the Homeric poems, under which the heroes of the Iliad are impersonations of the Sun and Moon and Stars, of Nature, of Night and Day, of the Seasons and the Winds.

Let us take the scheme of Saturninus. God, says this Gnostic, is one, unknown by all, ineffable, inaccessible. The Gnostic is less exacting than some writers, who have told us that the attributes of the Almighty are utterly unknown to man, and that the divine morality conforms to no human standard or experience. He allows that all beings, with their attributes, proceed from Him by way of emanation.

The highest power of God is His Wisdom or Word. This is the first-born Son of God, the ideal type by which the most perfect of all creatures, man, is created and formed. But the creation of man was committed to an inferior power — the Jewish God. He had received a mission to make man in the image of God, but in error he did not realize the Divine type, the heavenly Adam. Man was created a creeping thing. The Word, as pitying his unhappy condition, bestowed on him a ray of Divine life. But so feeble was the work of the inferior God, that the breath of the Word, by which humanity was enlightened, became powerless to effect his restoration to the Divine image. Christ therefore came down from heaven to put an end to the office of the Jewish God, and to save those who believe in Him — those, namely, who have preserved that ray of Divine light which was given to the first man, and transmitted to his descendants. The moment they have lost the ray of Divine light (and they lose it by the overmastering influence of evil spirits), the way of return to God is irrevocably closed. This heresiarch forbade his followers to contract marriage and beget children.

Bardesanes, one of these Gnostics, the chief of another sect, who wrote against Marcion, was the author of the first Christian hymnal. We are told that he composed a hundred-and-fifty sacred songs, which were set to music by his son, and were used by the orthodox, to their danger and detriment, till Ephrem the Syrian superseded them by other words, the tunes being retained, just as the English pietists of the last century adapted religious words to secular music. Nor is there much doubt that the ascetic Montanus, who won over the arrogant and fervid spirit of Tertullian, gathered his strange notions of the Comforter from the example, if not from the teaching of the Gnostic sects, who represented every form of mysticism, from antinomian grossness to ecstatic and morbid rigor.

We know these grotesque doctrines only through those who detested them, stigmatized them, and perhaps caricatured them. It is to be regretted that no single work has come down to us from those who taught what they called knowledge. Had such been our fortune, we might perhaps have been able to construct the system of these Syrian and Alexandrian mystics, and, however alien the scheme might prove to our habits of thought, have discerned that Valentinus, Basileides, Bardesanes, Saturninus, had at least as well ordered an imagination, as noble a conception of God, as rational a hagiology as those of many men who have challenged and obtained the reputation of orthodoxy.

This, however, at least is clear. The Gnostic idea of God was pure and even sublime. But the conception which assigns the work of the visible world to a malignant deity, because the Gnostic cherished an insane hatred of matter; the savage temper which discerns nothing in creation but misery, disorder and vice, and which shows its contempt for the body by fierce austerity, — or gross licentiousness, are grotesque misconceptions of that Providence which these enthusiasts allowed. Worse still was that sullen pride which limited the office of the Redeemer to a privileged race, to a few individuals, capriciously chosen, whose grant of this election was certified to them by some inward conviction, and was perfected by an absorbing contemplation; which, without the evidence of personal holiness, or the fulfilment of personal duties, transported them to the bosom of God; which, finally, asserted that the nature of the true Gnostic is like gold, the brightness of which no pollution can dim, no contamination affect. But, though the name of Gnostic, of Catharist, or Paulician, has faded away under the anathema of orthodoxy, it is doubtful whether the spirit has been exorcised. It is still possible for men to narrow Almighty beneficence, to arrogate to themselves redemption, to think that austerity is holiness, that an inward assurance is the Divine favor, to look bitterly on the beauty of God's creation, and see nothing but what is evil in nature, even though they may not people the world with Æons, and make their own system of belief a series of emanations from the Almighty and infallible exposition of His will.

We are told — though it is probable that the statement must be taken with caution — that the Gnostics, and particularly Marcion, accepted a mutilated gospel of St. Matthew, though with some additions, and most of the epistles of St. Paul, the pastoral letters being rejected; but that even those whose authenticity was allowed, were curtailed or interpolated so as to sustain the doctrines which Gnosticism affirmed. It is significant of the extent to which these tenets permeated Christian communities, that the Ebionites and Nazarenes — the bitterest enemies of the great Apostle, the persistent advocates of Jewish Christianity — are stated to have finally embraced the extreme Gnostic doctrine of a particular redemption, and the perfectibility of man by asceticism and contemplation. We are told that they said of the Redeemer, that "He was called the Christ of God and Jesus, because no one before Him had fulfilled the Law; but that if another had done so, he could have been Christ, and that they, by doing the like, would become christs, since He was a man like unto themselves." This wasted sect of Judaizers, who lingered on by the Dead Sea, was still open to the temptation which other sects have fallen into, and which are characterized by St. Paul in one of his pithiest and most prophetic sentences — Knowledge puffeth up, but love buildeth up.

The essence of the Gnostic system, whatever were the formularies with which it introduced its dogmas, was the saving power of knowledge or science. It matters nothing that the material of this knowledge was a long array of subjective or imaginary essences, the "bodiless expansions of a cunning ecstasy." They were, if we can believe that the votaries of this system propounded them all in good faith, as real to the Gnostic as the laws of nature, or the succession of geological epochs, or the development of species are to the physicists of our own day. The Gnostics wished to give an interpretation to a set of facts, or to an array of myths which had been accepted as facts, and believed that they had gained the key to their solution, by marshalling a progressive development of heavenly entities. They believed that by the steady contemplation of these great realities, the soul of man might be educated, ennobled, purified, glorified. The knowledge which they possessed separated them from the vulgar and perishing herd of men, made them the elect of a Divine wisdom, delighted them with the ravishing dream that they were the peculiar objects of the Divine favor, the self-made possessors of a saving science. The spirit of the Gnostic is found, not in what he knew, which a later philosopher declares to be visionary, but in the utter absence of that love of man for the sake of God, which is the practical side of religion, and of that clinging to a Divine ideal of moral excellence, and perfect holiness, which constitutes the contemplative side of the same religion.

There need be no antagonism between the religious sense and scientific method. A clear and keen intelligence, which observes diligently, and draws careful inductions from its observations, is quite compatible with that sensitiveness which stimulates and strengthens the sense of public and private duty, because it lives in the sight of God, and does its part in regenerating and purifying man for God's sake, according to its power. There is not, and there cannot be, any natural discord in the constituent faculties of man's being. All the forces which make up the identity of the individual may be, and ought to be, in harmony; may be made to assist each other in the work which each man has to do. In true and healthy minds such a harmony does exist. Nothing is more graceful, nothing more winning than the union of acute intellectual power, and the tender gentleness of an affectionate desire to do good, because the heart yearns after purifying and elevating the object of such goodness. Nor does experience lack examples of so noble a conjunction of energies.

But, as the religious sense may, unhappily, become harsh and bitter, may be perverted by narrowness, by spiritual pride, by sinister motives; so men may insulate themselves under a feeling of profound satisfaction at their own attainments in knowledge, and of contempt for those who are unequally instructed with themselves. Any kind of learning may suffice to effect this perversion, for the Gnostic professed to possess the highest and truest learning with which his age was supplied, and this on the most important and absorbing subject. The temper of the Gnostic does not cease to influence men, because the sciences of observation have superseded in exactness and interest the constructions of the Gnostic imagination. Any kind of knowledge may serve to inflate its possessor with an over-weening sense of his own acuteness and superiority. It may be the dry theory of the economist, according to which men are conceived to be held together by mutual interest, and individualized by an enlightened selfishness; or the method of nature, the knowledge of which may fill the student with a modish conceit of his own quickness; or learning; or philosophy. It may be impossible to construct a logical religion, and to give proof of the emotions by which man clings to a living God. But the religious sense, if it be just and loving, at least does this much. It binds men more closely together than any other force can; it gives, as long as it reigns in man, cohesion and duration to the unity which it creates; it constructs and purifies society; it makes man reverent towards his fellow-man, pitiful, tender, forgiving, courteous, graceful, gentle. If it dies or is perverted, Society becomes a camp, in which distrust is perpetual and panic is imminent; in which the enemy is at the gate, and the spirit of resistance is gone. So, at least, experience, past and present, informs us. It is possible, that, at the instant of this ruin, Archimedes still sits, poring over his problem, unconscious of the crisis, indifferent in the midst of his speculation to the crash, the havoc, the despair. After the agony is over, the same· sentiment will, unless a people be utterly lifeless, revive and renew the strength which has been wasted, and men will eagerly welcome the force which has hitherto been found to constitute the very soul of human society.

After all, the highest, worthiest, truest of all human knowledge, is that which is directed towards purifying and ennobling man. He who discovers the knowledge of this method, and, having discovered it, seeks to make it the law of social life, is the wisest savant, the truest teacher of mankind. The worth of the knowledge which analyzes a plurality of worlds is not disparaged when it is said that it is of little import by the side of that wisdom, if it can be found, and that understanding, if its place can be detected, which makes man happier, and stronger, and better. The greatest victories of science are little better than a thaumaturgy, if they have no effect on the well-being of society. They may become the instrument of conceit to him who wins them, the instrument of oppression to him who uses them. But, on the other hand, it is impossible for a science of social morality to make true progress, unless the whole race of man is bettered by it. It is impossible that it should influence mankind without making each successive generation stronger and more just. Like every other good force, it may be misused by designing persons, or parodied by charlatans, who mislead men into accepting the husk of a true wisdom, in place of its fruit. Whether Christianity has or has not finally achieved this science of social life, is a larger question than can be discussed here. But it is plain, that Jesus of Nazareth intended to propound such a science, that the Apostle of the Gentiles intended to affirm and expound the science, and that the permanent enemy of Christianity is the theory that the knowledge of God or nature, and the blessings of God or nature, are the heritage and privilege of the few, the elect, the fortunate.

Critics have detected traces of the Gnostic system in the pastoral epistles, and have, thereupon, discredited their authenticity. It is known that Gnosticism ripened in the early part of the second century, and it is inferred that the "falsely-named knowledge" of the First Epistle to Timothy is a reference to the Emanations of these sectaries. But the language of the Apostle is not necessarily directed against those whom we know as Gnostics. It seems rather to point to those Jewish or semi-Jewish sects, which are known to have sprung up in the cities of Asia-Minor, and to have attempted a compromise between the learning of the Rabbis and the tenets of Christianity, or, at least, to have overlaid the latter by the former. The Apostle was reasonably jealous of any addition which might be made to the simple creed which he had taught; for he well knew that nothing deadens the sense of religion so much, as the reduction of it to a set of formal definitions, the acceptance of which might be construed into an equivalent to that energy of faith and love, which his instincts and his experience assured him were the true constituents of the Christian temper.

Besides, though Gnosticism culminated in the second century, it does not follow that it was not existent, and even active, in the first. The earliest Christian controversialists give us the names of the Gnostic savants, but they do not expound to us the origin of the Gnostic temperament. If the exposition given above is satisfactory, Gnosticism, in some shape or other, is not of one age, but of all — is not the title of an extinct theology, but the equivalent of a permanent phase of human thought. That men busied themselves with the origin of evil, and recognized its antagonism to good, in a formal dualism, long before the apostolic age, is historically certain. That they had constructed a cosmogony on this principle is equally clear. That they had, according to the fashion of the time, realized the development of the universe by impersonating creative power in a series of angelic beings, is as plain as proof can make it. But this is only the shell of Gnosticism. Its kernel is the substitution of theology for trust in God, knowledge for religion, contemplation for duty, philosophy for love. The system of the Stoic and Platonist, as critics and rivals of Christianity, was only another phase of the same theory — was equally the substitution of the individual mind for the body of Christ, and the growth of the perfect man — the peace of the absorbed and enlightened intellect for the peace of God — the salvation of the few, by their own power and holiness, for the redemption of the world by the Passion and the Presence of Christ. We ought to be far from wondering that the Apostle detected and inveighed against this tendency. It is rather to be wondered at, that his writings do not contain frequent allusions to the danger in which, from his point of view, men might make shipwreck of their destiny in a vain and engrossing self-sufficiency. The early Church did recognize such a warning in the Apostle's statement, that the natural intellect of man does not receive the influence of God's Spirit.

Nor is there reason to think that the genius of Gnosticism is extinguished or evaporated, or that it ever will fail to assert itself in its own domain — that, namely, of exclusiveness, of spiritual or intellectual pride. It is true that no one now busies himself in constructing a dualistic hierarchy, or fills heaven, and earth, and hell with the fancies of an unrestrained imagination. The steady progress of phenomenal science — the regular method by which it has built up its inductions — the success with which it has interpreted the order of nature — have made men contemptuous towards imaginary systems, and sometimes even sceptical as to the existence of other than sensible forces. The cosmogonies of the Eastern sage, of the Greek philosopher, of the Western schoolman, have given way to the logic of facts, and the laws of nature which they exemplify. Those exploded theories were attempts to interpret the phenomena of Being; and for a time, at least, satisfied and delighted the mind. But they are abandoned only because other attempts have been made to interpret the same phenomena. Ptolemy retreats before Copernicus and Galileo; the scheme of elemental forms, by which Aristotle attempted to interpret nature, has been superseded by the chemical analysis of modern research; the humoral theory of physiology, by which the same philosopher tried to account for growth and decay, for health and disease, has been abandoned for a microscopic investigation into the circumstances of organic generation; creation is the formula of a bygone speculation, of which development has latterly become the scientific equivalent.

The thinkers and reasoners who lived before and after the commencement of our era were constantly busied with the philosophy of Being — with the laws of consciousness and nature — with the conditions of progress and change. To account for all those phenomena of sense and cognition, they invented a world of imaginary existences. Thus, for example, the appetites and passions, the reason and the spirit of man, were derived, according to some of these Mystics, from the four worlds of spirits. The characteristic words of this system are traceable even in the Septuagint — its terms are freely employed in the New Testament.

Childish and trifling as the system which these men constructed seems to us, it satisfied them. It enabled them to account for all they saw, knew, and felt — to give an exact and formal account of creation, and of the facts of nature or life. Deeply enamoured of their genealogies and cosmogonies, they wrapt themselves up in their contemplations — stood aloof from intercourse with the unenlightened world without them, and limited the possession of knowledge to those who were, like themselves, engaged in solving the problems of creation or development. Sometimes ascetic, sometimes licentious, but always for the same reason — because the body was only an accident to the spirit or intelligence of man — they lived in an atmosphere of spiritual and intellectual pride. It is Gnosticism in its rudimentary form, or in its tendency, which Paul contrasts with love in the First Epistle to the Corinthians. Gnosticism, in some shape or other, was invariably adopted by the heresiarchs of the first three centuries, as we see from Tertullian; and it was into an analogous creed that this father of the Latin church ultimately seceded, for the Paraclete of Montanus closely resembles "the great power of God" of Simon, and the mysterious Pleroma of Basileides.

"This people," says the Pharisee, "who know not the Law are cursed." The creed of the Gnostic was that of the Pharisee, without his Judaism, without that sense of nationality or patriotism which saved the Jewish devotee from being absorbed in the worst of egotisms — a belief in his own spiritual perfection, and a scorn for the mass of those who live outside the region on which the rays of divine light have shone. They who had learned the Law and its interpretation were harsh and fanatical, zealous for the maintenance of that empire which they possessed over the minds of their countrymen; but they did not forget that the nation was chosen as well as themselves, or repudiate the election of Israel in the ascendancy which they claimed for their own authority. They believed themselves to be an aristocracy of intelligence and education, but the collective Israel was as a nation, the soldier of God.

The seeker after wisdom, the Gnostic who inserted Jesus and the Gospel into his eclectic creed, believed that some men were illuminated, but that the great majority of mankind were consigned to impenetrable and unilluminable darkness. It was a favorite dogma of these idealists, that some were elect, and others reprobate. It is true that the Gnostic did not give himself up to a cold and apathetic fatalism, but demanded from those who were conscious of their election a fervid energy of the soul, which must be ever directed towards that Being from whom the illumination was derived. But he was the God of intelligence as opposed to the God of creation, insulated in his sympathies, haughtily indifferent to a world of sorrow and ignorance. The knowledge or wisdom which is not combative contributes little to the forces of human progress, is not the wisdom which is from above, because it does not aid in regenerating or redeeming mankind.

It has been stated that Gnosticism was the chief enemy with which the nascent church contended. It is almost certain that, in order to meet this enemy, the Pauline doctrines were affirmed by the western and accepted by the eastern churches, and that the rancor which the Jewish Christians entertained against the great Apostle was finally transformed into the reverence which has been for so many centuries felt towards him, as the great doctor of the primitive church. Marcion accepted his Catholic epistles, though in a mutilated form. What better weapon could be found to fight against these Mystics than the authority which their principal advocate recognized? Judaism was repudiated in order that Pharisaism might be combated

An effort, indeed, is made to proscribe Paul and the Gnostic under the same name, and, by the agency of Peter, in the imaginary discourses which are still extant under the name of the Clementines; but the effort failed.

The fantastic theosophy of emanations, æons, essences, and powers — the system under which logical formularies were represented as objective realities, and exhibited as a pedigree, which originated in a primeval pair called "depth" and "silence" — could have had no permanent influence on mankind, deserved no vitality. Even if this philosophy had rested on a real foundation, it would have done nothing towards the moral progress of mankind. No growth of mere speculative opinion has ever assisted in the development of virtue or morality, though such opinion may have, indirectly, retarded both. Man is the better by what he does, not by what he knows. The clearest and most confident avowal of belief may be, as we all know, unaccompanied by worthy service. Men may hide God's talent in their own napkin, keeping the talent diligently all the while, and even boasting of its possession. There is no theory more false than that which asserts that opinion and religion, belief and virtue, always co-exist; or, that those who cannot assent to a doctrine must needs fall short in the practice of godliness. But it is true that an opinion may be in itself immoral, because it contravenes, either directly or indirectly, that morality which lies under every religious life, or because it supersedes hearty obedience to it. To trust in God, and to do His will are the faith and obedience of the Gospel. In the absence of this faith and obedience, the true and the false in theology are equally virtueless. There is no allegiance to a definition, no loyalty to a formulary. Both are tendered to a Person and a Power, and are invariably offered on grounds which recommend themselves to the reason and the affections.

In the early age of Christianity, there was no field for that political action which may be powerfully allied with a great religious movement. The social life of mankind was, as we all know, governed by a jealous and irresistible military despotism, from which no one could escape. An attempt was made to maintain a religion and a nationality in the Jewish war. It failed after a prodigious effort, and Judaism was proscribed. To Christianity the importance of this event was enormous. It finally severed the new religion from the old, and transferred the centre of the Church from Syria to Italy and Egypt. But, even if the teaching of the early Christian fathers had not proscribed all resistance to constituted, or *de facto* authority, the example which the ruin of Jewry afforded would have been quite sufficient to deter the Christian Church from any organized hostility to the civil and military power of Rome.

Such an alliance, however, as that between political action and religious zeal, has been effected from time to time. This was the characteristic of Islam, and is the explanation of its amazing success. It accounts, also, for the force which Calvinism exercised during the sixteenth and seventeenth centuries. Men were not won over to the creed of the Geneva reformer by the attractiveness of the doctrines which he taught, but by the means which he employed to assist in spreading his creed. He appealed to republican sentiment — to that passion for political liberty which is always keenest when men feel the oppressiveness of institutions which cease to challenge their attachment, and to which they are no longer proud to be loyal. The most superficial glance at the history of the religious struggle, — in France, where Calvinism ultimately failed; in Scotland, where it triumphed; in England, where it ended in a compromise, — will detect how closely a political was intertwined with a religious movement. It may seem a paradox, but the great convulsion of the eighteenth century, which we call the French Revolution, was the product of this double energy — political and religious zeal.

The Gnostic was as little anxious to confront the military despotism under which he lived and dreamed as the Christian enthusiast was. But when a creed or a religion is debarred from alliance with political advocates, it can commend itself only by appeals to universal sympathy, and by the constancy with which it endures martyrdom. Christianity adopted both methods; Gnosticism adopted neither. It was a theology of particular salvation — confined to the elect and the illuminated only. Its adepts, as Tertullian maintains, shrunk from suffering on behalf of their tenets. Now a faith which incites neither love nor admiration will have no hold on the minds of men. A creed, on the other hand, may be harsh and severe, may distribute its rewards and punishments by no higher principle than caprice or chance, and yet may win its adherents by thousands, because it appeals to some profound and energetic sympathy. The Scotch Covenanters did not fight and die for the Westminster Confession, but for liberty of conscience. Besides, men may accept a faith which seems dark and forbidding, and yet find the profoundest consolation in it, because they look on themselves as the peculiar objects upon which its narrow favors are bestowed ungrudgingly, because they are able to die first.

As the Christianity of the apostolic age carefully abstained from traversing the authority of the political system under which it grew, so it shows no trace of any inclination to ally itself with the forces of a friendly government, should such a contingency arise. The maxim of its Founder, "My kingdom is not of this world, else would my servants fight," has its complement, implied but unexpressed, that the same kingdom declines the alliance of the civil authority in aid of its own pretensions to allegiance, or in effecting the extension of its sway. From time to time, a religious movement has enlisted political sympathies on its side, and may do so again. But the association must be temporary, unless the religion is to be enslaved and corrupted. For its own safety, it must make only a short treaty with material and social interests. The reason lies in the facts, that its influence and action cannot be narrowed to the limits within which political authority and social opinion are contained, that its agent is enthusiasm, and that this sentiment can have only an occasional connection with political utility.

The mission of Christ is to the world,— to save it, to renew it, to sanctify it. He propounds a general, why not a universal forgiveness? He suffered, the just for the unjust, that He might, as the highest example, commence that service which all those who ponder on His work, and thereupon would be His disciples, must needs continue. Like the runners in the Athenian torch-race, each man who is worthy of this office, and has set himself to the work, is to carry on, unextinguished, and with undiminished fire, his love towards the race of which he is a member. This is the glory of the noblest sacrifice which has ever been made on man's behalf. Do they, who, following His example, are willing to lose their lives trusting that they may find them,— whose hearts' desire and prayer is for the salvation of their people,— who can even, in the plenitude of their self-abnegation, wish themselves anathema from all hope, if by such means the whole race be enlightened, — shall they think that the majesty of God is at variance with the fatherly care with which He ever watches His creatures, or that it is not in His counsels that mercy rejoiceth against judgment? To have the mind of Christ, is to continue the work which He began, to save souls, to take part in the great battle against sin, misery, ignorance, moral death. Such a life is the best antidote against that morbid dread of God which clouds the religious sense of many, and that indolent egotism which claims to be illuminated, and is lazily confident in its own indefectible perfection.

## CHAPTER IV.

EARLY in the first century after Christ, a Christian living at Nablous, — a city better known by its ancient name of Samaria, — addressed an Apology to the Emperor Antoninus on behalf of his fellow-believers. This defence of the new religion was written by one who was well acquainted with the Old Testament and at least three of the Gospels, for he quotes abundantly from these books. The writer, who calls himself Justin, comments on the unfairness which treats the Christians with severity, while he defends them from those charges of impiety and licentiousness which were freely uttered against them. In giving a summary of their faith and practice, he informs the emperor of their method of common worship, and describes the ceremony of Baptism, and of the Lord's Supper or Eucharist. Justin gives the earliest account, after the Apostolic age, of the ritual observances peculiar to the new sect.

"Those," he says, "who agree with and confess our tenets are washed and regenerated in the name of God, of Jesus Christ our Saviour, and of the Holy Spirit. This washing is called illumination. In this baptism," he observes, "we do not use the ineffable name of God, for if any one did so, he would be forthwith seized with uncontrollable madness. When we gather for worship, we use common prayers in a loud voice, for ourselves, for the person who has been baptized, and for all others. Then we kiss each other. After this, bread, a cup of water, and another of wine are brought to the person who presides over the brethren. Thanks are offered to God. The president takes the viands, gives praise and glory to the Father of all, by the name of the Son, and the Spirit of the Holy One, offering general thanks because the worshippers were deemed worthy of such blessings from His hands. Then the deacons distribute the bread and wine to those who are present, and carry them to those who are absent. No person, however, is permitted to partake of them except those who are believers and are baptized. We offer alms, and are constantly together. We always meet on Sundays, when we first read the commentaries of the Apostles or the writings of the Prophets. When the reader ceases, the president of the meeting preaches. We then pray, and again receive the bread and wine."

The first account seems to describe the daily office, and the second to refer only to the Sunday service. It would appear that the common prayers were some set form, and that they were recited by the whole congregation. The method of worship corresponds, generally, to that which is alluded to in St. Paul's First Epistle to the Corinthians, though disorders and confusion had crept in upon the devotions of the Corinthian Christians. It may be observed, too, that at Nablous, — if Justin is describing the customs of the congregation in his own city, — there is no regular minister, in any modern sense of the word. The word which is translated "president" does not designate even a permanent officer. The solemnity of the Lord's Supper, and the preaching of the Gospel, are performed by a person who is not necessarily possessed of any thing but a temporary function. That such a president was selected by reason of his character and in consideration of his capacity for inculcating the doctrine and rule of the Christian life, may be expected; but Justin gives no hint of an order or a clergy set apart for this office, still less of any sacerdotal mediation, or judgment, or spontaneity. The primitive Church is a congregation, whose creed is excessively simple, whose ritual is an act of mutual sympathy, an expression of common needs. The author of the Epistle to the Hebrews tells us that there were believers who did not even collect together for common worship and mutual exhortation, though he advises the contrary practice.

The primitive Christians — Justin being taken as an instance of their customs — set great store on participation in the celebration of the Lord's Supper, or, as he calls it, in the Eucharist. The language which the Apologist uses about this rite is positive as to the belief in its being the means for associating the Christian with Christ, and of its being an essential to salvation or at least to religious health and safety. If the Apology of Justin be genuine, and its genuineness has been rarely disputed, and if Justin can be taken, as there is no reason to doubt he can, should the first hypothesis be satisfactorily accepted, as the type of the Syrian Christian at the beginning of the second century, the ceremonies of Christian initiation, baptism, and the Lord's Supper, are severally treated as illumination, regeneration, and a partaking of the body and blood of Christ.

The two characteristic offices of associated worship, which the testimony of Justin shows to have been generally practised in the earliest Christian communities, are obvious symbols of natural use. A ceremonial purification was not peculiar to Christianity. It is found in Judaism, in those Eastern creeds which influenced the religious sentiments over which Christianity was induced, and in the lustrations of the Greek mysteries. Physical purity was an apt emblem of moral sanctification, and its sign was adopted by the Great Master, as a means of formal admission into the covenant of His Gospel. Baptism in the name of Christ becomes, by a natural feeling, at once a symbol and a power.

One of the earliest, most lasting, and most widely-spread among the feelings of humanity, is that which exalts association into unity. Under the influence of this sentiment, physical objects which once belonged to some dearly-loved being, or physical acts which recall his presence to the memory, renew the pleasure or felicity which the presence of his being once gave. They form the link by which the soul can bind itself to that which has gone out of its sight, and after which it is earnestly longing. Relics and memorials are the means by which the sadness of separation is lightened, by which the reality of that which is so tenderly loved is certified and assured. Hatred, on the other hand, uses the same stimulants that love does. The tenderness which cherishes such mementos is akin to that fierce malignity which collects the relics of an enemy, in order to make them the material for the incantations of magic or witchcraft. As the solicitude with which deep affection gazes on that which it loves seems to guard or protect the object of its care, so men have believed that an envious or hostile glance may wound or weaken those against whom it is directed. Hatred is not only the counterpart of love, but it uses the same associations in order to glut itself.

Out of these sympathies, assisted by such reminders, men develop the permanent conceptions of family, country, church. It is because they are thus constrained to perpetuate what they have felt and known, that they are saved from that isolation, which may flatter men with a cynical sense of independence, but which would, if it were generally adopted, wreck society, and all the forms under which society is constituted and exists. To say that man cannot live alone is a platitude. But men may seek to gain all the advantages which social life affords them, and contribute nothing to the forces by which they profit.

The moral progress of man is not due to the fact, that in the struggle of life, the strong have supplanted the weak, or elbowed them out of existence. On the contrary, it has been effected by the fact that the strong have sheltered and cherished the weak, that they who can strive and conquer have used their power and their success for the purpose of succoring the feeble and the oppressed, for lavishing the tenderest feeling and action on those who cling to them for support and protection, and who have nothing to offer in return for these benefits but untiring and unchanging love. It may be that man has been developed to his present condition out of a mere animal savagery. It is certain, that if this be the case, he owes all his progress to actions which are the very reverse of that policy which gives the weak over as a prey to the strong. It is equally certain, that if he does decline hereafter into barbarism, he will owe his moral decadence to the spread of the temper which urges men to live for themselves alone.

The admiration, the worship, with which men witness the strength and wisdom which are used for the good of others, and not for personal aggrandizement,— the homage which they offer to courage, joined to gentleness,— are acknowledgments of the great part which such qualities play in the moral government of society. Nor is this admiration less enthusiastic because they who feel it are conscious only of the benefit which goodness and wisdom confer on themselves, and do not forecast their effects on mankind at large.

The memory of Christ was riveted in the hearts of His disciples and followers. He had largely availed Himself, in the teaching which He gave them, of the sentiment of Association, by the use of parable and analogy in His discourses and actions. He had instructed them in the doctrine that the unity of mankind was to be found in Himself, and had prescribed a ritual by which that unity should be perpetually suggested. When He was gone from them, the whole meaning of His intercourse with them became apparent and permanent. Before, their hearts were dull, and they could not understand Him, their eyes were holden that they could not see Him. Now every thing was clear.

But nothing seems to have been graven more indelibly on their memory than the scene of the last Supper. It is the one event in the life of Christ which St. Paul narrates. It is the central fact of the fourth gospel, the circumstance to which the discourses in that gospel tend, or round which they are arranged. It was recalled to the mind of all by the necessities of daily life, by the breaking of bread. The reminder was cumulative, the analogy natural. As human nature requires daily sustenance, so the spiritual nature which is contained in the life of man needs daily nurture. As the physical growth of man is due to his daily bread, so the growth to the measure of the stature of the fulness of Christ demands as imperatively the renewing of that spiritual food. The showing forth of the Lord's death is the source of the Christian's life. The five thousand are fed abundantly, and the fragments exceed the necessity. Nay, the practice of Christian man was prefigured in the Law. The heavenly food in the wilderness, the ever-flowing rock which accompanied the wanderers in the desert, are manifestations of the same spiritual force. Unseen but not undiscovered, He is in the midst. He is the Power of God and the Wisdom of God.

The readings in the Church, whose ritual Justin describes, are taken from the commentaries of the Apostles and the Prophetical books. The term employed to express these commentaries is that used by Xenophon to denote the collection of Socratic conversations which is known as the Memorabilia. It is clear that the Apologist was conversant with the three gospels, for he freely quotes from them, though he does not name the authors of these biographies. It may be that time has spared us only some of these compilations, and that the ruin which fell on Judea during the great war may have been followed by the loss of many apostolic compositions. The considerable space between the age of the first Apostles and that of the earliest Fathers is very imperfectly illustrated, is very inadequately filled by the reminiscences or collections of Irenæus. St. Paul may have adverted to one of these lost books, when he is said to quote, as a well known saying of Christ, that "it is more blessed to give than to receive," — a passage the more remarkable as the Apostle hardly ever refers to these doings and sayings.

The writings of the Prophets are those books of the Jewish Scriptures in which Justin was very well versed. Born a heathen, and bred a philosopher, Justin tells us that he was converted from metaphysical speculations to Christianity, by the conversation which he held with an old man who accosted him as he was taking a solitary walk on the sea-shore. These prophetical writings were carefully studied by the more learned Christians, as they formed the best polemical weapon against the Jews, their Messianic character harmonizing with the history of Christ.

St. Paul gives us some particulars about the ritual of the Corinthian Church. It had become necessary that the Apostle should put an end to certain disorders and confusions, and establish in Corinth a uniformity with the practice of other churches. There was one very notable peculiarity in the churches of this city, which is not mentioned as characteristic of any other church, which is not referred to in the subsequent epistle to the same church, nor in the epistle of Clement. It is the power of speaking in tongues, — a power, the manifestation of which St. Paul does not wish to forbid, though he plainly desires to keep it within the narrowest possible limits. It is probable that the discouragement with which the Apostle treats the faculty may have led to its disuse. It is clear that the faculty was abused, that it tended to disorder, and that its only possible value was that it might attract the favorable notice of unbelievers, though this advantage was counterbalanced by the risk, that an excessive or simultaneous exhibition of the power might induce an uninstructed audience to believe the actors mad.

The persons who possessed the power of speaking " tongues," uttered their sentences occasionally in a foreign language; but sometimes, it would seem, gave vent to unintelligible sounds. Some of these outpourings the Apostle compares to the irregular emission of such musical notes as have neither rhythm nor melody, or to the blare of a trumpet, which does not indicate any of the known calls to which soldiers give ear. It is probable, the Apostle says, that there is no sound, however numerous sounds may be, which is undevoid of meaning; but if one does not know what the sound may mean, the utterance will be a jargon. A man, indeed, may pray in language which he himself cannot comprehend, and the act of devotion will edify his spirit; but his mind will have no benefit from the sounds expressed, and perfect acts of prayer and praise must be intelligible as well as devotional. Five words which may be comprehended are worth more than ten thousand of those obscure sounds. If they must needs be uttered, a very few people should make the ejaculation, and one should interpret it, if it can be interpreted. If no interpretation be forthcoming, it is better for the person who possesses the faculty to be silent, as the sound neither profits himself nor others.

There is a danger that an honest enthusiasm may lead him who feels it into strange freaks — that it may be simulated by others for sinister ends — that it may be misinterpreted, even at its best. It is impossible to avoid the inference that the reasoning employed by the Apostle — containing, as it does, no small amount of suggestive irony — should have checked, and finally eradicated, the habit of speaking in " tongues."

Far superior, however, to this ecstatic, and somewhat superfluous gift, is that of prophesying, as St. Paul calls it. It is the most serviceable of spiritual gifts — edifying and instructing individuals and the Church. It may be communicated to all believers. Other gifts may be used with thankfulness when bestowed; this is that gift which all should desire to obtain; it is that, says the Apostle, which I wish that all of you possessed.

The names and history of those eminent men who had guided the public policy of Israel during the monarchy were familiar facts to both Jew and Christian. Some of them had written books. At least, their recorded sayings were collected and set in order by their disciples. These works, under the general name of "The Prophets," were esteemed highly by all who held to the Jewish covenant as a complete revelation, and were equally reverenced by those who believed that the Law was imperfect and typical — the shadow of that which was to come.

We are so accustomed to consider the prophet of the Jewish covenant as the expositor of the Divine purpose towards the chosen people and the rest of mankind, that we are apt to lose sight of his attitude towards his own generation — to forget that he rebuked and counselled king and nation — that he was a statesman and a jurist, who interpreted the politics of his age according to the law of God and the permanent interests of His people. The spirit of this law was expounded by the prophet, with breadth and boldness, with force and dignity, with exquisite poetry and pathos. The prophet was the preacher of holiness and righteousness, of religion and morals; for the Jewish kings constantly exhibited the traits of other oriental sovereigns, and the priests do not appear to have exercised any great social influence by the mere virtue of their office. It is by the prophets and their writings that Israel not only maintained the purity of his religion, but was saved from sinking either into one of those races which have been long since extinct, or from being degraded into a permanent, but a savage horde. The word of the Lord came to him, was spoken, and endures for ever. To the student of history it is impossible to exaggerate the influence which these men have exercised on the destiny of mankind. Though they were guided by such lofty impulses, and such profoundly religious sentiment, their life and action is intensely real. They were neither philosophers nor devotees, but politicians of the purest type, whose energies were devoted towards preserving the institutions of a petty Syrian kingdom, but whose principles of action were those of perfect political morality, and were therefore of universal significance. They believed in a public conscience, a public duty, a public religion, and they never failed to insist on the obligations which give society all its force and vigor. God had committed to them a great charge, and they dared not be timid or unfaithful.

History supplies us with no parallel to the influence which these men wielded. They were the leaders of opinion in a kingdom which was neither very large nor populous, at an epoch when their country was overshadowed by powerful empires, and was the highway of great contending armies. They had to preserve its independence by their policy. But they had a still harder task to perform, that of maintaining the purity of its religion. Even more dangerous than the political forces which threatened Judah, were the corrupting influences which tended to debase the Law by their contact; for no nature-worship was more gross than that of Phœnicia, no fetish more cruel than that of Moab and Ammon, and of the other old Canaanite races. They had to interpret the Law according to its spiritual meaning, to advocate a higher life than the corn, and wine, and oil, and honey of the older promise; and to set this loftier example before the State and the Man. Nor were the external difficulties of their position all that they had to contend with. Some prophets were found who, like Hananiah, apostatized from their calling; men whose time-serving falsehood extorted from Jeremiah that bitter complaint which contains in it a summary of ages in the world's history, — The prophets prophesy wickedness, and the priests applaud them, and my people love to have it so, and what will ye do when the end of these things comes?

These prophets were not ignorant enthusiasts, who owed their authority to mere self-assertion. They were trained to such learning as the times possessed, in certain recognized seminaries. These institutions were, it would seem, founded by Samuel, — for it is during the age of this Judge that the schools of the prophets are specially distinguished, — and were continued down to the great Captivity. At the Restoration, the prophet's place was supplied by the teaching which the Rabban gave his disciples. The Jews were ready to recognize the spirit of the older prophet in the teaching of the Baptist, and the discourses of Christ are the utterances of one who, trained as the prophets were trained, surpassed them all; completing the sum of Divine wisdom, announcing in all their fulness the counsels of God, and promising the continuance of the Spirit to his disciples.

As the part of the prophet was one of great honor and authority, so it was one of peculiar danger. Monarch and people were occasionally recalled to their duty by the warnings of these advisers, but as often turned savagely on the unwelcome or intrusive counsellor. The author of the Epistle to the Hebrews recounts the sufferings which these patriots underwent. Christ, with full foresight of His own destiny, charges the existing generation of the Jews with an aggregate of that blood-thirsty hate which prompted the death of Abel, and consummated the slaughter of Zecharias, — whose murder, says the Talmud, was committed during the time that Jerusalem was besieged by the Chaldeans, and was mercilessly avenged by Nebuzaradan.

It is the power, then, of interpreting religious duty in the various occasions of life, of bringing the Spirit of God which dwells within the believer to bear on the course of human action, which St. Paul prays that his Corinthian disciples may possess. **He** ranges the prophet after the apostle in the rank of usefulness. He would have them all obtain, and all use this gift for personal guidance and mutual counsel. Himself in the fullest sense a prophet, and enjoying abundantly this clear inward light, he longed that all his converts should be equally advanced in spiritual knowledge and wisdom, — should equally contribute towards the edification of the Church. He warns them against sectarian differences, reminds them that their allegiance cannot be divided or shared, and advises them to aid each other in the great work of wisdom and holiness.

The time was not come in which this function — to be performed by the members of an obscure and struggling sect — should be extended so as to fill the sphere in which the ancient prophets exercised their great ministry. And when the time did come, and an opportunity was offered in which Christianity, having interpenetrated the whole life of society, might constitute a Divine republic, a true *civitas Dei*, a state in which profound religious energy should go hand-in-hand with clear political sagacity, the Christian world was busied in logomachies, was ruled by monks and ascetics, by logicians and mystics. Then the Church eagerly completed a bargain, under the terms of which the successful portion was empowered to proscribe its rivals, provided only that the whole force of ecclesiastical government should ally itself with the temporary expedients of a demoralized and decaying government, with the degraded imperialism of the Constantines.

The worship in the Corinthian churches is strangely like that of the earliest Quakers. One man had a psalm to recite, another a rule of conduct to announce, a third some linguistic utterance, a fourth some revelation, a fifth the interpretation of some obscure passage of Scripture, or of some mystic declaration. To add to the confusion, the women were as eager in their contributions to this bewildering clamor as the men were. Hence the Apostle enjoins silence in the churches on the women, as is seemly, and to avoid scandal. The injunction, it appears, was peculiarly needed in the Corinthian churches, was special, perhaps temporary. Elsewhere, it is clear that women exercised great influence on the discipline of the Church, and that they busied themselves with the spread of the Gospel. Priscilla is one of these; so is Junia, whom Paul speaks of as an apostle; also Tryphena, Tryphosa, and Persis, and probably Julia, and the sister of Nereus, — to quote those names only which are found in the Epistle to the Romans. The notion that the Apostle discouraged the services of women on behalf of the Gospel is an exaggerated inference from the language of the Epistle to the Corinthians, and is contradicted by facts.

If the assemblies of the Corinthian Christians, when St. Paul wrote with the view of checking these disorders, resembled those ecstatic gatherings of the older Quakers, so the religious exercises which he commends resemble the decorous solemnities which have characterized the meetings of these sectaries, after the enthusiasm of teachers like Fox was controlled by the good sense of reformers like Penn. There is absolutely no hint given in the epistle of any organized ministry, still less of any hierarchy whatsoever. Every convert, as far as the text of the letter informs us, was on a footing of perfect equality with his neighbor or brother in Christ, was competent to raise his voice or expound in the Church. We do not even find a temporary president of the meeting, such as was set up in the church which Justin describes. The gifts of the Spirit were various, and every convert had some gift which he might employ for the general good of the Church. But this silence as to church government and an official ministry is not peculiar to the Corinthian epistles. Only one of the epistles addressed to churches contains any allusion to resident ecclesiastical officers; and this address to the bishops and deacons of Philippi, while it has made some persons suspect that the letter is of doubtful authenticity, has induced those who contend for its genuineness to assign it to the latest period of the Apostle's life.

But though the epistles to the churches afford little or no information on the subject of the Christian ministry, and present a mass of negative evidence as to the appointment of a regular order, the Apostle gives an account of what the office of the Lord's Supper was, and what it ought to be. The converts came together, each bringing his food and drink with him, though not, it would seem, with the intention of giving it to a common fund. Some were hungry, some indulged in excess; the rich enjoyed themselves, the poor were put to shame by their inability to vie with this profusion and ostentation. It would appear that the Corinthians imagined, provided they took their meal in the same building, that they were performing the rite which was commanded to believers as a solemn commemoration of Christ's death. St. Paul therefore narrates the circumstances under which the rite was instituted, enjoins its observance on Christians, shows the danger of a profane misinterpretation of it, and the consequences which have already ensued from careless malpractice, inculcates the rule that it is a feast in which all worshippers are equal, and promises to give further details on his arrival.

The First Epistle to the Corinthians gives some insight into the discipline of the Church. A professed believer had married his step-mother, and this, apparently, during his father's lifetime. Such a marriage was discreditable among the heathen. Under certain circumstances, it was, despite the prohibition in Leviticus, permitted among the Jews, in consequence of certain decisions in the Talmud, which professed to interpret cases like those of Abraham and Sarah, Amnon and Tamar, Adonijah and Abishag, where marriages between persons who were within close relations of consanguinity or affinity were either contracted or contemplated. The gloss of these doctors was, that in case the wife was of heathen parentage on the mother's side, the relationship need not be a bar: It has been suggested that the offender was a Jew, who had taken advantage of this opinion of the Jewish doctors, and had thereupon debauched and married his step-mother. It seems to me more likely that the wife had taken advantage of the easy law of divorce which prevailed among the Romans (for Corinth was a Roman colony), and had thus contracted a marriage which the Roman custom branded as incestuous, but for which, in so licentious a place as Corinth was, there was probably no punishment.

Apart from the consideration of its immorality, the act was dangerous to the reputation of the Church. The early Christians had every interest to maintain a character for purity, since scandal would be sure to be busy with them, however careful they were, if it could only catch at any fact. St. Paul therefore commands instant and severe measures. They are to suspend the culprit immediately, in the name of Christ, and by His power, from fellowship with the Church. They are to give him over to Satan, — the Apostle using this phrase familiar to those who knew the histories of Job and Ahab, to imply that the offender should suffer some severe bodily ailment, as a punishment and corrective for his offence. The object of the chastisement was not the destruction of the man, but the repentance of a sinner. We learn that the Church was roused to action by the Apostle's command, that it cleared itself of all complicity in the scandal, that it put public censure on the offender, that the offence was repented of, and that it was forgiven.

The Founder of Christianity was reproached with His lenity to offenders, was blamed for the readiness with which He welcomed repentant sinners. A scheme of religion which inculcated the doctrine of God's love, gentleness, long-suffering, which insisted on the impossibility of man's fulfilling all the requirements of a precise and searching law, and which taught that man was reconciled to God through the great sacrifice of Christ, could not be severe to those who sorrow over their sin, — could not but welcome back those who, roused by an accusing conscience, seek forgiveness and peace. If the Gospel declares all men to need salvation, if it warns men of the consequences which ensue to those who are impenitent, and even implies that a sharp and purifying fire is needed for them who have lived sensuously, though not sinfully, it is boundless in its charity to those who seek forgiveness. To grant this forgiveness is the very essence of the Christian religion; to refuse it is to be implacable, and therefore unforgiven; to inflict irrevocable punishment is to usurp the functions of God; to desire that such punishment should be inflicted is to be of a spirit of which no man should knowingly be, to league one's self with the accuser and destroyer. The scheme of Christianity admits the great value of human life, but it insists on the transcendent value of the human soul.

The generosity with which Christianity treated repented sin in primitive times has been permanently characteristic of its later discipline. It has even gone beyond the ancient rule, and has all but ignored discipline itself. But, however lax it has been in dealing with the practice of its followers, it has from time to time been implacably severe on their opinions. It has dealt with morals and belief respectively as the Index dealt with Lucian, — permitted the publication of all that is gross, suppressed every thing which it considered sceptical. It has, in the hands of those who pretended to be its fathers and doctors, committed the greatest cruelties which have ever polluted the world. The dark fears of tyrants have never devised such torments for their victims as the disciples of Christ have perpetrated, — and that without the tyrant's plea, without a word of justification from the teaching of Him whom they profess to adore, — in the face, even of His absolute prohibition. They who professed to be the stewards of God's mercy and grace, developed an insane fanaticism out of the fears which they stimulated, and led generations of mankind to believe that they were vindicating God's honor by permitting, encouraging, assisting a dark and merciless hatred against those who were suspected of heresy.

The Church of the earliest ages is not perfectly free from this attempt to usurp the functions of the Divine Judge. We shall see that the labors of Paul were seriously hindered by the narrowness of those who professed the faith of Christ; that the last days of his life were embittered by the apostasy of those who owed their knowledge of the Gospel to his unwearied energy; that for a time he was followed by angry calumnies. But the fervid zeal of the early Church was ready to welcome all who accepted the name, and strove to live the life of the Christian. It had not yet attempted those definitions which bewildered and rent it. It was busied with the belief that the work of all religion is to effect the association of man's soul with the undoubted Presence of God. It saw that the space between God and man, which might be infinitely small, and might be infinitely great, could be filled up by the person of Christ — a Humanity of perfect love, of unwearying providence, of such attractiveness that it occupies every affection, sanctifies every emotion, unites all men by a common bond, but is, withal, the power, the glory, the wisdom of God — the exemplar of all creation, the strength by which every thing is made, — one with God and one with man, — the one true Priest and Mediator. To accept His mediation is to satisfy man's most earnest longings — to guarantee the law of liberty, or, in modern language, the highest and purest civilization.

The Church at Corinth put a question of conscience to the Apostle. The worship of Greece and Rome involved the offering of sacrifices. The same nations practised augury by inspecting the viscera of slaughtered animals, these animals being the substitutes for a more ancient rite, which was common in Mexico at the time of Cortez, where human sacrifices were offered for similar ends, the body of the victim being afterwards disposed of in the same way. Having served the purpose of intercession or vaticination, the carcasses of these animals were sent to the butcher's shop. It is probable that by far the largest portion, if not the whole, of the meat exposed for sale had been previously employed for these sacerdotal objects, and that a conscientious refusal to purchase any of that which had been offered to idols would be equivalent to abjuring the use of flesh altogether. What is to be done in such an emergency? Can we purchase such food?

To a person whose early training led him to look with horror on any ceremonial defilement, however little it was coupled with a disposition to offend against the Law, the case was one which must have been instantly answered in the negative. The Jews were excessively strict in seeing every condition of ceremonial cleanliness satisfied in the preparation of all animal food, and would certainly have rejected this kind of flesh. But the Apostle thought differently, now at any rate. The idol is absolutely nothing. There is but one God, or, in case people believe there are powers in heaven or on earth, to us at least there is but One, who is the author of all, and to whom we revert, and one Christ, who is the Type of all, and by whom we subsist. They who really know and understand these facts have no need to find any difficulty in the case; or, as he subsequently tells the Romans, there is nothing unclean in itself; or, as logicians say, there is no objective impurity in any kind of meat. The uncleanness of food is a subjective impression.

In a later part of the epistle, the Apostle, after one of his characteristic parentheses, reverts to the case of casuistry which has been submitted to him. He is reminded of it by having alluded to the community of act, thought, and spirit, which are involved in the celebration of the Lord's Supper. He compares it to that fellowship in the sacrifice, which those who partake of the flesh offered at the sacrifice must needs reciprocate. And then comes before his mind the analogy which is presented by participation in flesh previously offered to idols. To participate in the sacrifice is devil-worship, and cannot be thought of. To imagine that the religious feast can be conjoined with an idolatrous symposium, a heathen revel, is to profane it, and cannot be endured.

The rule of life is, however, clear. What is lawful to an individual, and what is expedient or advantageous to a society are not always identical, and the Christian is bound to consider his neighbor's good. If you, who know that the act of idolatrous sacrifice is a mere farce, see meat exposed for sale, buy it without question or comment. If you are invited to the house of a man who is not a Christian, and you care to go, do so, and eat of any dish set before you, without question or comment. But if you are expressly informed that the meat has been sacrificed, avoid it for your own sake and that of the person who informs you. Better deny yourself than offend those for whom Christ died. Give no cause of scandal to Jew, Greek, or the Church of God. Take my example, who was a Jew to the Jews, and a Greek to the Greeks, in order to win them over. The example is that of Christ himself, who could not countenance intolerance of race or station — rebuking sin in all, encouraging what was hopeful in all.

Whether this liberty which the Apostle advocated was abused, or they who censured his system of generous interpretation were offended at such counsel, is not clear. But the author of the Apocalypse complains that the converts in the Asiatic churches eat things offered to idols, and that in Thyatira, the church listened to the woman Jezebel who claims to be a prophetess, and dares to counsel this practice. It is difficult to avoid the impression that part of the vision in Patmos was directed against the liberty which Paul demanded, though he gave counsel as to the limits of that liberty. It does not necessarily follow, that the writer of the vision was aware of the reasons which induced Paul to decide as he did, or of the cautions with which he surrounded his decision. But it was very hard to wean men from the traditions of the older faith, — to induce them to believe that a ritual which was merely symbolical was not of universal and permanent obligation. It is hardest of all to advise successfully, that the spirit of a law should be discovered, and its letter interpreted by such a spirit. It may be added that Justin Martyr comments unfavorably on those who give permission to eat the flesh of heathen sacrifices.

If the Apostle granted liberty in this direction, he refused it to those who would thrust the Jewish polity into the Christian Church. He hears that the Galatians are observing days, months, seasons, years, the Sabbath of the Jews, the new moons, the stated feasts, the times of the Jewish Law. He dreads that his labor may have been in vain, when men who have learned God's will, and, better still, were accepted by Him, return to such poor and contemptible observances. For Sabbatarian strictness the Apostle has no respect whatever. He tells the Romans that he is indifferent to the recognition of any such day. But when it is made obligatory by reactionary teachers, he even denounces the observance of it totally. The curious fancy which has intruded into some Christian societies a rigorous observance of Sunday, and which has transferred to it the extreme strictness of the Jewish Sabbath, was not only not countenanced by St. Paul, but spoken of as a matter of utter indifference, except when it is intended to suggest allegiance to the Jewish code. Then it was to be repudiated as delusive and dangerous. Even when that code was imperative, the Master had taught that the Sabbath had a purely human purpose; it could not be endured that prejudice should exalt it into a stringent obligation of religion.

The first day of the week had already been recognized as a convenient occasion for common prayer and mutual exhortation. According to Josephus, the days of the Jewish week were known over the civilized world; and the reason why Sunday was selected for the purposes of devotion is given by Justin. It was the day of the resurrection, and was thence called the Lord's day. St. Paul directs that on this day each man should lay up that which he can spare for the necessities of the poorer brethren, and observes that he gave the same direction to the Galatian churches. The wholesome and purifying custom of systematic charity characterized the Jewish synagogue, and was inculcated on the Christian communities. When men are taught to feel pity for poverty, distress, and sickness, they are insensibly schooled into that duty of forgiving injuries which Christianity has made an article of faith.

The Apostle insists that he is justified in drawing on this fund, or some similar resource, for the exceptional supply of his own personal necessities. Occasionally he accepted the spontaneous assistance of his converts, and particularizes some churches which had been eager to supply his wants. But his delicacy of feeling, his honest pride in the perfect disinterestedness of his missionary work, led him to dispense generally with such acknowledgments of his services. He abhorred the thought of making the Word of God a trade — of huckstering over the price at which his office should be compensated. A rare self-abandonment! It is as difficult to imitate the self-denial of an Apostle, as it is to achieve his vigor and success.

Paul and Barnabas put no charge on the churches, but the other Apostles did. Nay, they travelled in company with their wives, the Apostle specially designating the brethren of the Lord and Peter as having used this privilege. An early legend represents the wife of Peter as being led to death, and as encouraged by him to persevere. It is curious and instructive that this disclaimer of the Apostle, and contrast of his habit with the thoroughly lawful practice of the other Apostles, should inform us of the fact that the enforced celibacy of Christian ministers has no warranty in the conduct of the Apostles, and that the contrary custom is sustained by their example. But the time was not come yet in which worldly policy would recommend a Manichæan tenet as a part of ecclesiastical discipline.

The earlier epistles of St. Paul supply us with no information as to the form of church government adopted by primitive Christianity. It probably varied; its organization was not settled, nor was it important that it should be settled. Had there been any permanent, or even regular officers in the Corinthian church, it is impossible but that the Apostle should have made some reference to them. The Corinthians do not seem even to have established the diaconate; for the contribution which each is expected to make towards a general collection is not to be paid to some local treasurer, but is to be stored up in the house of the giver until the Apostle's arrival. Had the Apostle considered it important that the Corinthians should be supplied with a settled ministry, he would have ordained such officers at his previous visit, or in his first letter to them, which has perished, or would have directed them to provide themselves with proper officials from their own body. The disorders which he wishes to check — and the correction of which is the principal motive for writing the epistle — are not remedied by the establishment of a hierarchy, by providing a central authority to which disputes could be referred; and the same fact may be inferred negatively as to the other churches whom he addresses, with the exception of that at Philippi. St.

Paul must have been totally indifferent as to forms of church government, and would have rebuked any intolerance which might prescribe a uniform rule in all the churches.

With the exception of the deacon's office, the origin of which is narrated in the Acts of the Apostles, all that we know of ecclesiastical officers is obtained from the writings attributed to Paul. In his letters to Timothy, the Apostle instructs his favorite disciple in the qualifications which must be sought for in a bishop or overseer. These do not materially differ from those of a deacon. In the letter to Titus, the bishop and the elder or presbyter are identified. In the First Epistle of Peter, the word bishop is applied to Christ, and the Apostle describes himself as an elder or presbyter. The "angel" or messenger of the seven churches in the Revelation has been supposed, somewhat superfluously, to be the bishop, for it is difficult to see how a personage whose name implies departure from a particular locality should be identified with the resident governor of the Church.

There is not the slightest trace of any hierarchy in the New Testament, unless, indeed, it be discovered in the Apostolic College at Jerusalem, whose paramount authority St. Paul distinctly repudiated. The Church was a republic of federal congregations, bound together by no administrative tie, though closely united by a common faith and a common charity. Nor is any Apostle tied to a spot. Titus is sent to ordain elders in Crete; is spoken of, therefore, as its first bishop, but in the Second Epistle to Timothy he has gone to Dalmatia. Timothy is left at Ephesus in the first epistle, but is certainly not there at the date of the second, for the Apostle informs him that he has sent Tychicus thither. Where Timothy was does not appear, but he was to call at Troas on his journey to Paul, then in imminent peril at Rome, where, as it seems from the Epistle to the Hebrews, the disciple narrowly escaped his teacher's fate. It is an anachronism to speak of an Apostolic bishop, perhaps an anomaly. That this officer's appointment became general at an early period of Church history was due to causes which had no existence, or only an inchoate existence in the Apostolic age.

The silence of the New Testament on ritual and Church government contrasts markedly with the energy with which these accidents of later ecclesiastical history have been assailed and defended. It can be shown that the three ecclesiastical offices were all but universally recognized by the middle of the third century, — that the function of ordinary bishops was conferred by bishops only, that of presbyters by bishops and presbyters, while a less marked solemnity accompanied the appointment of deacons. According to Selden, however, who quotes St. Jerome, the bishops of Alexandria were elected and consecrated by the presbyters till the Patriarchate of Alexander, in the fourth century. But the ancient missionary did not delay his labors till he had received a bishop's license. The best claim to antiquity and independence, which can be put forward on behalf of the ancient Irish and Gaelic Churches, lies in the fact that St. Patrick appears to have received no ordination whatever, and that St. Columba was singularly independent of episcopal control.

It is not remarkable that authority, which is naturally apt to identify a fact with the form in which it is contained, or by which it is disguised, should, after the custom of episcopal government became universal, look on the advocacy of an alternative to such a form as disaffection, treason, or heresy. But, unless it can be shown that the form in question is absolutely essential to the maintenance of order, and the security of freedom, its expediency is always open to debate. The policy of episcopal government has been challenged, partly on account of the excessive zeal which its supporters have manifested in claiming for it a Divine authority, partly because it has been sustained by force against reluctant disputants. Now, in ecclesiastical as in civil government, a form of administration which resents criticism on its intrinsic authority is self-condemned; that which strives to suppress all opinion as to its validity, or value, is sure to provoke active hostility. Had the principle of episcopacy never affected to rest on Divine right, but had been content to found its claims on the obvious convenience of a graduated municipal system, it would have probably been accepted as the best way in which religious thought can be encouraged and tested, religious action assisted and guided. But its advocates attempted to make its acceptance a condition of Christian brotherhood; to force its establishment on unwilling minds, and even to inflict the worst atrocities of civil war on those sectaries who were dissatisfied with its regimen.

It is said that the establishment of a clerical order, and, in particular, of a permanent chief officer who should govern the Church in a town or district, was founded on a necessity for creating some organization against heretics and schismatics. The theory is plausible, but of doubtful proof. It is quite possible that, had St. Paul created some such officers in Ancyra, Ephesus, Corinth, his authority would have been more respected, and the churches of Galatia, Asia Minor, and Greece would have been spared some follies and scandals. But it was not the mission of the Apostle to organize a society, but to teach a religion. He did not fall into the common error of reformers and missionaries — that of setting up a precise rule of church government, for he knew well enough that such artificial systems are in the end constantly fatal to the movement which they are intended to further. The Apostle foresaw that his work would be, to a great degree, undone by intrusive tenets. Before his life was over, he witnessed more than once the partial or complete apostasy of churches which he had founded, and of disciples whom he had taught. But with the exception of a few, and these very general, directions to Timothy and Titus, he provides no ecclesiastical magistracy which should meet these imminent mischiefs. It cannot but be the case that he put no reliance in those adventitious aids to orthodoxy. It is certain, if he had no confidence in them, that he was guided by his customary prescience. The schisms, heresies, religious parties, of the second and third century were innumerable. It was only when State and Church were allied that outward uniformity was achieved under the mechanism of an episcopal system.

Apart from the natural tendency to organization which a common belief and a common practice engender, the social habits of the early Church rendered some form of church polity necessary, and even spontaneous. The primitive Church of Jerusalem was poor. It adopted a strict communism, an ascetic, contemplative life. In time, when the resources which its first disciples threw into the common fund were exhausted, it lived on the alms of the faithful, adopting finally the custom of the Jewish hierarchy, who levied first-fruits on their dispersed brethren. Hence the early necessity which arose for establishing a treasury, with officers who should be appointed to distribute the funds, and who should obviate the charge of favoritism. These, we are expressly told, were the motives for establishing the diaconate. In Nablous the duty of distributing the common fund was intrusted to the president.

St. Paul was far too wise to attempt the introduction of this communistic system among the Gentile converts. He knew well enough that such a scheme would be fatal to energy, would be fatal to the Church. For the sake of peace, and as part of his compromise with the Judaizing party, he recognized their claim, that the Gentiles should remember the poor, adding, with some irony, that he was ready enough to do so. Nor did he neglect to carry out this promise, for he was engaged in this work of charity, or at least generosity, when the rabble set on him in the temple at Jerusalem. He had no objection to assist the poverty of those pious ascetics, of putting their claims before his converts, though he shrunk from taking any compensation for his own services.

In course of time, it was inevitable that distress should arise within these Gentile churches, and it was notoriously the duty of Christian men to relieve the wants of their brethren, and indeed of all men. The profound sense of this generous obligation was one of the best gifts which Judaism bestowed on Christianity. The establishment, then, of officers who should collect the alms of the richer, and assist the wants of the poorer brethren was necessary. The office was not limited to the male sex, even when the poorer congregation asked the aid of some rich and distant church. Phœbe, the deaconess of Cenchrea, gets an introduction from St. Paul to the churches at Rome, just as a colonial missionary might be introduced to the benevolence of a wealthy English congregation. The text implies that her mission was an application for some pecuniary assistance. It is to be regretted that Pliny, in his celebrated letter to Trajan, admits that he felt it expedient to put two of these pious women to the torture, in order to extract the truth from them. But the fact shows the important position filled by the Bithynian deaconess.

K

The bishop and his presbytery bear an obvious resemblance to the great or the little Synedrion of the Jews. The former of these was constituted in imitation of the seventy elders who were selected by Moses and associated with him; the latter, containing twenty-three members, was supposed to be indicated by certain passages in the book of Numbers. The chief of this assembly of elders naturally became the bishop. Among the heretics, says Tertullian, the bishop's office was temporary, as was also that of the presbyters. The function of such officers was to keep order in the Church, to admit the catechumens, and subsequently to see to the instruction of the young, to preach, and to govern. The office of a judge in matters of doubtful doctrine, in heresy, and in any breach of the Church's law, was a later development of the episcopal office, but was in course of time naturally annexed to it, as the organization of the ecclesiastical system was more exactly elaborated. It may be added that, as persecution became more general, the post of bishop was that of danger, and, among men who were reproached with a passion for martyrdom, that of honor. The reader need hardly be reminded that men who have been persecuted are not always tolerant. In the history of Christianity, it has frequently been found that they who have suffered most, and most patiently for their creed have, when enabled to give effect to their own judgment, been distinguished for a savage and relentless orthodoxy.

Again, familiarity with the local magistracy and

council of the Roman colonies may have suggested analogous institutions in the Church. The earliest churches, when Christianity was so far tolerated as to permit the erection of permanent buildings (and we read of such buildings as early as the time of Alexander Severus), were built in the form of the Roman basilica, or court of justice. On the raised apex of the building was the bishop's throne, while, arranged in a semicircle, on either side, were the seats of the presbyters — the altar being placed just before the bishop. So the emperor dispensed justice from his tribunal, while his assessors and advisers sat on either side of him, and delivered their judgments on the case before the court. So the Pope sits still during the highest ceremonies. The name by which the area of the bishop's jurisdiction is designated is a word denoting a secular administration. Diocese is used by Lysias, Demosthenes, and Aristotle, to imply the control of expenditure. It was transferred to the Latin language, and in Cicero means the civil divisions, or shires, into which a province was parcelled out.

We shall search in vain, then, for the details of ecclesiastical government in the authority of the Apostolic age. They were developed from the necessities of the position, and from the convenience of adopting a process of administration which was familiar in secular experience. Rapidly, episcopacy became one of the conservative forces of the Church, and so formed a barrier against novelties in speculation and practice. In time, the conflict of opinion, which raged through the fourth and fifth centuries, was waged by episcopal champions — the success of the combatants varying, the vehemence and violence of the battle increasing. After a while, the patriarchal see became the unit in the Church, and the bishop a suffragan to the metropolitan, as the presbyters had been made the subjects of the bishops. Last of all came the struggle for the primacy, and the submission of the whole Christian republic to a theological Cæsar.

It is not difficult for us to anticipate what would have been the judgment of the author of the Epistle to the Galatians on those who would limit the gifts of God to the subjects of one ecclesiastical administration. We can easily imagine what he would have said of those who assert that a missionary effort is neither successful nor valid, unless it be accompanied with some definite hierarchical organization, and who would therefore intrude on the labors of others, — not that they may plant or water, but that they may clip the tree into some set shape. With a strong effort he had disengaged himself from the trammels of a precise and formal education, and, though willing enough to concede to the prejudices of others, he insisted that the shibboleths of ecclesiastical parties were vain in themselves, and might be tyrannical, reactionary, and even fatal to religious truth altogether. The heathen have been converted and enlightened. In place of some gross fetish, dark rite, or debasing superstition, they have been told of a Father who forgives, of a Brother who leads them to the Divine presence, dwells with them, and familiarizes them with that for which heretofore they ignorantly and fruitlessly longed. They feel a new nature — are new men — have been born again. Then, in the freshness of their faith, some come down to trouble them, and say, — Except you adopt the ceremonial, the ritual, the forms, the government of the church to which we belong, ye cannot be saved. Can any one doubt what advice Paul would have given in this crisis, or that his zeal for Christian liberty would have forced him to repeat that contemptuous wish which he uttered when he heard of those who troubled the Galatians?

We can, with no great stretch of fancy, realize the gathering together at the house of Justus, hard by the synagogue. Prayers are said by the assembled converts. Psalms are sung, perhaps those with which the Jews commenced their devotions. Then follows the reading of the Scriptures, and in particular those majestic compositions which, full of dignity, wisdom, warning, hope, have come down to us under the names of the great Jewish prophets. Then some of those present narrate their experience of the new gospel, recount the visions, the ecstatic reveries, the heavenly sounds with which they have been favored, — such, for example, as are told in the Shepherd of Hermas. Others give, in turn, to the whole assembly, or to groups collected there, short exhortations on the Christian life and the Christian hope. Afterwards follows the feast in memory of that which Christ held on the night that He was betrayed; then thanks are given to God, and the assembly disperses with the kiss of peace.

## CHAPTER V.

THERE is probably no man who doubts the historical existence of The Person some of whose acts and words are narrated in the gospels. But to many minds He is represented as an idealized being, the real lineaments of whose life and teaching it is impossible to discover in the cloud of myths by which the figure is enveloped. This opinion has partly risen out of a disbelief in the supernatural — a disbelief which has been growing for the last century, and which has been strongly assisted by the progress of physical science, — partly out of the impression that the miracles of Christianity are at once essential to its truth, and manifestations of an absolutely new power, instead of being, as they profess to be, the exercise of exalted energy, — partly from antagonism to that dogmatism which, professing to be based on certain positions, the acceptance of which is necessary to salvation, has inflicted, and still inflicts, prodigious injuries on mankind. The theory that the narrative of the gospels is generally mythical is further supported by the fact that it contains discrepancies and contradictions, which, on the commonest rules of historical criticism, ought to throw grave doubts on the genuineness of the story. This latter argument seems to me to have very little weight. The notion that genuine history is characterized by an exact and minute attention to details, is wholly modern. It may be doubted whether — since no narrative can give all particulars — this method of historical composition does not, with all its affectation of reality, present a more unreal presentation of the past, than the artless tale of an interested, but uncritical observer, — whether, in short, syncretic history is not exceedingly apt to be untrustworthy or deceptive. Thucydides is the type of an exact and patient historian. Had, however, another author, of an equally critical turn of mind, devoted his attention to the same events, we should, most probably, have two very different stories of the Peloponnesian war. The more accurately two persons narrate their impressions of the same great events, the wider is sure to be the discrepancy between them. No two men see facts in exactly the same light, or direct their attention to exactly the same circumstances.

Be this as it may. If the narrative of the Evangelists is a myth, it is the most magnificent myth ever invented. Assume, if you will, that the Jesus of the gospels is a Jewish doctor, who united in His person, and at that time, the wisdom of a Rabbi and the enthusiastic genius of a Hebrew Prophet, and that two parties — the Jewish hierarchy and that bureaucracy which got the party name of the Herodians — combined against Him with a trumped-up charge of treason against the Roman government, and threatened

Pilate — a creature of Sejanus, who might be alarmed at the prospect of being involved in his patron's ruin — into getting this inconvenient teacher put out of the way by a legal murder. It is plain that this is the ostensible ground of procedure before Pilate, and it is equally plain that offence, taken at the unsparing reproofs which Jesus uttered against the chiefs of Jewish society, was the motive which weighed with the traditional parties of Christ's day. Such an event is no way remarkable. An oligarchy conspiring against a reformer, and using every effort to crush him, is a familiar historical occurrence.

But this, though it is, in brief, the prominent fact in the life and death of Christ, and though it is seen clearly in the story of the gospels, is not the conception which occupies the minds of the Evangelists, and absorbs those who have studied their narratives for eighteen centuries. In the epic of the Gospel, if we are to consider these compositions as so many poems, there is one hero. There are other characters drawn in very slight outline, but with great clearness, with rare beauty and nature. The fervid unsteadiness of Peter, the habitual dejection of Thomas, the tenderness of John, the indecision of Nathanael, the zeal of Zacchæus, the womanly worship of the Magdalene, the contrast between the sisters of Bethany, are portrayed in a word or two.

But in the centre of all this is the figure of Christ. It is not a colossal form which dwarfs the other actors in the drama, or a prodigious force by the side of which ordinary human energy is lost, or an overmastering will whose resistless action compels submission and obedience, but it is an effulgence which extinguishes every other light. It is said that the sun at its highest makes all other flame cast a shadow. Now the Evangelists were so profoundly conscious of the luminousness of that Presence, that, to the reader of the gospels, Christ appears always in the radiant garment and with the visage of His transfiguration. He is as the sun in the splendor of which other luminaries are extinguished. The Humanity of Christ is never lost sight of, He is always Jesus of Nazareth, but He is surrounded by an indescribable and mysterious clearness, which we seem to gaze on as the disciples did. In the simplest and most familiar acts of His life among them, He is with them, but not of them. Their relations to Him are not those of a Rabbi to his pupils, but of men necessarily following and wondering at a Person who is wholly superior to themselves, whom they saw constantly, whom they reverenced profoundly, but whom, as they confess, they understood imperfectly. He taught as one having authority, and He spoke and acted with all the authority of His teaching. If the Christ of the gospels is a hallucination of the Evangelists, it is the most amazing and the most attractive conception which the imagination has ever framed.

Attempts have been made more than once to invest an historical personage with ideal characteristics. Two such attempts were notoriously undertaken in rivalry of the Christ, as described in the gospels. These are the life of Apollonius of Tyana by Philostratus, and that of Pythagoras by Jamblichus. The most unfriendly critic of Christianity would not contrast these narratives favorably with the gospels. Besides, both personages are unreal. The existence of Apollonius is doubted, and the first historian of Greek philosophy, Aristotle, though he often speaks of the Pythagoreans, never mentions the name of the sage who was in after times reputed to be the founder of the sect.

But the draft of an idealized portrait has been once made, and by the greatest master of dramatic language which the ancient world produced. Every effort of his imagination was lavished by Plato on completing the picture of his Socrates, and the works of this incomparable writer have come down to us entire. We know that the picture is ideal, for we have a homelier portrait of the wisest Greek from the pen of another disciple whose sketch is much more true to nature. But Plato did for philosophy what the great sculptors of antiquity did for the human form. As they invested their statues of gods and heroes with their highest conceptions of human beauty, so Plato conferred on his imaginary Socrates the possession of the loftiest ideal philosophy.

The parallel between Christ and Socrates has often been drawn. Both were reformers of society, both suffered on a false charge of impiety, and in deference to a false patriotism. But here the parallel ends. Socrates is the purest example of heathen ethics, and the Platonic system of ethics is sustained by a scheme of emanations which are intended to have the force of a religious authority, and to be confirmed by the laws of thought. But Christ is the founder of a religion. Nay, He is the religion itself. Other men have been shadows of the great Original. Here is man in the image of God, — man as the ancient seers conceived him to have been originally framed, — man as modern optimists conceive him capable of becoming. Here is the type of humanity. Henceforth religion is the imitation of Christ, because the nature of God has shone forth in the person of man. If this conception is a myth, the grandest poetical character is dwarfed into nothingness beside the narratives of the reformed tax-gatherer, the attendant on Paul and Barnabas, the physician of Troas, and the fisherman of Galilee, who, whatever may be their discrepancies in detail, agree in this magnificent ideal of wisdom, holiness, loveliness. If this conception be a myth, humanity is better in its myths than it is in its verities.

The easiest road to saintship is by asceticism. Men are instinctively so enamoure l of self-denial — are so pleased by a contrast to the wretched clamor of self-interest, which is always stunning them with its pretentious noise, that they will honor a fool if he can show himself disinterested. They will even acquiesce in a system which is certain to induce moral and social evil, even if it furthers the worst ambition which a sinister organization can gratify, provided only that an ascetic tinge is imparted to those who found the system. Buddhism is the worship of asceticism. Brahmanism owes its continued existence to the austerities of Fakirs and devotees. The founders of the Roman orders have been almost invariably rigorous ascetics. Some of them have been crazy, or almost idiotic. There is nothing which is more cardinal in the discipline of the Roman Church than the celibacy of the clergy. A married minister of the Gospel is inconceivable to the most liberal layman of the Romish Church. Nothing puzzled the contemporaries of Talleyrand — secularized as he was by the highest authority, so much as his marriage. And yet the truest critics of the social state in Roman Catholic countries have deplored the celibacy of their clergy — have seen that the surrender of all domestic ties gives a vigor to ecclesiastical organization and usurpation which is eminently dangerous to society, and is wholly inimical to liberty. And in another manner, though the Græco-Russian Church enjoins marriage on the parochial clergy, all authorities — latest among them, Dr. Eckhardt — concur in stating that all ecclesiastical influence is with the monks, and that the secular clergy are despised and degraded.

Christ totally repudiated asceticism. He is continually represented at the home of rich men. When He entered on His mission His first appearance is at a wedding. He avows that He came eating and drinking, and we are told that He was calumniated because He did not decline the hospitalities which were offered Him. He recognizes the stern courage of John the Baptist, — asserts that he was a prophet, nay, even more than a prophet, — but speaks slightingly of his pretensions and position as compared with those who are within the kingdom of heaven. He taught, to be sure, that men who follow Him must deny themselves, — He put a sharp test to the rich young man who would be His disciple, — He avowed that wealth was a danger, and inculcated reliance on the providence of God for the supply of daily necessities. The sacrifice of one's own interest may be a condition of the highest morality and religion which the Gospel inculcates, but Christ never makes asceticism the end of life, as the purifier of the soul.

It is evident that the disciples who walked with Christ were struck most of all with His insight into men's hearts. He knows man thoroughly. He divines the thoughts of individuals, anticipates their words, reads their very soul. This is the power which is always present in Him. Such a conception is perfectly true to nature. To know mankind is the greatest manifestation of what we call genius. To interpret public opinion, and thereupon to guide it, is the highest effort of statesmanship. To know all this, and to be able also to exercise the same power in particulars, — to discern by an instant intuition all that passes through the mind of another, — is to be possessed of the Wisdom and the Power of God. Now this was what the Evangelists perpetually recognized in their intercourse with Christ.

Joined to this marvellous insight into man, Christ had another notable characteristic, — that of profound sympathy for suffering, infinite tenderness for the weak, boundless charity for the penitent. The reproach was cast at Him that He was the friend of publicans and sinners. The rich man who made Him a feast is amazed at His gracious bearing to the penitent woman who shed tears on His feet. His parable of the Prodigal Son — a story which has taught repentance and hope to thousands — is the narrative of His own bearing to the sinful soul which yearns for pardon. So, again, with His commiseration for the widow at Nain, His compassion for the bereaved parents in Galilee, His sympathy with the sisters of Lazarus, His unceasing benevolence to the sick and ailing. There is nothing more touching in the life of Christ than His welcome of children to His arms, and His sorrow at the impending fate of Jerusalem. Now, if wisdom is divine, love joined to wisdom is even more divine. It is the rarest of conjunctions, but the most winning of forces. It turns a terror into a Providence. This exact scrutiny into motives, this distinctness with which thought or purpose is known, would frighten and deter man from companionship with so acute and clear-sighted an observer. But when this knowledge is interpreted by love, it becomes infinitely attractive. And the Christ of the gospels is a personage in whom these qualities combine. He has even a word of compassion for the miserable Judas, He utters a prayer for the forgiveness of them who crucified Him.

The Jews, nineteen centuries ago, were keenly expecting the coming of the Messiah. The teaching of the Rabbis had discovered this manifestation in such phrases as "the Word of God," "the power of God," "the wisdom of God." Some speculated on the mystic numbers in the Book of Daniel. Some, mindful of the glorious era of David and Solomon, materialized the promise made to the Fathers. This was the popular view. The multitudes were ready to make Jesus a king. They joined gladly in His processional entry into Jerusalem — an act which evidently alarmed the chief men in the city. The last expectation of the Twelve, according to the narrative in the Acts of the Apostles, is that He should restore the kingdom to Israel. But the wisest men anticipated only a moral revolution — a fulfilment of the prophecy of Zechariah, "The Lord shall be King of the whole earth. In that day there shall be one Lord, and His name one." The doctrine of Christ, "The kingdom of God is within you," had no strange sound to Jewish ears. The office of the Word, according to the Talmudists, is to enlighten the man. The young man who fulfilled the Law was not far from the kingdom of God. The Jew could read and understand the words of Hosea, — "What does the Law demand of thee, except it be to do justice, and to love mercy, and to be ready to walk with the Lord thy God."

During the life of Christ the two characteristics which I have referred to were constantly before the view of His disciples. Of course they did not believe that such a person could be delivered into the hands of His enemies. When Peter repudiated the suggestion, he, no doubt, spoke the thoughts of all those who were with him. It is probable that Judas did not intend to do more than take money for assisting in an attempt which he was persuaded would fail. Is it possible to believe that John the evangelist, who was the especial object of Christ's favor, and who was known to the high priest, could have witnessed what went on in the pontiff's palace and the prætorium, and have been silent, if he had not been convinced that this judicial procedure would have ended in an acquittal, or in some manifestation of power, by which Christ would have passed out from the midst of His enemies? Had not Christ said that He was greater than Solomon and Jonah — the king and the prophet who severally affected the imagination of the Jew most powerfully? For the one was the most splendid monarch of Eastern story; the other was the prophet who, having by his counsel restored the kingdom of Israel to the dimensions it reached in the days of the great king, left unwillingly his office of chief minister at the court of the second Jeroboam, in order to denounce the sin and predict the fall of Nineveh the great — of the rival, and finally, the conqueror of Israel.

The narrative of the gospels testifies to the consternation of the disciples at the judicial murder of Jesus. But their sorrow soon gave way to joy. They were informed that He was risen again from the dead, and this by eye-witnesses of His revived Presence. The body was no longer in the tomb.

They who do not believe that death has ever loosed its hold on those whom it has once occupied are constrained to adopt the hypothesis, that the narrative of Christ's resurrection is a fraud, or a delusion, or both. If the disciples did dispose of the body of Christ, and persisted in proclaiming that He had risen, till they were overpowered by an hallucination which had its beginnings in deceit and falsehood, and if, while occupied by this imagination, they adopted a severe and ascetic life, an exact and precise morality, it is not easy to find the parallel to such a delusion. No rational person can doubt, that the belief in the resurrection of Christ was entertained as firmly by all those who professed His religion, as the belief in their own existence was. It is proclaimed before God and man, not, be it observed, for any material end, — such as a scheme of conquest, or the foundation of a spiritual despotism, to be exercised by those who could induce their hearers to acquiesce in a supernatural authority, — but by men who are charged with advocating so spiritual a system, that they ignored home, friends, country, life itself, for the sake of Him whom they said was risen.

It seems impossible to doubt the good faith of those simple and devout men, who could have had no possible motive for committing a fraud, and perpetuating a falsehood. Writing twenty-five years after the event, the apostle Paul states that Christ was seen by Peter, by the Twelve, by five hundred at once — most of whom, he added, were still alive at the time of his writing; by James, and again, by all the apostles. Belief in the resurrection of Christ is not made to depend on the testimony of one or two women, who have visited the sepulchre at the early dawn of a spring morning and been deceived by some appearance and sound, or upon the assertion of some ecstatic visionary, whose imagination has represented the Person whom he had followed so long, the voice which he had so often listened to. The evidence is cumulative; and, as far as one hears, no single person who had averred that he had seen the risen Christ ever shook off the impression or conviction, or discovered that he had been in error. There is no parallel to so general, so persistent a delusion.

According to the narrative in the Acts — given three times over, and purporting, on two of these occasions, to come from Paul's own lips — the conversion of the Apostle was due to a vision of the risen Christ. Without relating the circumstances, St. Paul tells the Corinthians that he had an interview with Jesus, and was thereupon an independent witness of His resurrection. Elsewhere, he rests his equality with the old apostolate on the ground that "he had seen the Lord." The author of the Clementines disputes the fact, in order to dispose of his claims to such a dignity. It is clear, then, that when Paul wrote his epistles there were very many persons who were ready to give their testimony to the resurrection of Christ, — to their having seen and conversed with Him.

The affirmation of the death of Christ is the basis of the doctrine which asserts the redemption of man. The means by which man can be restored, or be created anew, or can commence the process of perfection, is the suffering of Christ. That the progress of humanity is achieved by the self-sacrifice of those who devote themselves to its good, is a tenet in every religion, and is confirmed by overwhelming experience. The sacrifice of Christ is the apotheosis of this principle. Whether one considers the merit of the sufferer, or the excellence of the doctrine which he taught, the example of Christ is the chief illustration of the seeming paradox, that society gains by its losses, that it conquers by its sacrifices, that a righteous cause triumphs because it spares neither life nor labor in the prosecution of its claims, in the vindication of itself. Christ was the great atonement, but man is always engaged in the work of atonement for his fellow-man, as long as vice, sin, ignorance, have to be combated, wrong redressed, right done. Too often, indeed, the sacrifice and suffering are wasted because the immediate end is false or unworthy. Whatever else may be its merits, Christianity, in the hands of Paul, puts prominently forward the statement of the condition under which man may be regenerated, and declares that this sacrifice is vain, even in the person of its highest Exemplar, unless the same course be followed by those who accept the Gospel. Other apostles had affirmed the doctrine that the sacrifice of Christ is the salvation of man. Paul recognized the ethical significance of the statement, extended and developed it, and made it a permanent rule of conduct. The atonement of Christ is not in the hands of this Apostle a magical purification, but an example, the imitation of which is the duty, the glory, the hope of them who would be like Him; and if stress is sometimes laid on the immediate effect of Christ's death in those who are enlightened, and less emphasis is put on the continuity of the work which man does for man, it must be remembered that the apostolic generation confidently looked forward to the termination of the world within the lives of those who had witnessed the crucifixion.

To do unsought and unrewarded benefit to mankind for the sake of God is the essence of the Christian life. It is that which gives perpetual vitality to Christianity, which enables it in spite of its having been often enslaved to a coarse, harsh, false, political system,—in spite of its being perverted by dogmatic logomachies, and presented as a set of opinions,—to assist and retain the foremost place among civilizing agencies. The essence of Christianity is not in the priest, but in the sacrifice. It is to Christianity that we owe school, hospital, reformatory, and other allied agencies by which it is hoped that sin and vice will be discouraged and diminished. It is very possible that many of those who are virtually under its influence, decline, as far as words go, to acknowledge its authority. But men are constantly, for good as well as evil, controlled by traditions, habits, associations which they do not recognize, or which they even repudiate. Other religions have inculcated beneficence, almsgiving, charity; but Christianity is peculiar, in having taught that man can save man, and that he ought to save man. The civilization of man is not an induction, but an experience, a harmony, an adaptation of those forces which may enlighten him, and leave him free.

The sacrifice of Christ, and the significance of that sacrifice, are deduced from the admitted facts of His trial and execution. Both trial and execution were due to personal animosity on the part of the leading Jews, who stirred up the populace to demanding the death of Jesus. People talk of the fickleness of a mob, and ignore the deliberate malignity of an oligarchy. There is reason to believe that the mob was not one of native, but one of foreign Jews, who, coming up to the temple in crowds, that they might celebrate the Passover, were easily wrought to madness by hearing that Jesus had said He would destroy the temple. Another mob of foreign Jews, twenty years or more after this time, was roused to the same madness when they were informed that Paul had brought Greeks within the Jewish precinct. In these days, the Russian of the Greek Church, and the Frenchman of the Latin, are more easily driven to frenzy by tales about the profanation of their churches in Palestine, than the resident Christians of Jerusalem are. When they visit the sacred places, they are far more fanatical than those are who habitually dwell on the spot. Nor is the more sober judgment of those reformed churchmen who do not stimulate the religious sense by symbolism or local feeling free from liability to similar impressions. Facts, says the Roman poet, have far less influence on the ear than they have on the eye. But distance lends intensity to sentiment.

The resurrection of the body was a fixed article in the creed of the orthodox Jews. It was affirmed by Christ generally. He predicted it of Himself. As has been stated before, it was believed to have occurred in the person of Christ, and there were a host of witnesses who were ready to affirm that they had seen Him in life and in the body whom the chiefs of the Jewish nation had persuaded Pilate to crucify. It may be said that the body of Christ was not identical in its physical qualities with that of His life and passion. He appears suddenly, and disappears as suddenly. The corporeity of the risen Jesus was unlike that of ordinary men, but it could, according to the narrative of the fourth gospel, be touched and handled. According to Luke, the risen Christ actually ate with His disciples, and soon afterwards disappeared, being carried away to heaven. But no other gospel ascribes to Him those peculiarities of ordinary life, and the authenticity of the passage in St. Luke's gospel is not free from doubt.

Paul was by education a believer in the resurrection of the body, and had he remained constant to the faith of his youth, he would have insisted as energetically on this tenet as a necessary part of the creed of a spiritual religion, as he did after his acceptance of Christianity. Then he had seen a Person who had certainly been dead. The tenet had been verified by a prerogative instance. Accepted as a fact, the resurrection of Christ became the basis of that doctrine according to which Christ unites and permeates all those who are His redeemed. This is His grace, His peace, His presence or indwelling. So strongly is the resurrection of Christ identified with the spiritual life, that the Apostle cannot conceive the death of Christ to be effectual for the regeneration or salvation of mankind, except on the hypothesis of His subsequent resurrection. "If Christ," says he, "has not risen, that which we preach is valueless, and your trust is delusive. We too are found out to have given false evidence of God, for we have borne our testimony of Him that He has raised Christ, whom he has not raised, if there be no resurrection of the dead. — If Christ be not raised, your confidence is vain, ye are still in your sins; nay, they who have slept in Christ, have perished. As it is, however, Christ is," he adds (using a metaphor familiar from the custom which prevailed among the dispersed Jews, of forwarding offerings to the temple in Jerusalem), "the first-fruits of the dead."

Paul gives no reason for this connection of the resurrection of Christ with the hopes which he held out in his gospel, beyond this statement, that the resurrection is the guarantee of man's immortality, and thereupon of that compensation for the sufferings of life, in which the religious sense assures men. He held, it would seem, that unless there be some fresh garment for the spirit of man, unless it be clothed on by some eternal vestment, it has no individuality, no existence. The body is the instrument of natural life, and the spiritual life of the hereafter needs some similar instrument by which to exhibit and continue its energies. In short, if the death of the body be not a prelude to its resurrection under some new and perpetual organization, death annihilates the spirit simultaneously with its separation from that physical being which manifestly perishes. To die is not to live, unless the life finds some other dwelling-place. "We know," he says, in his Second Epistle to the Corinthians, "that if our earthly house, which is a tent, be dissolved, we have a habitation from God, a house not made with hands, eternal in the heavens. In this we groan, longing to put on our heavenly home, to be found clothed, not naked. We who are in this tent groan under our burden, since we do not wish to be stripped, but to be clothed fully, that the mortal part of our nature may be absorbed by life."

The immortality of the Greek philosophers was vague and shadowy. That force, genius, virtue, could be irretrievably lost with the death of the man in whom they were existent, was an intolerable suggestion. That the outrageous injustice with which the life of antiquity was too frequently acquainted, with which all social life is too familiar, should not be rectified by some Power, and at some future time, was so shocking a sentiment, that it could not be entertained without imperilling even that measure of justice which existing society has been able to secure, and without which society would come to an end. But how, and in what form, the soul's immortality and felicity were to be secured, was left indefinite. Plato expounds his conception of the soul of man after death in the form of a vision, vouchsafed to Er the Armenian — a myth which, probably, had a Syrian origin. But, while the psychological existence of the human soul was affirmed, the physiological conditions of its existence are ignored. The good are rewarded, the bad are punished. But how do the former apprehend their felicity? how do the latter become sensible of their misery? To know and to feel, to enjoy and to endure, to be sad and to be happy, require the existence of some organization, through and by which the man receives his impressions. The road of knowledge is by experience and sensation. How can a disembodied spirit preserve its consciousness, which is its being? The instinct which refuses to acknowledge annihilation is intelligible, but what is the process by which identity is secured?

With this difficulty Paul attempted to grapple. Nothing appears to indicate more clearly how the Apostle's mind was impregnated with the formularies of the Peripatetic school, than the exposition which he gives of the means by which the personality of the man may be secured in the life to come. Here, however, it may be necessary to say a few words on the psychology of that school of ancient thought, from which, as the writer believes, the phraseology of the Apostle's statement is derived.

In the Aristotelian philosophy, all the phenomena of life and consciousness were comprised in one word, for which ($Ψυχή$) there is no English equivalent. Perhaps the nearest is "the vital principle." The word is applied to the spontaneous development of any organism whatever with which Aristotle was experimentally familiar. Had he been acquainted with the laws of crystallization, there is every reason to think that he would have extended the application of the word so as to include this development, for he does not confine his term to the phenomena of volition only.

The Aristotelian philosophy takes cognizance of the facts of life and nature. But it takes no note of the transcendental and supernatural. It is entirely subjective, — entertaining no other evidence than that of sensation and consciousness, if, indeed, it makes any marked distinction between these two terms. It is possible, the philosopher argues, that there may be a life of the man which transcends experience. It is certainly unpopular to dispute the opinion that the man is immortal, though the body perishes. But of such an existence there is no evidence. Nay, it is impossible to conceive how it may be, however much we believe that it is, because we are familiar only with the machinery by which impressions are received and by which thought is evolved from those impressions. The instrument of thought is in the body, and the body perishes.

The general principle of life, or of spontaneous as opposed to derivative motion, exhibits various stages of development, from mere growth to appetite and will. The highest manifestation of life, that of man, includes the phenomena of the more imperfect forms of existence. Man, besides his own proper organism, has that of the brute and the plant; he grows and feels as well as thinks. The Aristotelian psychology, in brief, is incomplete Darwinism, differing from it mainly in the fact, that the progression of existence is conceived as co-ordinate, instead of being due to natural selection, —this phrase being a euphemism for the fact that the strong prey on the weak, or at least narrow those opportunities of life which the weak would have in the absence of the strong.

Such an organization Paul recognizes as a " natural body." But he assumes that this natural body contains the germ of a higher organization, which is destined to receive that part of man's complex nature, " his spirit," and which survives dissolution. The difference between the man of physical creation, and the man of the new or spiritual creation, lies in the fact that the former is life, the latter spirit. The former is of the earth, is the vessel of the potter. The latter is the Lord from heaven. The realities of physical existence are distinct from those of the heavenly nature, though Christianity is the exaltation of the former to the latter. To them who are regenerate the higher life is potentially present, whether they have died or are alive. This only is sure, that when He comes, the transformation will be instantaneous and complete. The dead will rise in their new nature, the living will be changed. The risen Christ is the exemplar and prototype of that glorious body which man will receive in exchange for the weakness of his present habitation, and in which he will preserve his individuality. The hope, however, of this resurrection seems to be limited — for the language used by Paul is sometimes perplexed and ambiguous — to those who are regenerate, in whom is sown that germ of a new life which endures beyond death and the grave, and in the consciousness of which the Christian can exult over his last and his greatest enemies.

St. Paul does not accept that coarser theory of a resurrection which confers on the spirit of man the same organism that he had and used during life. It must be something wholly different. It seems likely that this idea of the spiritual body — though it had not been unfamiliar to him in the school of Gamaliel — was framed on the vision which he had seen on the road to Damascus, and which was impressed so indelibly on his memory. Christ is in the heavens, the place of light, from whence comes life. Hence, relieved of the ordinary conditions under which the human body is limited by the grossness of its nature to one spot, He can show Himself in his glory to the furious enemy who is afterwards to become the faithful Apostle — can warn, reprove, console, instruct him. And though we have no knowledge of what that nature is, we do know this, that we shall be like Him. It is plain that the Apostle had identified the doctrine of man's immortality with the resurrection of Jesus, and that he therefore holds a middle position to that immortality of the pure intelligence which the Greek philosopher and the Jewish allegorist of Alexandria accepted, and to that perpetuity of physical impulses and feelings which has been frequently held by Christian teachers of a later epoch, and also believed by many uncivilized races, to constitute the only true immortality of man. Many of these creeds, which strongly affirm the spirituality of God, as strongly affirm a material, and even sensuous resurrection. This, as is well known, is peculiarly the case with Mohammedanism. Our own age and race have developed a still grosser theory in Mormonism, which asserts the being of a material god, and promises its devotees a voluptuous immortality.

The researches of modern science have shown that the earth is a vast graveyard, wherein are buried not only the bodies of innumerable creatures, but where extinct forms of life, more numerous by far than all existing organisms, lie entombed. Man, the latest born of these forms, has inherited for his portion the sepulchre of a thousand successive worlds. The eternal hills of his experience are, in comparison with regions which look far less permanent, recent structures, built by some vast upheaval out of the bed of a deep but geologically modern sea. The only unchanged form is the ever-shifting ocean, which has at one time engulfed, at another relinquished the land here and there. And the succession of these epochs involves so prolonged a period of time, that the mind is wholly lost in attempting to give reality to that which is as illimitable as space. Creation reaches back through an incalculable series of years, during which the earth, now shaken by internal fire, now reeking with a continuous summer, now bound in permanent winter, was rushing round the sun, and hurrying with the company of its fellow-planets through space. The beginning is infinitely distant. Man is a being of yesterday, even when the remotest period which modern speculation suggests is assigned to his appearance on the earth. There are a few inhabitants of the primeval seas which have preserved their organisms, which have remained unaltered through these multitudinous cataclysms which have overtaken the earth, through those furious storms which at various periods have desolated creation. But man has only appeared in the most recent epoch of the world's history. Can his existence be the sign of the world's last renovation, of a peaceful and steady growth, the consummation of which is a new heavens and a new earth? To the men of the apostolic age, the earth had waxed old, and was ready to pass away. If we, so many centuries after their time, hold to their faith, the race of man was in the infancy of its true destiny, was commencing its career, when they taught that the end of all things was at hand.

Had the facts of modern science been unveiled to the eyes of Paul, it does not appear that his exposition of the resurrection would have been different. It may be true, he might have answered, that the experience which we have of life connects it with an organism which is born, grows, decays, perishes. But the experience which we appeal to is assuredly bounded. We may assert, but erroneously, that no other being exists beyond that which we can comprehend. There are, may be, other forms in which life is continued, nay is exalted, of which our faculties are not and cannot be cognizant, but after which the soul, the heart, the spirit of man strives, in which it trusts that it may escape annihilation. This eager search after life and immortality is the germ of that perpetual and unchangeable existence which resides in this body of death, which ever prompts the man to treat his present life as the preparation for an unlimited eternity. Such a longing for the perfection of God is a gift of unspeakable value to the possessor, is a cause of immeasurable benefit to man, is by its very presence a pledge that it will be certainly satisfied, however little its fulfilment comes within the range of experience, or agrees with its inductions.

The Gospel of redemption and immortality was, according to Paul's teaching, to be preached and offered to all men. It is evident that the Apostles at Jerusalem shrank from carrying the tenets of Christianity beyond the pale of the Jewish nation. The Acts of the Apostles gives no color to those legends which scatter the Twelve in various parts of the earth. St. Paul's words in the Epistle to the Galatians indicate that the Apostles were at Jerusalem at the time of his conversion; that they were there three years later, when he went up to visit Peter, but stood aloof from them; and suggest that they were there still, fifteen years after the first visit, when the mission of Paul to the Gentiles was finally admitted, the teaching of the Jewish converts being reserved to Peter. The absence, too, of any allusion to any other apostles in the other epistles and writings of the Apostolic Age, seems conclusively to show that the Twelve lived together in poverty and prayer at Jerusalem. At last, Jerusalem having been destroyed, and nearly all having been removed by death, John, in extreme old age, is said to have migrated to Asia Minor.

The sincerity of conviction, the flexibility of character, the sagacity which discerned what was essential, the rigor with which the essentials of Christianity were insisted on, the tact with which men are treated, and the perfect catholicity of Paul's mind, gifted the Apostle with peculiar influence in commending his doctrine to the Gentile world. He is troubled with no scruples about race, rank, sex; and he does not hamper himself with any attempt after effecting a uniformity among his disciples or converts. Critics have affected to discover evidence compromising the authenticity of certain epistles — as, for example, those to the Philippians, one to Timothy, and to Titus — in the fact that a hierarchy, or, at least, a scheme of general office-bearers, in certain churches is recognizable in these epistles. By itself, the objection does not seem to possess the least importance. Had a particular form of church government been prescribed in any of these epistles, the acceptance of which was to be deemed necessary, or even important, grave doubts might well be thrown on the document, or, at least, on the passage in which such a rule might be found. But Paul was absolutely indifferent to the mere organization which a Christian society might adopt. The man who bade that the service of the Church should be conducted decorously and in an orderly fashion, set no store by any particular process for effecting these ends. He even puts little stress on the sacraments. He did not, it seems, practise baptism himself, except in rare instances. He makes, except on one occasion, no marked allusion to the Lord's Supper. With him religion was no outward form, however venerable or sacred it might be, but an inward light, bright enough to guide the whole heart and conscience, and yet capable of being diffused over the nature of the humblest and weakest.

The Christianity of Paul was the first religion which invited all men into the brotherhood of the Faith. It is true that it did not pretend to attack the prevalent usages of society, to counsel resistance to the imperial system, to seek reform through political agencies, to construct the secular life of the existing generation anew, to prescribe a form of polity, to break down any customary habit which is not in itself morally vicious. It was intended to be a community within a community, which was aggressive only by passive resistance to errors of opinion and grossness of practice, which was intended to absorb, not to reconstitute society. To use a modern phrase, Christianity trusted to moral forces only, and trusted to them without making any reference to their indirect significance. As has been before observed, the conduct of the early Christians was exceedingly like that of the Quakers of Penn's age. They took no active part in opposition to popular practices, but protested passively against them. Hence, at first sight, the Christianity of the Pauline gospel seems to be wanting in that force which reprobates or checks social and political wrong. Nay, some have gone so far as to argue that it condones or encourages the evil which it does not directly attack. Thus, it has been said to have counselled acquiescence in slavery, to have justified the extravagances of despotism, to have substituted a dreamy quietism for that active resistance to the coarse excesses of insolent power which may be the highest duty that man can fulfil for his fellows.

But this charge is in many particulars unjust, and even unintelligent. It ignores the circumstances of the age in which Christianity was developed. It ignores the fact that the triumphs of passive resistance are more numerous, and have been more lasting, than those of energetic opposition. It fails to notice that a creed, which puts all men on the same level of necessity, and offers all the same magnificent hopes, is the heaviest discouragement to secular distinctions. It does not acknowledge that the genius of Christianity is a perpetual assertion of the equality of man, nor see that it meets that haughtiness which affects superiority over the general lot of humanity, — or which disdains to acknowledge any right or any justice which has not been conceded by power, — with the example of Christ, who made Himself of no reputation. It is the essence of Christianity, as taught by Paul, that man is bound to consider his duty before he asserts his rights, and that there is no claim which he can set up for eminence, which he ought not to substantiate by the service which he has done for it. Hence, the natural tendency of the Christian temper is towards political and social equality. The Judaizing teachers would have made it communistic, and Paul's good sense detected the peril of such a theory. If we look at his teaching from a modern point of view, the Apostle, in so far as he contemplated the reconstruction of society by the aid of Christianity, accepted the two leading conditions of what is called popular government, — that all social distinction should be personal, and that it should be won by public service.

A sufficient refutation of the statement, that the social theory of primitive Christianity sustained or encouraged the harshness of the relations which subsisted between master and slave, is to be found in the eagerness with which the latter accepted it. Slavery, it is true, was a far less bitter lot in antiquity than it has been made within societies which are professedly Christian. The emancipation of slaves was common. They were frequently treated with kindness and consideration. They were permitted to acquire property, and even to purchase their own freedom. Their condition improved under the empire; for slavery is never more cruel than when it is practised by a people having free political institutions, is always least onerous when all classes of society are in the grasp of a common despotism. It was made a social reproach against Christianity that it enrolled such numbers of slaves among its members. Bishops, in early times, were elected from this class of persons. Thus, Callistus, bishop of Rome 218-233, was, according to Hippolytus, a slave of one Carpophorus, a confidential person in Cæsar's household; and, if we can trust the report of this author, who vouches for his personal acquaintance with the facts, he was a swindler and knave. There will be no great attraction in a religion which does not seek to ameliorate the condition of those who embrace it. Besides, it is known that from early times, the possession of slaves was considered by Christian writers and teachers as contrary to the Christian notion of justice, which imposes the duty of doing as one would be done by. It is certain that this notion has finally succeeded in proscribing the practice as antichristian and inhuman, and that oppressed races have to thank the teaching of the New Testament for immunity from slavery.

This doctrine of absolute equality between the members of a common religion was accepted in a still more practical form by Mohammed and his successors. As the promoters of this religion appealed to the sword, they were able to enforce such a general equality. It must be allowed that the success of Mohammedanism was as much due to the promise of equal privilege, in the case of all who accepted the new faith, as it was to the valor and enthusiasm of primitive Islam. The facility with which this religion is even now extended is to be accounted for by the fact that it is constantly brought in contact with a system of privileged castes and races, and that it effects the destruction of all these distinctions by conferring equal dignity on all its converts. It does not fall within the compass of this work to discuss the causes which have arrested the civilization which the Mohammedan creed achieved, and which have even caused it to retrograde from the height which it reached ten centuries ago, at Bagdad and Cordova. It is sufficiently clear that the doctrine of the natural equality of man within the limits of the faith, and the comparative tolerance with which Islam treated dissentients from its tenets, account for the remarkable phenomenon of a few Bedouins establishing a mighty empire, and developing science and philosophy, when these were almost unknown names to a mediæval Christianity. Nor is it less clear, that the chief reason of the decline of Islam does not arise from its contact with European civilization, but from the barbarism of its later political system, and from the fanaticism of its Rabbis.

As, according to Paul, the beginning of the Christian life was trust in Christ, so the perseverance of the Christian was due to the grace of Christ, or as it is sometimes called, the Spirit of Christ. The teaching of the book of Proverbs personified the wisdom of God; the communications made from the Almighty to the Prophets of the Jewish monarchy, of the captivity, and of the restoration, were effected by the instrumentality of the Word of God; and these conceptions were still more fully solidified in the book of Sirach, in the Wisdom of Solomon, and in the Alexandrian theosophy. That God therefore visited man by the instruments whom He had created or chosen, was a familiar form of thought to the Jews of the Christian era; and when Paul speaks of Jesus as the power by which the union between God and man was achieved, he is using language which was perfectly intelligible to his hearers. In course of time the Word of God had ceased to be an abstraction, and was conceived to be a Person. But the Personification was complete when this conception was united to an historical man, who alone among men had, after suffering the common lot of humanity, vanquished the common enemy, was risen, was glorified, was out of the dominion of death, and had become the assurance of life and immortality.

If men have any belief in God, and if they acknowledge, in their relations to Him, any thing beyond what is purely secular — if they do not allow His personal existence to disappear in Pantheistic generalities, they are forced to recognize some mediator between themselves and Him. Thus, in the language of Paul, Moses was the mediator between the God of the Hebrews and that people, as Mohammed is said to be to Islam. So, in a far higher sense, because gifted with a far more exalted being, Christ is the Mediator of the new covenant, as well as the great atonement for mankind. And just as, during His life on earth, His gospel formed a perfect rule of life — a sufficient exposition of the faith — a full ground of hope, so He is present by His power, His Spirit, His grace, though He no longer appears to the ordinary vision of men. He is known better to the believer than He was known to His disciples in the days of His flesh. Whatever other intermediary there might have been previously between God and man, such agencies are superfluous in the spiritual presence and life-giving power of Christ. He unites all the imperfect and divided functions of priest, angel, spirit, in the intercourse which he holds with his people, — in the grace, peace, strength, hope, which He gives them. No phrase is too strong to express the power which He wields, the authority which He possesses, the gifts and graces which He can bestow. He lifts men from the sin and weakness of their mortal nature, bestows on them a new creation, reconciles them to God, supports and strengthens them in the toil of a transitory life, and conducts them finally to the presence of His Father and theirs.

Paul dwells but little on the alternative to this picture of the Christian life. The world around him was full of sin and wickedness, of ignorance and deformity. There are those who have no place in the kingdom, who have no inheritance with the saints, — with those who have been made holy by the sacrifice of Christ and by trust in Him; but very little is said of such persons, apart from reprobation of their life. The Apostle does not dwell upon the lot of the unblest — does not attempt to describe the condition of those who are cast away. He is not responsible for those theories of endless torment inflicted on unforgiven sin, still less for that scheme of the Divine justice and mercy, which would, in accordance with no moral sentiment whatever, capriciously condemn some persons to eternal banishment from the sight of God, to the perpetual company of mocking and malignant fiends. Christ died for the godless; His love is sufficient for the salvation of the whole human race. It is enough to know how great is His mercy to those who love Him. It is superfluous to inquire into the future condition of those who disregard His Gospel, still more so to speculate on the lot of such men as have never heard the Word. Nay, if love be the most enduring of the Christian graces —living when trust is realized, and hope is satisfied— and if this be the chief attribute of God and His Son, it is incredible that he should be pitiless who commands pardon and pity as the best offering which man can make Him. The Gospel which Paul preached has much to win men, little to terrify them. The presumptuous insolence which seeks to make the Almighty the author of uncharitable and merciless judgment was unknown to the man who was all things to all men, in order that he might gain some, and who believed that he had the mind of Christ.

Christianity owes the form which it has assumed, when it has been best interpreted, to the Pauline scriptures. The gospels give us a history, in which the facts of a life, the sayings and lessons of a great Teacher are narrated. But, except in the fourth gospel, the theology of the narrative does not develop much more religion than can be found in the pages of the evangelical prophets. With the first three evangelists, Christ is the last, though incomparably the greatest, of those to whom the Vision of God was vouchsafed, in whom the Spirit of God was manifested. In the fourth gospel, He is the Word incarnate, in whom exist the loftiest powers, — who is with God from the beginning,

— who is in full communion with the Everlasting Father, — who has life from the Father in Himself, as the Father Himself is the source and centre of all life.

In the gospel of Paul, Christ is an Example, but also a Power. He is the source of man's salvation, and the origin of all graces. Paul tells us that he announced a simple creed, — that " Christ died for our sins according to the Scriptures; that he was buried, and rose again the third day, according to the Scriptures;" and that abundant evidence was supplied to the fact. This is his gospel. Out of it he constructed his theology, by it he insisted that the reconciliation between the creature and Creator was effected. This is the chief element which he imports into the ancient doctrines of the Hebrew Scriptures, as they were understood by the doctors of the Christian era. God is still there, as He is described in the Prophets, a Being of infinite love, patience, gentleness. The commandment of God is still imperative on man, and must be interpreted, as heretofore, by its real spirit. Only the Law is done away — the ritual of Moses — its ordinances, sacrifices, ceremonies, with all the glosses of tradition. Not, indeed that the repeal of these enactments, the abandonment of this symbolism, is to inaugurate a period of license — to release man from his allegiance to that spiritual religion which purifies the heart. Far from it. The epistles of Paul abound with directions as to how man may live holily, reiterate the obligations of those who ally themselves to this new religion. Every one of the relations of domestic and social life pass under the

Apostle's review, and are commented on repeatedly. The Christianity which he taught does not inform men that the acceptance of certain tenets can be made substitutes for the regular fulfilment of moral duties — that obedience to stated ceremonies is the obedience with which God is satisfied, or is in itself a purification. He allows no man to say *Corban*, and thus pretend that a gift to the altar is a release from human ties. He exacts honest, persevering, intelligent work, as strictly as a political economist does. He knew that the largest power of doing good was contingent on the fulfilment of very homely and every-day offices — that few men are able to do real public service who neglect their ordinary business, and sacrifice common sense to some ideal wish. He had too much practical wisdom to be ignorant of the fact, that a man is not the worse Christian because he masters the cares of this life by his diligence, and that the best way to use one's substance well, is to earn one's substance honestly. That which binds the whole of Christianity together — which effects the unity of redeemed humanity — which constitutes the Church — is the presence, the indwelling of Christ. In this Christ are united all the power which God has given or will give, and all the tenderness of that devoted and ceaseless love which made Him a sacrifice for man. But the gospel of Paul is neither ascetic, nor contemplative, nor dogmatic. Man is illuminated, not to dream, but to labor. He is to earn his living — to seek by the toil of his life the means for conferring benefits on others, — to work out his own salvation, to seek the salvation of others, and, as he best may, to commend his faith by the diligence, holiness, and perseverance of his life.

It has been said truly by M. Vacherot, that Paul was the greatest of innovators and the least of sectaries. His gospel was intended for all mankind. The hopes which he held out to those who believed were not bounded by caste, or race, or sex, or condition of life, or age, or habit of thought, or power of thought. Had it been possible for those who constructed a theology from his writings to have apprehended the spirit in which those writings were composed, the world would have had a different history. The disciples of a great teacher, however, are not those who learn his formularies, and busy themselves with methodizing his principles, but they who seek to gather to themselves the mind of the teacher, who are followers of him in his attempt to evangelize the world.

But, in fact, the dogmas which have been defended by the teaching of St. Paul, are not contained in his writings, but are developments for which those who propounded or accepted them strove to find proof or warranty. The Christianity of many modern sectaries is like the Salaminian ship, which, still pretending to be the vessel which carried Theseus, has now, by reason of perpetual repairs and additions, little left of the original timber. For Paul is not, technically speaking, a theologian, since his theology is, except in one important particular, that of Gamaliel and the other orthodox teachers of later Judaism. Even after his conversion he could call himself a Pharisee. Upon Judaism he induced the office of Christ, as the only and the complete solution of the question which had long agitated all religious minds, — How can man be saved? This question is still asked by those who have repudiated Christianity, and, denying the immortality of the individual, assume the immortality of the race. And these persons answer the question in the same manner that Paul does, — that man in the aggregate is made perfect by the sacrifice of man, — that humanity gains by them who offer themselves as victims for its moral progress. Both agree that no good deed is wasted; but the Apostle of the Gentiles, while he insists on the conditions which govern the regeneration of mankind, claims that a recompense remains for them who have devoted themselves on behalf of their fellows, and that the identity of the agent is as enduring as the force of the action.

It is part of the irony of history, that men are often credited with opinions and motives which never controlled, or even influenced them. Of this perverse judgment, popular ideas about the Apostle Paul are conspicuous instances. He is sometimes considered as the author of those subtleties which took their rise in Alexandria, after Christianity was made to contribute to the syncretic philosophy of Philo, and which culminated in the dialectical refinements of the fourth and fifth centuries. He is really a preacher who took Jewish monotheism, engrafted on it those limitless energies which he recognized in the mediation of Christ, and inculcated an intensely spiritual, as well as an exactly practical morality. He is occasionally spoken of as an egotist. But he was really a man of great judgment and gentleness, of attractive manners, of immense activity, — one side of whose nature was occupied by an absorbing love of Christ, the other by a passionate longing to communicate the joys and hopes which he entertained as widely as possible throughout a suffering world.

## CHAPTER VI.

THE apocryphal or legendary literature of early Christianity is very copious. Much has been already printed, and additions are constantly made to what is known. Dr. Tischendorf has lately collected a fresh volume of these writings. But his publication probably embraces only a part of that which still exists in manuscript. If all these relics of theological romance were collected, they would form only a small fragment of what has been written. Some of these writings enshrine historical facts and genuine traditions. According to the modern canons of criticism, the fact that a story is unknown out of the particular region in which it is current, rouses a suspicion of its genuineness, which is quite distinct from its intrinsic likelihood or improbability. But modern criticism is, perhaps, apt, in interpreting the genuineness of records, to be led into conceiving that the writings of ancient authors were constructed on the method employed in our own day. In much ancient history, when the writer lives amid or near the events which he narrates, the facts are subordinated to the inference, or colored and selected to assist the inference. But the narrative may still be a real reflection of the age in which it is written. It seems an extravagance of scepticism to look on the Annals of Tacitus as little better than a political romance, the biographies of Suetonius as a mere epitome of court scandal.

These apocryphal writings of early Christianity may be subjected to one easy test. The dramatic tendency which certainly influences the authors of these narratives generally supplies the means for detecting the age of the story, and sometimes the motive for its composition. We have historical evidence of the growth of theological dogma; and when divisions arose in the Church, during the time that dogmas were being crystallized, the temptation to make the story a vehicle for the transmission or defence of a dogma was irresistible. The absence of dogmatic coloring is not a proof of the authenticity of such writings, but is good evidence of their antiquity.

Some of the most ancient of these compositions, — as the Pastor of Hermas, and the epistle of Barnabas, — were introduced into early manuscripts of the New Testament Scriptures, and, for a time at least, were received as authorities. Some of these, which a later criticism accepted as canonical, were rejected or suspected in an earlier age, as for example the Apocalypse. It is not unlikely that this acceptance or rejection was due, in the first instance, to the fact that some had been widely distributed and others had only a local circulation.

Among the earliest specimens of this legendary

literature, is a story entitled the Acts of Paul and Thecla. The story, alluded to by Tertullian, has latterly been republished in the original Greek, by Dr. Tischendorf. It is a narrative of the sufferings undergone by a damsel of Iconium, who had heard the preaching of St. Paul, and who resolved to abandon all — lover, home, friends — for the sake of the gospel which he preached, and in honor of the preacher. The earnest and self-denying attachment which the early Christians bore to their teachers in the Faith, is frequently alluded to by the Apostle, and is scornfully commented on by Lucian, in his narrative of the exploits of the charlatan Peregrinus. Thecla, like Lydia, was one of those female converts of primitive Christianity, whose heart the Lord opened, and who ministered to the wants of the apostles.

The Acts of Thecla give a portrait-description of the Apostle's person and physiognomy. This description is probably the origin of those other accounts of Paul's appearance in the flesh, which are found, for example, in John Malalas and Nicephorus. He was, we are told, short in stature, almost bald, bow-legged, stout, with eyebrows meeting, and with a prominent nose. Other accounts add that he had small but piercing gray eyes. His manner was, it is said, singularly winning. His face and figure must have been markedly of the Hebrew type. He has himself commented on the meanness of his personal appearance, and the unattractive delivery which characterized his speech. To translate his homely phrase, his oratory, he says, was nothing to speak of. But he, nevertheless, could call to witness the success of his ministry, when he claimed to possess a transcendent treasure, enclosed though it was in an earthen vessel. The poverty of the casket served to assist the lustre of the jewel it contained, the plainness of the setting called attention to the worth of the gem.

The great Apostle, then, was a man who did not possess the two gifts which were most prized in the ancient world — personal beauty and fluency of speech. He did not command attention by the majesty of his person, or rivet attention by the eloquence of his utterances. To outward appearance, he must have looked like some common-place travelling Jew, whose rapid and confused speech provoked the Athenians into calling him a blabbler, when, quitting his ordinary province, — that of arguing with the Jews and their proselytes in the synagogue, — he essayed to dispute with the polished loungers in the Athenian agora. But this speech, homely, unadorned, rugged as it might have been, possessed two characteristics which are more persuasive than the subtlest oratory. The speaker was thoroughly convinced of that which he said, and profoundly in earnest when he commended his convictions to others. The great master of ancient eloquence said that dramatic action was the first, second, third requisite of successful pleading; but no art can rival in its effects the outspoken utterances of disinterested sincerity, no address is more certain to command the sympathy of an audience, than that of a man who pleads from his heart.

Paul was born at Tarsus, a city of Cilicia, — no mean city, as the Apostle called it, with the natural feeling of a man for his birthplace, and the home of his childhood. The city was built on a plain at the foot of Mount Taurus, and through it flowed the stream of the Cydnus, which, rising in the snows of the mountain, and gushing through deep ravines, was notable for the coldness of its waters. The river, says Strabo, divides the town, and the gymnasium of the youths was on its bank.

The same author informs us, — writing at a time when St. Paul must have been a child in this Cilician city, — that the inhabitants of Tarsus were so addicted to philosophy, and took such a general interest in every branch of education, that the reputation of the city exceeded even that of Athens and Alexandria — the great centres of intellectual activity and of high culture. And it is remarkable, continues this authority, that the students are not strangers who visit the city, as they do at most of these ancient academies, but are the natives of the district; most of whom, when they have gained the learning which the schools of Tarsus supply them with, migrate to other places, and rarely return.

There is very little recorded about the family of Paul. He tells us himself, that he was of pure Hebrew descent, the phrase that he uses being probably the equivalent of that which a Spaniard took pride in when he called himself an old Christian. He was of the tribe of Benjamin, and was perhaps named after the gallant, wilful king whose chivalry, comeliness and lofty stature were so exceptional. We are informed that his father belonged to the strictest school of the Pharisaic sect, and that his son was reared in the same discipline. We know further, that his father was a Roman citizen, either by purchase or grant. Add the facts that his sister had a son, who either lived at Jerusalem, or, as is equally probable, had come up to the holy city at the time when his uncle made his last unfortunate visit there, and that he had five other kinsmen, two of whom had become Christians before himself, and all that we know of his family is told. The alternative name of the Apostle, that by which he is best known, was apparently part of the Gentile name, by which, in conformity with Roman usage, the citizen was designated. Paulus is a cognomen shared by many families, as might have been easily the case, for it means a person of small stature, and such nicknames were common in the days of republican Rome. Silas or Silvanus, a companion of St. Paul, was similarly a Roman citizen, and so, it would seem, was Lucas or Lucanus, whom we know as the third Evangelist, and the author of the work called the Acts of the Apostles, in which are contained a few selected incidents of the Apostolic age. Paulus is only one of three Roman names which the Apostle bore. We know nothing of the other two.

The fact that St. Paul learned a trade in his youth gives us no hint as to the social circumstances in which he was born and brought up. It is well known that the doctors of the Jewish law prescribed the instruction of every male child in some handicraft. Eastern nations have no conception of an hereditary aristocracy,

— of a class which is made leisurely by the possession of inherited wealth. As among Mussulman communities at the present day, so among the Semitic races of the Christian era, a king might lift a beggar from the dunghill to set him among princes, and as easily compel him to revert to his original condition. Some occupation, therefore, was universally taught to the youth, by which, should misfortune overtake him, the man might earn his bread. "He who does not teach his son a trade," said the Rabbis, "teaches him to be a thief" — *i.e.*, a Bedouin, or a brigand. So the young Saul, living at Tarsus, was instructed in the craft of a local industry — the manufacture of goats' hair into a strong cloth for tents. This cloth was called cilicium, from the province in which it was first manufactured, and in low Latin was used — perhaps is still used — to designate the hair shirt worn by ascetics and devotees. There was a time in his life when the Apostle found his skill useful, though it does not, I think, follow necessarily, that he was actually engaged in the manual labor of a hand-loom weaver at Corinth.

After a time, — but at what time we know not, — the youth was sent to Jerusalem, to be taught by the most eminent of the Jewish doctors, — the last and the greatest of the Hebrew schoolmen. Gamaliel was the grandson of Hillel. As the Acts of the Apostles tells us, he was an honored teacher among the Jews, and a man of good sense and moderation. The Gemara is full of stories about him, illustrating his influence, orthodoxy, and wit. Thus, he is made to talk familiarly with Cæsar, — by whom is probably meant Augustus, — and to have vindicated the Jewish narrative of man's creation, and the doctrines of the soul's immortality and the body's resurrection, by citations of Scripture and ingenious parables. It is possible that his pupil Saul was one of those Cilician Jews who disputed with Stephen. We know that he was in that furious rabble which, goaded by the reproaches of the eloquent and zealous deacon, shed the first Christian blood. As Paul obtained his knowledge of Greek literature in Tarsus, so he learned the mysteries of Jewish casuistry at the feet of Gamaliel in Jerusalem. It appears, too, that Paul had some permanent home in Tarsus, for there Barnabas sought and found him, when the two Apostles of the Gentiles set out on their first formal mission.

It does not seem that Paul's circumstances were mean. He constantly travels by sea, and with some retinue. That he freely spent his substance on his companions, and on those who might need his assistance, is to be expected from the generous character of the man. That he was intensely sensitive to any suspicion of mercenary motives, is well known. That he did not hesitate to assert his right to the assistance of his converts, and that he was exceedingly averse to insisting on the satisfaction of that right, are perfectly consistent traits. But this jealous love of independence did not deter him from accepting assistance which was urged on him, nor did any false shame prevent him from acknowledging such gifts with affectionate gratitude. He knew distinctly that any service, however great it may be, is instantly suspected, and certainly tainted, if any charge of self-interest can be alleged against the doer of it. That he suffered occasional privations, due to temporary causes, was to be expected from the missionary life which he undertook. But a pauper could not have lived for a long time in Ephesus. It was the most frequented city in Asia, and therefore was a place where no one could have resided except at considerable expense. Besides, during his residence he made acquaintance, in a somewhat intimate fashion, with some of the "chiefs of Asia." It appears that when he was imprisoned at Cæsarea, Felix expected that he might make offer of a bribe, so as to procure a release from his confinement, and the bribes which corrupt Roman governors took were large. Nor again at the closing period of his recorded history, when, if at any time, his circumstances would have been desperate, does he seem to have been impoverished. Some of his friends accompany him, apparently as passengers, in the ship whose sign was Castor and Pollux; and in Rome, where Juvenal tells us the cost of subsistence was excessive, the Apostle lives in his own hired house, the soldier who kept him in a kind of free custody being quartered on him. We find that this house was large enough to receive such visitors as waited on him, and to contain an audience.

These facts have been commented on, not with a view to attempting a life of the Apostle, — an undertaking which has been frequently essayed, and never with success, but because the circumstances which have been adverted to should be stated, in order to form an estimate of St. Paul's character as a man, and his work as a missionary. For he is really the missionary-Apostle, — chosen, set apart to carry the good tidings to all the nations, to found churches, to train preachers. It was he and his disciples who " turned the world upside down." With three exceptions, the names of those who had followed Jesus up to his passion disappear from sacred history after the catalogue is given in the Acts of the Apostles, — always occupy an inferior place to Philip, Stephen, and James. In the infancy of the Christian Church, John is associated with Peter; a little further on, and James the brother of John drinks of the cup and undergoes the baptism, which Christ, with affectionate sadness, predicted would be the lot of the sons of Zebedee. Later legends give us the history of the apostolic dispersion, and at last assign his mission to each of the Twelve and describe the acts of his martyrdom. In all likelihood, however, as they were at Jerusalem on the occasion of Paul's first visit, so most of them remained there as an apostolic college, under the presidency of James, known as the brother of our Lord, till death removed them one by one, or till the survivors, foreseeing the fall of the Holy City and the ruin of their race, fled to some place of refuge beyond the Jordan. It is probably at this time that the voice from Patmos is raised, and the Christian Church is instructed in the mystic vision of the future Providence of God. Last of all, the gospel of Christ's discourses is published.

ZEAL OF THE DISPERSED JEWS. 217

It seems clear that the resident Christians of Jerusalem excited little animosity on the part of those rival sects whose hatred toward Christ was so furious and so inveterate. It is true that immediately on the formation of the Church the boldness of men like Peter, and John, and Stephen brought persecution on the faithful. But at that time the death of Jesus was fresh in the memory of men, and the hierarchy became alarmed and indignant at being charged with his murder. Nor do we know what were the causes which led to the execution of James and the imprisonment of Peter.

The author of the Acts of the Apostles tells us that the execution pleased the Jews. It is possible that, for a few years after the crucifixion, the events which preceded the Easter of His Passion may have recurred to the memory of those who took part in that crime, and that the hate which, as the Roman historian tells us, is felt by the wrong-doer to his victim, may have roused the people to acts of hostility against the companions or disciples of Christ. During the middle ages, it was a common thing for the populace to be roused to excesses against the Jews by inflammatory orations preached on the Passion of Christ at Easter time. It is seen, too, that the dispersed Jews who did pilgrimage to Jerusalem at the Passover were more easily stirred to fanatical outbursts of rage than the settled inhabitants of the city; and they who profited by their first-fruits and their offerings were not unlikely to conciliate them by zeal against those who might be supposed to be unfriendly to Jewish nationality and the

10

Law of Moses. It may be, too, that James and Peter — one of whom, by reason, it seems, of the vehemence of his character, was surnamed, with his brother, " the son of thunder; " the other, the chief witness of Christ's life — may have provoked this sudden onslaught by reproaches similar to those which were uttered by Stephen, and have led Agrippa to consider that policy demanded the sacrifice of these troublesome sectaries. It was the last attack on the Apostolic college, as far as we have information in the Acts of the Apostles. Afterwards, we are told, the Word of God grew and multiplied. There was nothing, indeed, in the character and practice of the Jewish Christians which could cause permanent hostility to the Church of Jerusalem.

Agrippa had been one of those adventurers of royal blood, who swarmed at the courts of the Roman emperors. Following the traditions of the Republic, the emperors maintained a number of dependent monarchs in the outlying parts of the empire, as in the interior of Africa, in Syria and in Asia Minor. They set up, and deposed these puppets at pleasure. They encouraged pretenders to plead their rival claims at Rome. Sometimes a kingdom was made a province, and afterwards constituted anew into a kingdom, with the same or altered boundaries.

The imperial house had hitherto shown great favor to the Jews. Julius Cæsar had received important assistance from the nation at a crisis of his fortunes, and he had not been ungrateful. Augustus followed the same policy. He confirmed Herod the Great in his sovereignty over Judea, and, during the reign of this astute king, the Jews prospered and preserved a form of independence; for Herod's wrath fell mainly on his wives, his children, and his nobles. The jest of Augustus, that he would rather be Herod's hog than his son, is well known. Either by design or from caprice, the monarchy of Herod was not continued to his sons, for they received only small portions of their father's extensive dominions, while the greater part of Palestine was committed to the rule of a procurator who was subordinated to the proconsular governor of Syria. Such a procurator was Pilate, who was in the first instance a creature of Sejanus, and had, perhaps to please his patron, as well as to indulge his natural savageness of temper, treated the Jews with extreme harshness. The fall of Sejanus occurred a little before the murder of Christ; and the affectation of justice, the comparative gentleness of the procurator's manner in dealing with the Jewish authorities, the symbolical protest against the iniquity of condemning the righteous, and the concession to the threat of being represented as unfaithful to the jealous and suspicious Tiberius, point to the alarm and anxiety which Pilate felt at the crisis when the priests led Christ before the governor.

Agrippa had been the friend and companion of Caligula, and the confidant of his secrets. He had shared those furtive pleasures which Caligula ventured on, during the lifetime of Tiberius, when the man's real nature was unknown to any one but his closest associates, and to the dark, shrewd old emperor. In order to maintain his appearance at court, and to further his intrigues after the throne of the great Herod, Agrippa had involved himself terribly in debt; for in those evil days, nobles and princes borrowed largely in order to find the means for profligacy and bribery, with the certainty that they would be able to recover their fortunes from subjects or provincials if they could get a kingdom or the administration of a province. Thus, Agrippa borrowed largely of Alexander Lysimachus, the rich Alabarch of Alexandria, stipulating that half the sum should be paid at Alexandria, the other half at Puteoli (another illustration, by the way, of the manner in which the Jews carried on their banking operations); of Antonia, the mother of Claudius; and, finally, of a rich Samaritan who lived at Rome and was a freedman of Claudius. But, up to the time when Tiberius died, Agrippa had been the unluckiest of adventurers. His prospects were then at the worst, for the emperor had not only slighted his suit, but had cast him into prison.

On the accession of Caligula, he was instantly released and loaded with favors. The emperor gave him a chain of gold, the weight of which was equal to that of the fetters with which he had been loaded. He made him king of the Jews, bestowing on him that which he had so long sought for in vain. Agrippa hastened to take possession of his kingdom, but was imprudent enough to exhibit himself in royal pomp at Alexandria, where the Jews were at that time exceedingly unpopular. The last recorded circumstance of his public life — a similar but a more scandalous exhibition of vanity — is well known to all who read the Scriptures, and is also narrated by Josephus.

Agrippa seems to have been the only man whom Caligula really loved. When the emperor became insane, and the whole world was subjected to the caprice of a cruel and sensual madman, Agrippa still influenced him. At last, Caligula declared himself a god, and bade the empire worship him, and the empire submitted with alacrity to the amazing degradation. The Jews alone refused to commit this act of impiety, and Caligula ordered that a statue of himself should be forthwith set up in the Temple at Jerusalem. Had the command been obeyed at once, there is little doubt that the outbreak which tasked the energies of Vespasian and Titus would have been anticipated by thirty years.

At this crisis, Agrippa threw himself in the very path of the madman, as he was on the full course of his frenzy. He addressed a letter to him, in which he implored him not to take this step. The letter is preserved in that work of Philo which narrates the sufferings of the Alexandrian Jews, and the attempts they made to conciliate the emperor. The effort must have cost Agrippa infinite anxiety. It was certainly an act of singular heroism; it was as if he had cast himself to the wild beasts of the circus, for he risked life and all that he had lived for. Agrippa had been a voluptuary and an adventurer; he had been the meanest thing the world had ever seen — a courtier of the early empire; but in this act he showed the courage of the Maccabees, from whom he was descended. It is only justice to him to believe that he counted the cost, and that he deliberately ventured every thing to save the Temple from profanation, the Jews from an inexpiable insult, and the empire from a desperate war. He gained delay by his remonstrance, and Caligula's death put an end to the danger.

These facts in the life of Agrippa have been mentioned because they show that, although he had been corrupted by the influences of the Roman court, and had flattered the worst vices of the worst men in the worst age of the world's history, he was yet saved from utter degradation, and roused to courage by the religion which kept its hold on him. That motive, which was strong enough to make a hero of Agrippa, and which might have made him a martyr, if the dagger of Chaerea had not shortened the career of Caligula, animated every Jew. The Jew was of a race, according to Cicero, that was born for servitude. But no race ever struggled more earnestly for its faith and its nationality than that of Israel did; and, dispersed and broken as it is, none has ever maintained both with greater fidelity, none has illustrated more clearly how powerful passive resistance may be.

It has been observed that from the days of the elder Agrippa, the Church at Jerusalem enjoyed unbroken quiet. Its chief officer was a devout ascetic, for James lived according to the strictest rules which the Law prescribed to the profession of a Nazarite. His mode of life resembled that of those anchorites, the Trappists of ancient history, who lived by the Lake Mareotis, under the name of Therapeutæ, and were probably the representatives of the Buddhist mission which was sent to Egypt in the days of Ptolemy Philadelphus. The knees of James became horny by the constant attitude of prayer. Josephus, who narrates the circumstances of his death, states that the man was highly honored and respected. Strict in the fulfilment of those obligations which the Law imposed, the college at Jerusalem may have been looked on as a mere offshoot of the Pharisaic sect, which provoked no antipathy on the part of the Jewish hierarchy, because it advised no innovation on the practice of orthodox Israel.

The physical constitution of St. Paul was weakly, — as in the case of many men who have been characterized by great mental vigor and unsparing energy; his bodily powers seemed wholly inadequate to the task which he undertook. Besides, he underwent labors and hardships which were sufficient to try the endurance of the strongest frame, of any frame; for it is often the case that certain privations are borne better by the weakly than by the robust. It is well known, moreover, that he speaks of some peculiar trial to which he was subject, a trial which he designates as a messenger of Satan. It has been suggested that this was some sensuous impulse. But this interpretation is erroneous as well as offensive. The "thorn" is some sudden racking pain; some constitutional infirmity which agonizes or prostrates the sufferer for a time. The word which has been translated thorn, is properly a sharp stake. A verb formed from it is used to denote crucifixion or impalement. A paroxysm of such pain would leave the patient "buffeted," *i.e.* sore and uneasy; the word expressing, in popular language, the feeling of having been bruised or beaten. It may be observed that such bodily afflictions were supposed, in accordance with the language employed at the commencement of the book of Job, to be injuries inflicted by Satan — the accuser, who is permitted by God to stretch forth his hand against the servants of the Most High, but who cannot touch their life. The dominant notion of modern theology, which makes the incitement to sensual impulses, and other sins against the holiness, the majesty, the providence, and the will of God, an act of an ever-watchful and malignant spirit who tries to drag down into his own misery those who are ordained for a higher destiny and loftier hopes, was at least an undeveloped opinion in the Apostolic age. St. James tells us, that sin is the spontaneous following of a man's own lusts and appetites. The devil of St. Peter's epistle who goes about, seeking whom he may devour, is plainly a human, and not a spiritual foe — a persecutor, but not a seducer.

The Apostle suffered, then, from some intermittent or recurrent malady. It was probably to this disease that the pallid look, which all his descriptive portraits specify of him, was due. I have little doubt that the disease was neuralgic. One conjecture as to its nature has been made, which appears to be plausibly supported by certain passages in the epistles and elsewhere. It is that he suffered from weakness of sight. It is supposed that his writing to the Galatians "in such large letters" is one hint. Another is in his saying, that some who loved him would have plucked out their right eyes for his service. A third is gathered from his mistake about the high priest. But not one of these passages is conclusive, and none suggest the strong fierce pain which the word employed by the Apostle to describe his suffering naturally signifies. It is, however, a matter of obvious interest to know what was the physical hindrance which Paul suffered from, and from which his resolute and devout spirit gathered consolation and even strength. The honor we entertain towards those who have conferred inestimable benefits on mankind is not lessened when we learn what were their physical ailments, what were the personal hindrances which they had to battle with, in addition to the enormous toil which must be undergone by those who, in God's name, and for man's sake, strive to teach an ignorant, and purify a corrupt world. We do not care to know these things because they show that such eminent persons are so much like ourselves, but because we would understand how the power which stirred and strengthened them was so vast, so effectual, so divine, as to overcome what seem to be insurmountable obstacles.

It was an early question whether the Apostle was married. The passage in the Epistle to the Corinthians, in which he speaks of himself as unincumbered, with domestic cares, does not preclude the notion that he might have been a widower — does not even prove more than that he went on his missionary journeys alone. On the other hand, he speaks of his assent to the death of Stephen, and of his commission from the Sanhedrim, — functions and powers which could not well have been exercised by a man who was not a member of that council. But we are expressly told that this great assembly of the Jews included only fathers, in order to secure a merciful interpretation of the Law. An early explanation, too, of the "true yoke-fellow" at the Church in Philippi, — whom he bids labor to reconcile or assist Euodia and Syntyche, — recognizes the wife of the Apostle in the phrase. The epistle was, it may be said almost certainly, written from Rome, and during the time of that imprisonment in which the perils of the Apostle's situation were aggravated by sorrow, and ultimately by the desertion of many among his friends.

The ascetic spirit which has induced men to forego domestic ties, and with them the reciprocal gentleness, unwearied love, unvaried patience, persevering energy, which should belong to the relations of husband and wife, parent and child, — which do belong to them generally, and which constitute the strongest sanctions of social life, — has been developed and inculcated for various reasons. There are persons who have, deliberately and of purpose, shut themselves out from those attachments that they may serve their fellow-men the better, and so serve God. The very purity and beauty of these relations, and their paramount value in the organization of society; the fact that they are commended at once by clear reason and tender affection, make the sacrifice of him who could delight in them, but who resolutely avoids them, that he may give his undivided will and powers to the good of mankind, the highest effort of self-abnegation. Christ recognizes such a sacrifice; but with the significant hint that the sacrifice must be made with a real and intelligible purpose.

Again, the celibate state was recommended by St. Paul expressly for temporary reasons. In view of the "present distress," — the tempest which was threatening the infant Church, — it might be expedient to lessen the trials of life by diminishing the number of its ties. The Apostle's advice is simply that of a prudent man, who foresees the strain which human nature will be put to, and who dreads the risk. It is counsel given in aid of human weakness, while the case which Christ puts is of that strong and persistent heroism which knows no weakness. The Apostle bids men avoid suffering; the Master contemplates the example of the man who resolves to give his undivided and unimpeded energies to the highest ends.

A third series of arguments in favor of celibacy was derived from that dualism which characterized Arian theosophy. In the view of this scheme, the body was an evil beast, to which the soul was linked, and from which it should seek freedom by a continual practice of austerities. The Creator of man had, forsooth, bound him, Mezentius-like, to a corrupt and loathsome nature, from which he must strive to liberate himself — from which, in thought at least, he must live apart. The body was not, from this point of view, the instrument of life — the mechanism by which God's will might be done — but an evil and insatiate power, an ever-present enemy, which must be beaten down and crushed. That it should be allowed any pleasure, however innocent and pure, was to concede something to a foe who would seize every opportunity for mischief. It is not unnatural that this morbid misconception of human life should have its reverse, and that there have been individuals, and even sects, who have carried their theory of the dual nature of man to such a length, as to believe that the indulgence of any appetite, however gross — of any practice, however debasing, — may leave the soul untouched and untainted. Such a sect, we learn from the Gemara, existed among the Jews in the time of Gamaliel. "There are men," it is said, "who assert that they cannot sin, either with the soul or with the body. If the spirit is divested of the body, it flies away like a bird. If the body is separated from the soul, it lies as senseless as a stone." The answer of the Jewish schoolman is in the form of a parable. "A certain king had a rich garden, full of ripe fruit, and he put as guardians into it two keepers — one lame, the other blind. The lame man, however, climbed on the blind man's back, and together they robbed the garden. When the owner came, and found that such a deed had been done, both culprits denied the act. How could I see the fruit? said one; how pluck it? said the other. The wise king, however, was not deceived. He bade the lame man get on the blind man's back, and, binding them together, thus judged and punished both."

And, lastly, the practice of celibacy has been advocated, because it has been found to suit the policy of religious despotism, and has aided in establishing an organization which has subserved a factitious object, by denying the affections any natural centre. It is almost superfluous to urge how entirely this practice has been enforced for sinister ends, how completely akin it is to the ultimate authority on which the Christian polity is founded. It was unknown to the Jewish discipline, it was a mere accident of the Apostolic age. It owes its sanction to the worst ambition which has ever perverted men, — the desire to control the religious sympathies of humanity in the interests of intolerance and aggression.

The revelation of the Almighty, in describing His love for His creatures, can use no more expressive word to denote His Providence than that of Father; with all that it suggests of unwearied patience, forethought, goodness towards helpless infancy, trustful childhood, inquiring and impetuous youth. It has sanctified that affection which belongs peculiarly to mankind, by transferring it to the nature of God. And, similarly, the relations of the great Evangelist, the Mediator, the Saviour of Humanity, to the nature which He has exalted and redeemed, are figured under the similitude of that other tie which constitutes home, with its affections, its reciprocal duties, its graces, its labors, its purposes. They who employed those facts of social life to illustrate the dealings of God with man, were, we may be sure, wholly devoid of that perverse spirit which has enslaved men to a morbid asceticism, or to a politic scheme of ecclesiastical government. Certainly, if Paul remained a celibate after his conversion to Christianity, his motive must have been that which Christ recognized and commended under such exceptional circumstances.

As the Christians of the Apostolic age held marriage in honor, so they emancipated woman. The equality of all believers in the sight of God tolerated no social difference, no pride of race, no theory of an inferiority of sex. The Apostle would not break down the subordination of a wife to her husband in the household. To have announced the domestic equality of the sexes would have been too violent a paradox for the age in which he lived, and Paul is at the pains to warn believing matrons against presuming in temporal matters on account of their equality with men in the Church.

In the world outside the Christian Church, women were generally in a position of marked inferiority. They were, according to the custom of Semitic nations, carefully secluded among the Jews, — for Philo reckons it among the grossest injuries which Flaccus did the Alexandrian Israelites, that he permitted the mob to break open the harem of the Jewish family, and to compel the women to remove their veils. What the

Jews thought of women generally may be gathered from the Book of Ecclesiasticus — a work written during the time of the Syrian domination. The civilization of Greece never extended to her women. It is true that the haughty Roman heiress and matron had assumed great independence — custom allowing an easy divorce. But this independence had become in many cases synonymous with licentiousness — if we can credit satirists and historians — though occasionally there might have been wives who deserved such grief as that of Paullus, whose virtues are celebrated in the exquisite elegy of Propertius.

But Christianity raised women at once to the level of men. They presided over churches, they travelled as evangelists, they formed the earliest permanent order in the Christian ministry, under the name of deaconesses. It is true that at Corinth Paul would have silenced their preaching, but the command is probably local, and founded on special reasons. Tryphæna and Tryphosa are the types of a class. Aquila and Priscilla — always mentioned together — were the founders of the Church in Rome, the teachers of the learned Apollos, and continued their joint labors so long that they were the object of Paul's latest greetings. In Lucian, the old women and the widows take up the case of the impostor Peregrinus, and importune for his release.

This equality of women with men, this honor paid to devout maidens and matrons, this dignity assigned to them in the domestic life of early Christianity, led, of course, to scandalous and malignant calumnies at the hands of unbelievers. The apologists of Christianity engage themselves in refuting these slanders. Justin tells a story of a young man of Alexandria who wished to publicly demonstrate his personal morality by the severest test. There was a little color for suspicion in the fact that Christianity was necessarily a secret society, and it was only too notorious that, among the heathen, mystical religious rites, to which only the initiated were introduced, were often a veil for gross debauchery. The circumstance which induced the expulsion of the worship of Isis from Rome was, if we may trust Josephus, a scandalous intrigue furthered, in consideration of a heavy bribe, by the priests of the Egyptian goddess.

It is almost superfluous to say, that the Pauline epistles, in common with the rest of the New Testament Scriptures, are full of exhortations to purity — full of warnings against unchastity in deed, word, and thought. It was an age of excessive grossness, of coarse licentious speech, and the Apostle would have no compromise with it whatever; prescribed complete seclusion from its practices as the only preservative against its contagion. He exhorts his disciples to remember the pledge which they have given to their Maker and their Redeemer, and to utterly put away from themselves every thing which might lure them back to the wantonness which popular Paganism permitted, or even commended — which was suggested publicly, and practised openly. The discoveries at

Pompeii confirm the description given of the morals of Antioch.

The powers which the Apostle possessed for the furtherance of his mission were not, as has been stated, those of an imposing presence and rhetorical skill. He did not win his converts by impetuous denunciations, or by magnificent promises, or by practising on morbid fears. To the Jews he argued as one of their doctors would, that Christ was prefigured in the Law, and in the Prophets, and in the Holy Scriptures, — in the three divisions of the Jewish Bible. It was not difficult to do this, partly because the habit of interpreting these writings in an allegorical sense was very familiar, as we may see from the Talmud and the writings of Philo; partly because the Old Testament is full of Messianic anticipations, of unfulfilled, but glorious promises. Doubtlessly, the history of the Messiah, His rejection by the Jews, His condemnation by priests and council, His crucifixion by the Roman governor, was a vast difficulty, a perpetual stumbling-block. Some of the believers in Christ met the difficulty by denying the reality of the crucifixion altogether. But great as the crime was, it was a crime of ignorance. It was due to the fact that God's counsels were hidden from the princes of the world, who would not otherwise have crucified the Lord of glory. To those, however, who rightly understood the revelation of God, it was clear that Christ must suffer, in order that such glory should be won. The condition of all progress, all growth, all restoration, all perfection, is suffering. It was a cardinal tenet in the morality of Judaism, that the just are the expiatory victims of the wicked, that the regeneration of the world is to be hoped for and obtained by the self-abandonment of those whom God raises up for this high end. Hence, the Apostle could speak of himself as one who was helping, by his own self-sacrifice, to fill up what was not even completed by the death of Christ, — the perpetual expiation which man makes for his fellow-man — the waste which is demanded from the believing soul, in order to compensate for the waste which is caused by the sinful soul. As far as humanity is concerned, the sacrifice, the crucifixion, the shame, the loss is still going on, in order that humanity may be exalted and redeemed. The Apostle appeals to the consolations which must be afforded to those who are convinced that they are aiding the work of human redemption, by identifying their efforts with the supreme effort of Christ's Passion. Christ, I grant (it is as though he should say), was crucified, but ye are crucified also. Your life-long struggle with the temptations and trials which beset you, with the passions which are crowded into your mortal nature, with the foes within you and the foes without you; your work for your own salvation and for that of others, — are similar to that grief which He endured for you, which He suffered whom I preach to you as your Saviour and your Example. The shame of the death is done away by identifying it with the most ardent struggles after the purification of your own souls, and the regeneration of the world. Met by the scandal of the crucifixion, — and it was an overwhelming scandal, — Paul boldly made it a matter of satisfaction, and insisted that it was not only the initiative in the redemption of man, but the type of that great struggle in which death and the grave are baffled at the very moment of their apparent victory. The difficulties which afterwards arose as to the nature of Him who suffered, and as to the part which men play in their own salvation and that of their neighbors, were as yet latent.

With the heathen world there was another difficulty. St. Paul tells us that to the Greeks — the name is generic — the Gospel he preached was folly — a sheer absurdity. To common habit it must have seemed so. We can imagine such persons arguing as follows: — Here is a well-informed man, who has travelled much, and seen much of the world. He is, to be sure, a Jew, and therefore believes in such a conception of God as is just and pure, though the belief is overlaid by a host of antiquated observances and superstitions. We can accept the monotheism which the Jew teaches. The best and wisest men of our own race have held such opinions, and have repudiated those vulgar ideas of the Divine nature which are current with a mob of profligates, with illiterate villagers, and with the rabble of towns. But this is not a teacher of monotheism. He proposes to us a deified, or, at least, heroic redeemer of mankind — a new incarnation of the Deity. And who is his strange God? It is a Syrian peasant, who possessed certain powers which were probably magical, and who ended his career by a violent death, inflicted by judicial sentence, and, as we may reasonably suppose, for having taken part in some local insurrection. That a wise and holy person should suffer death for his opinions is not without a parallel — that such a person should have sprung from an ignoble origin is not without precedent; but that he should have sprung from such an origin, in such a people, have limited his teaching to a section of his own race, have perished by the hands of those he instructed, and should now be held up before us as an object of reverence — as a person who, having died, has risen, lives, and is a God — passes the bounds of credulity. What Festus uttered as Paul pleaded before Agrippa, what the Athenian Literati said, when they invited him to expound his doctrine on Mars' hill, must have been in the mind of many who heard him speak.

With such persons the Apostle dealt by teaching the common interests of mankind, the universality of the Divine Providence, the certainty of the Divine judgment, and the appointment of a Person by whose agency that judgment should be declared; who, having lived among men, and having died the death of men, was recalled from death in order to fulfil this inevitable purpose. To live is to prepare for death, to die is to enter into the vestibule of the Divine judgment-seat. So he reasons with Felix, and with the Athenians. No part of the Greek theology exercised a more powerful restraint on the conduct of men, than the tribunal of the stern, strict judges before whom the dead were arraigned, and by whose sentence the pious and the guilty were rewarded and punished. But, in the scheme which the Apostle proposes, and which affirms those elements of a primeval faith, there is coupled the tenet, that he who is to be judge is also advocate, that he who will hereafter utter the sentence is renewing the nature of those who will appear before his tribunal. To the Greek mind, initiation into sacred rites, — the knowledge of which was confined to those who were fit to receive the revelation, and who would be purified by the knowledge, — was a familiar process. The Apostle appropriates the word which designates this purifying knowledge to the Christian faith, and the Gospel becomes a mystery.

All the descriptive portraits of the Apostle affirm that, whatever may have been his physical appearance and utterance, his manner was singularly graceful and winning. Of the attachments which he inspired we have abundant proof. Of the affection which he felt for his converts and disciples we have similar evidence. If he endured enmities he consolidated friendships. His intense personality makes his associates or disciples shadowy and almost impersonal. At first, indeed, Paul seems to be subordinated to Barnabas, whose name (two occasions excepted in which active hostility is shown to these fellow-laborers) is always put before that of his great colleague. But after the quarrel between them, when Barnabas disappears from the narrative, and Paul becomes almost the only personage in the history, the associates of the Apostle are his disciples, probably his converts. Such were Silas, Luke, Timothy, Titus, and others.

Nothing, it has been said, illustrates the grace of Paul's manner more completely than his letter to Philemon. Very likely it is the sole remaining example of many similar epistles, written as occasion arose to those with whom he was united in the double bond of teacher and friend. The circumstance which gives occasion to the letter is well known. The fugitive slave of an opulent citizen of Colossæ — as we may surmise the master was — has been converted by the Apostle, and is employed as a messenger to the Church which Paul had planted there. The master had also been a convert, and St. Paul writes by the slave's hand at once to the Colossians, and to the master, with a view to disarming the anger of the latter against the runaway. Nothing can show greater tact than this epistle. The writer begins by thanking Philemon for the kindness and generosity he had shown to the Christians in his neighborhood. Then he introduces the subject of his letter; alludes playfully to the name which the slave bore — "the Profitable;" states that he would have gladly kept him as an attendant on himself, but could not do so without consent; and prays that he may not only be forgiven, but treated hereafter as a fellow-Christian. Then he offers to pay for any loss which has occurred to Philemon by the fraud or misconduct of his servant; hints at the relations which have already subsisted between Philemon and himself; assures himself that more than his request will be granted; and expresses a hope that he may be spared to pay Philemon a visit. Nothing can be less intrusive, less importunate in its tone, than this letter, and yet nothing can more earnestly express the wishes of the writer, and avow more courteously his assurance that the favor will be granted.

Equally marked is the sensitiveness which appears in the Epistles to the Corinthians. In his anxiety to restore unity to the distracted Church in that city, and to cure scandals which had infested it, the Apostle uses the greatest caution in administering rebuke and counsel. We learn from these epistles what were the leading characteristics of those primitive Christian communities, what were the internal dangers to which they were exposed, and how great was the tact needed to direct and control them. And we can also learn from the genuine portions of the Epistle of Clement to the Corinthians, that the Apostle's advice had the effect of quelling their disorders, though they broke out with redoubled mischief after St. Paul's death. The Corinthian Christians were only too apt to imitate those faction fights of the Jews and Romans (for the Corinth of the Apostolic age was hardly a Greek city), which are described as having been waged before the tribunal of the philosophic Gallio.

But though the Apostle was notably discreet in his treatment of those with whom it was important to be conciliatory, his temper was not absolutely imperturbable. It is fortunate for the future of the Christian religion that his patience had its limits. He was too sagacious not to see that the attempt to fasten Judaism on his followers would simply ruin Christianity, and that the attempt must be met resolutely and at once. And as a man in whom the feeling of self-respect was heightened by the consciousness of his own energetic temperament, by the knowledge of his prodigious success as a missionary, and by the ever-present conviction of a special revelation from Christ, — to which revelation, and to which alone, he owed his knowledge of the Gospel he taught, — he was thoroughly exasperated by the attempt of his adversaries to disparage, to even deny his apostolic authority. The result of this anxiety for the future of Christianity, and this necessity of self-defence, was the Epistle to the Galatians, in which the Apostle vehemently asserts the authority of his mission, gives the history of his call to the apostolate, and his early resolution to act independently of the college at Jerusalem, attacks the consistency of two such men as Peter and Barnabas, and then announces the necessity of separating, at once and for ever, the Christian Gospel from Jewish practices. He plainly declares the ceremonial parts of the Mosaic covenant to be abrogated, annulled, antiquated; nay, that obedience to them is inconsistent with the fellowship of Christ, — taking a position from which retreat was impossible, affirming a principle which nothing could explain away or qualify. He rebukes the levity with which his converts had supplemented his teaching; assures them that his gospel needed no addition; and expresses a wish that he could be with them instantly, and solve his doubts as to their attitude towards him and his gospel by speech, rather than by the slower process of communicating to them by letter, and waiting for a reply, — to change his written word for word of mouth. A man of warm affections, Paul always preferred to treat men with gentleness and consideration, even when he was prescribing a strict rule of spiritual life; a man of strong convictions, he could not suffer the essentials of his ministry — his independent authority as a teacher, and his complete knowledge as a missionary — to be disparaged or trifled with. He affirms the former by an unwonted and emphatic adjuration; he pronounces an anathema on those who change his gospel, — add to it, or substitute any other teaching for it.

The method of the Apostle's reasoning is often obscure, generally abrupt, never, in the technical sense, logical. He expressly repudiates the use of such an instrument of persuasion as the formal method of demonstration. The subject did not admit it, except in so far as, in dealing with Jews, he appeals to the authority of the Old Testament Scriptures. For religion is not an affair of evidences, does not admit of demonstration. It may be questioned whether faith has ever been aided, or doubt resolved by the logical apparatus of theology. It has been proved that the religious sense may become nearly extinct in an age to which dogmatism has supplied the strictest definitions, the most elaborate conclusions. To win a man over to God's will, to instruct his heart in the belief that God is a real Being whom man can love, and loving, will obey, and to nerve him for the struggle which such love and obedience invite him to, against the sin, the meanness, the selfishness, the arrogance, the vanity, the ignorance of a mere worldly life, — is not the function of logic, which may perhaps raise a man to a passive acquiescence in a Power, or at best to the cold admiration of some unvarying Law. "The affections believe," says Paul, and reason takes the impulse as a principle of action. And what is true of a religion which gains man to God, is even more manifest in the exhortations by which the Apostle bids men believe in Christ. He appeals to loyalty, — to that mysterious sentiment, which, apart from the prospect of past and future benefit, binds men to the incarnation of perfect love, wisdom, gentleness, purity, — the power and the wisdom of God. If men do and can claim this loyalty because they exhibit in faint and imperfect outline some of these divine attributes, or evoke it because they merely represent the cohesion of social life, how much more should He claim an all-absorbing devotion who was on earth a pattern of perfect goodness, and has given infallible guarantees of future perfection to His disciples. Such a loyalty, ever present, ardent, untiring, but glowing more brightly, working more fervently as his experiences accumulated, governed the Apostle's nature from the day when he drew near to Damascus, to that in which he saw the time of his departure at hand. This he commended to his converts, not by any weight of reason or wisdom, but by his perpetual experience of Christ.

Even, however, if every allowance is made for the

subject which the Apostle treated, and for the pregnant brevity of his phrases and expressions, it cannot be denied that the method of the Pauline epistles is singularly inconsecutive. The style abounds in parentheses, inserted argumentations, recollections of topics, which are introduced into matter foreign to them, or diverse from them, in the most puzzling fashion. Sometimes, also, so many words are omitted from a sentence that it requires the boldest conjecture to supply the missing terms. It seems as though the clause had been inserted between the lines of the manuscript, and that space failing for the whole sentence, the expression was condensed into inextricable ambiguity. Thus, for example, in the case of that celebrated passage, "a mediator is not of one, but God is one," it is said that at least two-hundred and fifty renderings have been given of the eleven words in the original. The sentence bears every mark of having been written in. It is not essential to the argument. The Apostle is stating that the mission of Christ is the fulfilment of a promise made through Abraham to mankind, ages before the Mosaic covenant was promulgated and confirmed. The Law, on the other hand, was not an immediate revelation, was an addition to existing promises, and was added in order to obviate sins of disobedience or recklessness, was communicated by subordinate authority, was put into the hands of an intermediary, plenipotentiary ambassador, or mediator. Then, to emphasize the difference between the earlier promise and the later law, he defines such an agent as Moses was by a parenthesis.

A mediator implies the existence of two separate parties, between whom the person delegated to such an office acts. But God is an original Power, — He is one of the parties to the covenant or promise, and His direct relations with the person to whom He makes the promise are of a far higher significance than the revelations which He communicates to man by man.

Instances could be multiplied of these after-thoughts, parentheses, recollections, glosses on what has been already written down, and is being read to the Apostle by an amanuensis. Let us take an example. The Corinthians ask him what they are to do in the case of purchasing meat which has been offered to idols, or is suspected of having been offered. He commences his reply in the eighth chapter of the First Epistle, and in the course of this states his own feeling, that if any act of his, however innocent in itself, were to shake the faith of his brother, he would in conscience abstain perpetually from the act. This leads him to comment on his apostolate, and his claims to consideration. This suggests his right to maintenance at the hands of his converts, did he choose to claim it — a right which he vindicates at length, and by many analogies. The fact that he makes no claim leads him to expound the principles which have guided him in his public career, and to insist on diligence and consistency in the Christian life. Here he illustrates the risk of falling away by showing how large was the Divine favor to the Jews in the wilderness, and again parenthetically detects a spiritual significance in the Providence which supplied their wants. In the face of these benefits they fell into idolatry, and, as the Apostle is reminded, into other offences against the majesty of God. Their example is your warning, for your trials are not beyond your endurance. Then, reminded of the idolatry of the Israelites, and simultaneously of the food and water in the wilderness, he abruptly speaks of the feast which is held in remembrance of Christ and His betrayal. He justifies his statement that this rite is a communion of Christ, by the community which exists between them who partake of the sacrifice; and this brings him back to things sacrificed to idols, on the use of which he now gives a full opinion at the conclusion of the tenth chapter. The course of the reasoning is traceable, — it is not incoherent, for it is associated; but no better illustration can be given of what Aristotle calls inconsecutive utterance, as contrasted with methodical statement, than this passage does. With very rare exceptions, it is always possible to discover the connection of thought in St. Paul's dictations to his amanuensis, or in the copy which the amanuensis made; but the association between the connected statements, though real, is vague.

If the reader of the Pauline epistles can disengage himself from two superstitions, — one which urges him to discover a Divine revelation in every sentence and word of these writings, and another which seeks to tie a hearty, earnest, shrewd, religious man to some prim system of composition, such as might be congenial to a literary pedant; the one dictated by a spirit of divination, the other by an unnatural affectation, — he will find more freshness, spontaneity, and reality in the epistles of St. Paul, even in their obscurest and most involved passages, than in any more exact compositions. The writer understands what he is talking about, and means what he says. If he staggers under the greatness of his subject, if he is distracted by the infinity of the interests which he treats, if every word which rises to his lips suggests a host of profound and large associations, if his care of all the churches gives every fact a varied but a real significance, — the intensity of which is heightened by the energetic affectionateness of his nature, and the vivid way in which he sees the bearing of every thing which occurs in the course of his ministry, — human speech must be blamed for its poverty, human experience, which has developed speech, for its narrowness. His life was in his hand, his heart was on his lips. The heart was often too great for the speech. It learnt much and suffered more. Short of those mysterious hours which were passed between the garden of Gethsemane and the darkness on Calvary, the world's history has uttered nothing more tragic than the words of this aged missionary, — "At my first defence no one came to my assistance, but all deserted me." Is this to be always the lot of such men as Paul? He has his consolation, — "The Lord stood by me and strengthened me."

Though the general style of the Pauline argument is obscure and involved, there are passages of astonishing beauty scattered up and down these epistles. Such, for example, are the magnificent episode on Christian love; and the exposition of the resurrection. Nothing can be more clear and succinct than the narrative of Paul's early apostolate, which is contained in the Epistle to the Galatians, or his *résumé* of the depravity into which gross superstitions had degraded the Roman people. So, again, the letters to Timothy are full of affectionate solicitude and fatherly counsel, as that to Philemon is a pattern of high breeding and tact.

The antecedent likelihood, that many of the Pauline compositions are lost, is strengthened by distinct evidence. One at least, which was sent to Corinth, has perished. It is probable, that in his care of all the churches he despatched many other letters to the numerous cities in which he had planted his gospel, from Antioch in the east to the extreme west — where, as Clement of Rome informs us, he preached after his first trial. Tradition gives him as wide a missionary enterprise in the West as history shows him to have accomplished in the East and in the centre of the then known world. We could have wished that the vigorous sketch which he gives of his earlier labors had been continued in the last epistle which came from his hand, and that we had been informed in his final charge to Timothy of the conclusion of that noble struggle, that complete race, on which he congratulates himself at the consummation of his career.

## CHAPTER VII.

THE conversion of St. Paul is the greatest fact in the history of the Christian Church. Other men, from having been persecutors, have become preachers, have cherished that which they previously wasted. The zeal of a convert is proverbial, and the zeal of the early Christians, certainly of the Gentile converts, was unwearied. Nothing can exceed the boldness with which the Fathers of the Apostolic age, and their successors during the days of persecution, defied the power which crushed them, but could not root them out. Every age has witnessed the heroism of martyrdom; and Christianity counts her confessors from the days of the Neronian persecution to those of the slaughter in Madagascar. It is impossible to coerce the human will, except it be first debased; and Christianity made the human will divine in the sacrifice and glorification of Christ. He was the Example as well as the Redeemer of humanity. By the grace of God, men could be made like Him who is the Captain of their Salvation. No sex, no age, no rank, no race, was excluded from this great emancipation. On the one side was a despotism, vast, unavoidable, all-embracing, iron, — a military occupation of the world, — at the head of which was some scion of a worn-out aristocratical family, which in its best days was notorious — even among the Roman nobility — for hardness and licentiousness. Four emperors of the Claudian race occupied the triple function of commander-in-chief, chief judge, and high priest. Beneath this system lay a world of despair. There was no refuge from the violence of government except obscurity, no opiate by which to forget the terror except sensual indulgence. On the other side was the promise of God, the new light of a glorious future, which faith affirmed and hope made near. The coming of Him who had ascended was daily expected. He would be seen in His glory before the generation in which He lived had passed away. And when men murmured because He delayed His coming, and said that His promise was slack, they were comforted with the assurance that He was not slack, but merciful; they were told that we who are alive and remain shall be caught up with the dead to meet Him in the bright region above them and to dwell with Him for ever. To interpret the zeal of the early Christians we must measure not only their hope, but the contrast which experience presented to that hope, — the dead, hateful, cruel world of sight, the fresh, lovely, joyous world above. The heathen called them mad, but they knew that their hope was sober truth. In the world, they were most miserable; in Christ, they are already blessed. Woe to man, when such enthusiasm vanishes. The mission of humanity is over, if the Judge comes, and finds no faith, no trust, no confidence in the world, nothing but blank apathy, or easy self-indulgence. This was the temper of the early Church.

Of this zeal, hope, endurance, faith, Paul was the most conspicuous example. He had always been eminent for his activity. In the days when he persecuted the Church his energy was unbounded. Having harried the Christians of Jerusalem, he journeyed to strange cities, taking advantage of the general anarchy which the furious despotism of Caligula permitted. In those times of darkness his hope was in all that the Rabbis had taught, or could teach, of the immortality of man's soul, of the resurrection of the body, of angel and spirit. In misdirected faith, in impetuous endurance, he travelled madly over the plain which leads to Damascus, under the burning mid-day sun, eager to vindicate the law of Moses on those recreant Jews.

The narrative of St. Paul's conversion, — the vision in the way, the light from heaven above the brightness of the sun, the voice from heaven, the solemn question, — not the less solemn, because it used a familiar metaphor, — the summons to obedience, and the acquiescence in the command, the change of heart, purpose, life, though not of character, — is given three times over in the Acts of the Apostles. St. Paul does not in his own writings refer to the circumstances of this great crisis in his life, but simply states that he persecuted the Church, that God revealed the Son to him, and that Christ appeared to him last of all. And this omission is the more remarkable, because there are several occasions in the epistles, in which reference to the supernatural event would seem convenient or apposite — as, for example, when his claim to the apostolic office was challenged, or questioned, or impugned. For the Apostle was assailed from two quarters. The Jews never forgave him for his desertion of the cause in which he exhibited his earliest activity. His name, his person, his mission, were odious to them. They did not forget that this ringleader of the sect of the Nazarenes had once been the bitter foe of the society to which he had apostatized.

They who recognized the mission of Christ, but clung closely to the Jewish ritual, were little less hostile to Paul. Shortly after the death of Christ, there arose a sect which went by the name of the Ebionites, which still existed in the days of Jerome, perhaps in those of Justinian. Some traced these men to a teacher called Ebion; others said that the name meant nothing but "the poor," and that they were those Judaizing Christians who gave so much trouble in Antioch and Galatia. These men hated the Apostle, and denounced him as a heretic and latitudinarian. They circulated a wild story about his conversion. They said that he was a pagan, who, for love of the high priest's daughter, became a Jew, but that, being disappointed of his wish, he abjured Judaism, and wrote against circumcision, the Sabbath, and the Law. The story is told by Epiphanius.

Among the relics of early Christian literature is

a narrative, referred to already, which gives certain imaginary conversations between St. Peter and other Scriptural personages on the one hand, and Simon the magian on the other. The authorship of the work is ascribed to Clement of Rome. But this is a manifest absurdity. The date of the composition is probably the middle of the second century. But, though the title of the book is a forgery, it undoubtedly depicts the opinions of those sectaries who existed up to the fourth century in the neighborhood of the Dead Sea, and who, recognizing the twelve apostles as the only source of authority, united Judaism to Christianity. At one time they were a powerful party, and, as they combated with Paul in his lifetime, so they succeeded, for a century at least, in overturning his authority in the Eastern churches. The Homilies of Clement represent Peter as arguing against, and demolishing the sophistries of Simon. Some of these are the fantastic tenets of Gnosticism. But, in many particulars, Paul is plainly glanced at. Thus, the authenticity of a personal revelation is distinctly repudiated, — Peter alleging that even an angel could not address man except through the interposition of a human body; and, when Simon replies that a vision is given to none but the good, Peter quotes examples to the contrary from the Old Testament. "If," says he to Simon, "you have been visited by him, taught by him in an hour, and made an apostle; utter his words, interpret his sayings, love his apostles, and do not proclaim war against me, who have lived with him. You have withstood me, who am the solid rock and foundation of the Church." It is difficult to avoid concluding that St. Paul is referred to in these expressions.

It is not easy to detect the extent to which Judaism dominated in the churches of Palestine. But it appears certain that the measure of its influence is the measure of hostility to St. Paul and to his pretensions as an Apostle. The extreme party denied his authority altogether, and even circulated fables to his disadvantage. Even the more generous were not without fear at his boldness, and suspicion as to his motives and acts. This is shown by the language used to him by those residents in Jerusalem, who persuaded him that he should make a show of respect for the Law, by associating himself with certain Nazarites, and presenting himself in the Temple with them. This concession was followed by disastrous consequences, — by the riot in the temple, and the interference of Lysias, the imprisonment at Cæsarea, the voyage to Rome, and the captivity there. Every one can see how constantly Paul strove to conciliate the Jews, and how constantly he was repulsed.

Two defects were discovered in his claim to the apostolic office. He had been a persecutor. He did not satisfy the definition which the college at Jerusalem gave to the status of an apostle — that of one who had been in the company of Christ during all the course of his ministry, from His baptism by John till His final disappearance. This was the qualification of Matthias. It is probable that as long as there remained any alive who had seen and followed Christ, vacancies in the Apostolic College were filled up from their number, and that, even afterwards, they who had conversed with the apostles were treated with peculiar respect, as the recipients of these memorabilia which the apostles narrated or compiled. In course of time, it is true, all these witnesses would be removed by death. But the prospect of this cessation of ocular testimony to the facts of the Divine life did not disturb the early Church, for it always looked forward to the speedy reappearance of Christ upon earth. When this hope was delayed, many adopted Chiliasm, and believed that the personal reign of their Saviour, to last for a thousand years, was close at hand. Such, for example, was the belief of Justin. Here, then, was the great difficulty in the case of Paul. Even if it were possible to exalt to the eminence of an apostle one who had persecuted the Church (and at first the disciples seriously distrusted him), how could they admit the claims of one who had probably never seen Christ during His course on earth, who certainly had never listened to His teaching or witnessed any of these great facts which were certified by the other apostles. In the first instance, these difficulties were overcome by Barnabas, who introduced Paul to the other apostles, sought him out at Tarsus, whither he had departed, and was for a time associated with him in the ministry, till the friends were estranged at Antioch.

But Paul was distinctly resolved to own no man as

his superior in the work before him. He insisted, that in every particular he was the equal of those who were acknowledged as apostles; he asserts that he did not for an hour yield to any dictation. To have done so would have imperilled every thing, — his own authority as a teacher, the reality of the revelation delivered to him, the liberty which he assured his converts in the Gospel. There are some who may see in this resolute attitude of the Apostle, the inevitable egotism of a strong will and a clear purpose; but it is more reasonable to discover in such a temper, an unshaken conviction in the reality of the mission which was intrusted to him, and a distinct persuasion that this mission was to be fulfilled in one way only, and by those specific means which he had been already adopting. And, to us — who can understand the effect of this uncompromising temper upon the history of Christianity — it is manifest that the Apostle's persistency is the reason why Christianity did not become a mere Jewish school, which might have had a faint existence in the Ana of some Talmud or Cabbala; or would, more probably, have been completely lost in the general havoc of the great Jewish war. As it is, the teaching of the Pharisee of Tarsus has given method to modern civilization, has erected religion into a social system, and has constantly been a standard by which the Christian republic has been measured and reformed.

The Epistle to the Galatians contains the most emphatic declaration of St. Paul's authority and independence as an apostle, though it is not the only protest against those who might impugn his right to the position which he had assumed and vindicated, for nearly every epistle of the Apostle contains allusions to the same subject. The most sceptical critic has never questioned the authenticity of this composition, or hinted that it is affected by any of those canons of forgery which have been so very variously affirmed about the sacred writings of Christendom. Rough and plain-speaking to excess — as might have been expected from a man whose anger was roused at the intrusion of mischievous busy-bodies and pedants among his converts, and at the foolish facility with which the former had imposed, and the latter had acquiesced in, a vain and superfluous ritual — the letter is full of gentle passages and affectionate appeals. It is to be observed, too, that no name is associated with that of the Apostle in the preamble to the epistle; that no salutations from individuals, or to individuals, are found at its conclusion. The grievance of which the Apostle complains is his own — though shared by his companions — but he could not, or would not, associate any individual with himself in the expostulation which he addressed to these vacillating disciples. He wrote too, we may conclude, hastily, even impetuously, immediately on receiving the vexatious news of which his communication treats, and he has had neither time nor inclination to collect and send the messages which are so general in his other epistles.

In preparing the way to an exposition of the authority under which he spoke and acted, the Apostle reiterates a statement that the Gospel which he had preached was complete, that it needed no addition, and that no alteration in it could be permitted. He couples with this assertion an emphatic excommunication on those who hold the contrary. He varies the expression in the fifth chapter, announcing that he who troubles them shall bear his judgment, whoever he be, — the phrase seeming to denote that the emissaries of Judaism alleged the authority of some persons in the Apostolic College, and that the Galatians were overawed by the pretensions of those who "had seen Christ," or at least were the mouth-pieces of those who had enjoyed such important experiences. And then he asserts that his announcements which he had made to them were not received from men, but by the revelation of Jesus Christ. By this he appears to imply that he had not accepted the traditions of the teachings which Christ uttered, nor had ranged himself as the disciple of any apostolic master, but had interpreted the circumstances of Christ's life and death by the spirit of Christ which dwelt within him, and which sufficiently revealed the significance of these great and absorbing facts. It is unnecessary to argue that this knowledge was conveyed to him in any supernatural manner. The facts were patent enough. St. Paul could appeal to the younger Agrippa as to the absolute notoriety of the events which attended the life and death of Christ. The importance of the revelation does not consist in the mere fact that Paul knew the events. In all likelihood, he had heard them over and over again during the days in which he was a persecutor. What was significant, was, that knowing them he interpreted them, and that they ceased to be a stumbling-block to a man who had made such advances in the knowledge of Judaism.

St. Paul was resolved immediately on his conversion. He understood that his mission was to the Gentiles, and, as he tells us, he associated himself with no man whatsoever, not even taking a journey to Jerusalem in order to confer with the apostles, but withdrew into privacy to some part of the region which was vaguely called Arabia, and which was sometimes made to include Damascus, just as Xenophon extends the district of Syria so as to contain the Euphrates. After a time he returned to Damascus, and announced himself as a convert and a missionary of the Nazarenes. Thence, as he tells us in his Second Epistle to the Corinthians, he escaped by being let down in a basket from the window of some house which overhung the wall of the city.

Three years after his conversion he went to Jerusalem. But, faithful to his determination not to involve himself with the Jewish Church, he saw, as he asseverates with an oath, only one of the Twelve, and James the brother of Christ. Those, indeed, were men of the highest eminence and consideration, whom it was at once seemly and prudent to acknowledge. But he saw no other apostle, and remained in Jerusalem fifteen days only, during which time he was in the company of Peter. These days were doubtlessly spent in conversation about the mission and life of Christ; and it seems certain,— though St. Paul repudiates the presumption that he derived any part of his authority, or of the exposition which he gave of the Gospel, from any person whatsoever,— that he must have heard during this fortnight many of those facts of the private life of Christ, which were so well known to the chief of the Twelve, and many of those discourses which Peter so clearly remembered.

The Apostle of the Gentiles returned to his work. For a time, according to the Acts, he resided at Tarsus; whence he set out with Barnabas on those early journeys of which we know little, but which, probably, extended over Asia Minor, and, in particular, over Galatia. During this time he was absolutely unknown by face in the Jewish churches. He was only reputed to be a preacher of that very Gospel which he had previously harassed. After a lapse of fourteen years from his first visit, he went again to Jerusalem with Barnabas, in order, it appears, to appeal against the importunity of those who wished to bring the Gentile Christians under the ceremonies of the Jewish law. Titus, also a Greek, accompanied him. It seems that the Apostle gave way in the case of Titus, as he took the initiative in that of Timothy, only as a means of conciliating prejudice, though he protests that this concession was not of necessity. The debate at Jerusalem led to an amicable separation. The Twelve saw that Paul was really and generally the Apostle of the Gentiles; Peter, of the circumcision; and that both were eminent in their calling. The chiefs of the Church sided with him no more than he did with their local customs; but the most eminent among them — James, Peter, and John (and St. Paul speaks somewhat disparagingly of their pretensions to hierarchical authority) — admitted the mission of Paul and Barnabas, leaving them to carry out their function without let or hindrance, and reserving the teaching of the Jewish race to the Twelve. They exacted only one obligation, — that the proselytes of Gentile origin should not forget the poor, ascetic, contemplative Church at Jerusalem. The risks of rupture were avoided, and Paul and Barnabas returned to Antioch.

But the inveterate passion of the converted Jews, which urged them to reduce all men who agreed with them on doctrinal points to the same ceremonial and ritual, was not extinguished by this compromise. The college at Jerusalem might acknowledge the wisdom of conciliation, might concede to the energetic and resolute bearing of St. Paul, might find it impossible not to "glorify God in him," seeing how successful had been his mission. But, with the rank-and-file of religious sectaries, uniformity is every thing; and ambitious men, those who "wish to glory" in the largeness of their following, know that they can always stimulate the rank-and-file to demand uniformity, — just as politicians can trade on a sham patriotism, — and that they can always, by watching for their opportunity, precipitate a crisis. The believing Jews at Antioch waited for such an opportunity.

Meanwhile, St. Peter went down to Antioch. The fact is mentioned, but not the occasion. For a time matters went on smoothly. St. Peter had himself, according to the Acts of the Apostles, preached to the Gentiles, attended on their conversion, baptized them, eaten with them, been reported to the apostles at Jerusalem for a breach of the ceremonial law, had explained matters, and had been exonerated from blame. Now, a further decision had been given in favor of liberty, and Peter was not slow to acknowledge and act on it. But the unfortunate facility of being ashamed of his duty at a crisis, — which seems to have been a special weakness of this apostle, which led him to deny Christ after vehement protestations of loyalty, and which is implied in the legend of his martyrdom at Rome, — misled Peter in this emergency. Certain emissaries came to Antioch from James, and apparently reproached Peter for having abandoned the exclusive rule of the Jews. He was afraid, and withdrew himself from Gentile company. The other Jews, we are informed, played the same underhand part; and, worst of all, even Barnabas, who had been chosen as an apostle to the Gentiles, and had labored with Paul for years, joined the secession. For this unworthy conduct, Paul rebuked the chief apostle publicly, charged him with inconsistency, and reminded him of the grounds on which the Gospel was founded, as compared with those on which the Law rested. We do not know the effect of this rebuke; but, judging from the character of St. Peter, we may be certain that it caused no real division between the two great apostles. If Peter was rash and timid, he was affectionate and ready to repent of offence committed. It is exceedingly probable, too, that the persons who had perverted the Galatians were some of these Antiochene Jews; and that, when St. Paul tells the story, the Galatians were not at a loss to identify the emissaries who had unsettled them.

The narrative, whose leading characteristics have been stated and commented on, was intended to prove three things. St. Paul wished to show that his apostolate, both in its origin, and by the tenor of the facts which preceded his second journey to Jerusalem, was independent of the Twelve, and derived no authority from Jerusalem. He could not brook rival, still less superior, in the work which was before him, nor submit to any control whatsoever, on the part of any man, however eminent he might be. This had been his constant determination, from the first day of his Christianity, and he was not likely to forego it after so many years of missionary labor, and in the case of persons who owed all their knowledge of the Gospel to him, till such time as these meddling emissaries had striven to misrepresent him, had repudiated his authority, and called in question the completeness of the Gospel which he preached.

Next, although he protests against having sought it, or sacrificed any thing to gain it, he asserts that the Twelve made the concession, or arrangement, that the Gentiles should not be constrained to accept Jewish rites, and implies that a division of labor was effected, by which he had the guidance of the Gentile, Peter of the Jewish converts. This compromise seems to be indicated as still valid in the introduction to St. Peter's first epistle, which is especially addressed to the dispersed Jews. Not, indeed, that St. Paul would object to any association with the special ministry of Peter, — on the contrary, he frequently addressed the Jews, — but the rule was a general one, and in effect most important, because it was a formal acknowledgment of Paul's mission, and of its total independence. Henceforth the two churches were to be one in faith and mutual good-will, but different in their ritual, ceremonies, and government. The church which Peter was to instruct was national, that which was put under the guidance of Paul was œcumenical. The story that Peter ruled the Church of Rome for a quarter of a century is, of course, contradicted by the facts told in the Epistle to the Galatians, and is plainly a baseless, though ancient fable, which has been maintained and amplified in order to serve particular ends, and to justify ecclesiastical Cæsarism.

In the third place, St. Paul intends to imply that the circumstances reported to him as to the state of the Galatian churches justify a suspicion of bad faith on the part of the college at Jerusalem, and, in particular, of James. It is plain that the agents of this eminent person disturbed the peace of Antioch, brought about the vacillation of Peter, and even perverted Barnabas. It is difficult to avoid the conclusion, that the same authority had been employed to sanction the Propaganda in Galatia. What else is the meaning of those allusions to some great personages in "the angel from heaven," "those who seemed to be something," who "seemed to be pillars," they "who would shut you out of the Church that they may be the objects of your admiration," of him "who is to bear his own judgment whosoever he be?" These expressions can hardly apply to obscure and unauthorized preachers, who, without any personal or external recommendation, were traversing the Apostle's doctrine. Impressible as the Galatians might have been, they would hardly have been turned from the freedom which St. Paul's gospel gave them, at the hands of such a missionary, to submit to the Jewish rite and the Jewish ceremonial, and this by the arguments of strangers, unless those persons had come armed with very full credentials. Luther does not denounce Tetzel, but the Pope whom Tetzel represents. St. Paul is not thinking of nobodies, when he is so exceedingly plain-spoken in the wish which he utters against those who troubled his converts.

Nothing can be more false and more delusive than to imagine that the first teachers of the Christian religion were men whose harmony of opinion and action was complete, who entertained one view only of the Gospel, and who had neither difference, nor debate, nor quarrel. They were not unconscious mouth-pieces of a supernatural inspiration, automata of some uncontrollable enthusiasm, unanimous machines, but were men of like passions with ourselves, men with characters, impulses, affections, fears, dislikes — were human in the mistakes they made, and in the truths which they embraced and enunciated. It is sheer superstition to treat them as more than men, as other than men, however highly we may value their labors, and reverence the spirit which generally guided their thoughts, their actions, and their words. If we make them unreal and transcendental personages, we do them a great injustice, and ourselves a certain mischief, because all free inquiry into their motives and feelings is suspected as a challenge of their authority, and every other form of commentary becomes mere verbiage shed around a foregone conclusion. They are not stars fixed round the great central Light, and differing only in glory and goodness from Him who is the centre of their system. But they have what light they possess from reflection, and feel themselves immeasurably distant from the Power which illuminates them.

Such men as St. Paul, who have seen much of the world, — have made human nature and human character their careful study, and who know how much of both nature and character is due to circumstances, education, association, habit, — are inevitably tolerant, invariably indifferent to mere varieties of feeling and peculiarities of manner. When men of St. Paul's intelligence are animated by a desire to do good to those with whom they are brought in contact, they use these differences discreetly, and easily accommodate themselves to idiosyncrasies of race and character. In a word, they possess tact, and a conscientious, self-denying, earnest, active, generous nature, which is also gifted with tact or discretion, wields among those with whom it is conversant an irresistible influence. And, on the other hand, they who live in a little world of their own, — be they apostles or ordinary men, — contract a narrow and exclusive temper, set great store by trifles, are conservative and tenacious on minor points, insist on literal obedience, are passionately fond of conformity, are jealous for the letter, are slow to understand the spirit. As time went on, and Paul became more catholic in his teaching and manner, the ascetic college at Jerusalem became more scrupulous, precise, rigorous, exacting. In the presence of a great and comprehensive genius, they are willing to effect a compromise, will acknowledge that there is a world beyond their experience. But when he is gone, the old exclusiveness usurps its place anew in their minds, they forget their concessions, they torture themselves with the idea that they have gone too far, and seek to retract what they have granted. When St. Paul was at Jerusalem, James gave him the right hand of fellowship. When he is gone to Antioch, the emissaries of James follow him in order to revoke in detail all that had been previously allowed.

The spirit which influenced the apostolic society at Jerusalem is by no means extinct. It is possible to conceive the case of some missionary who has spread the light of the Gospel among the heathen, and has won over abundant converts. These converts run well, suffer many things. They may even submit to martyrdom with courage and constancy, braving death and torture on behalf of the creed which they have embraced, and in the faith or confidence which they entertain. A persecution as bitter as any to which the early Christians were subjected, may fall upon them, and they may perish numerously — man, woman, child — under the hand of pitiless enemies. They may be exposed to the most dangerous calumny which can be raised against one who wishes to reform or restore the society in which he lives, — that, namely, of unfriendliness to established institutions — of being unsocial, unpatriotic, traitorous. The remnant which is left after the hurricane may win tolerance from its persecutors — may even convert them. Unluckily, however, when the heroes of this spiritual warfare attract the attention of such Christian societies as have lived at ease, it is found that they are destitute of some form, or mode of government, or ritual, which is accepted among certain other communities. They have, it is true, faith in Christ, and have obeyed the law of the Gospel, striving unto death. They have never heard of the form, ritual, or mode of government, for the Scriptures are silent on such topics, and they have learned little beyond what is written in the New Testament. But they are now to be informed, that unless they accept the system of which they now hear for the first time, they cannot be saved; that faith in God and His Christ is nothing except they have faith in a hierarchy and a liturgy. It is easy to anticipate what would have been the attitude of St. Paul towards such intruders. He has left it on record in the Epistle to the Galatians. He tells us his own practice when, in the Epistle to the Romans, he repudiates building on another's foundation.

In quitting this topic of the vexations which St. Paul had to endure at the hands of the Church in Jerusalem, it is proper to remark that, if we can trust the genuineness of the First Epistle to the Thessalonians — and the weight of internal evidence is overwhelmingly in its favor — there was a time in which the example of the Jewish churches might be held up to Gentile converts. St. Paul speaks of the Thessalonians as followers of the churches of God which are in Judea. But it is not likely, after he had borne the provocation which was given him in Antioch and Galatia, that he could have used such language of those "who came from James."

St. Paul rests his claims to the apostolate on the providence of God, and on the marks of favor with which his mission had been supported. In these particulars he did not fall short of those who affected to be specially apostles. He uses a term familiar in the nomenclature of the Aristotelian logic, to denote his destination for the high office which he fulfilled. He was separated as an Apostle, defined, so to speak, to the duty. Christ was revealed to him, not, as has been suggested, to tell him the facts of the Master's life, or to implant in him the discourses of the great Teacher, or even to narrate to him the wonders which He wrought, — for it is impossible to doubt, that had this been the case, frequent quotations from such a literal revelation would have been given in the epistles,— but to inform him as to the spiritual significance of Christ's coming, and to impart to him the Gospel which he should convey. Except, therefore, in the passage where he describes the institution of the Lord's Supper, Christ is not a man who lived among men and taught them, but a Divine being who wields the power of God, and by Himself associates man with his Maker. In the Gospels, Christ is perfect Humanity. He is deified Humanity in the Apocalypse. But in the Epistles of Paul, though He is intensely personal, He is a Power, an Illumination, a Lord of dead and living, a Redeemer, a Judge, a Being whom men tempt, whom men love, reverence, serve. In the gospels, He is the highest of Teachers; in the epistles, He is the Son of God and the Brother of man.

The intense and unvarying loyalty which St. Paul felt towards Christ, the profound faith or trust which he had in Him, were his hope and consolation, the guarantee of his mission, the absorbing object of his life. This comfort was clouded only by one recollection,— the fact, namely, that he had once persecuted those who believed in his Master. Hence, in no tone of hyperbole, but in sober and sad earnest, he speaks of himself as chief among sinners, because he had blasphemed Christ, persecuted His followers, insulted His Gospel. He can excuse himself, nay, can explain God's mercy to him, only on the ground that he was ignorant, and had none of that trust in Christ, which is now his safety and his comfort. Similarly, he speaks of himself to the Corinthians as the least of the apostles, as unfit to be called an apostle, and for the reason that he persecuted the Church of God. He refers to his previous career in his energetic letter to the Galatians, and again in the last epistle which he wrote to any company of his converts — that to the Philippians; when his mind was most completely absorbed in the retrospect of his ministry, and when, having seen that his life was Christ, he reckoned that his death was gain. In the midst of his consolations, in the best season of his hope, this remorse was always before him.

It is quite in nature that this memory was far keener to the Apostle than it was to those who a few years before were persecuted by him. Men forget the wrong done to them more easily than the wrong they have done. They remember the latter in one of two fashions. They either hate energetically the object of the injury — rousing themselves by every motive they can frame to excuse the wrong, and continuing it; or they are full of tenderness towards those whom they have dealt unjustly by — eagerly seeking out occasions, long after all other recollection of the facts has faded, to relieve themselves by showing kindness, by accumulating benefits on those whom they have injured. It is in keeping with this feeling, that Paul speaks so lovingly of those who were in Christ before him, that he declares he would lay down his life — nay, even be rejected from the Divine favor, if he could only secure the salvation of those by whom he would have dealt so savagely if they had embraced the Gospel in the days when he "breathed out threats and murder."

What does he mean in the Epistle to the Galatians when he speaks of the excessive persecution and havoc which he inflicted on the Church of the believing Jews? Does it not seem as though he had tortured them, as he had himself been tortured, when he reckons up the sufferings of his apostolic life? Once in the history of the Israelite nation, the tribe to which Saul belonged had nearly been exterminated, and the survivors were thereafter no way lacking in zeal. The fugitives of Rimmon, the residue of Gibeah — the remnant of men, women, and children, who escaped that terrible slaughter — were headstrong and fanatical in future. Paul had the spirit of his ancestor, who sought to slay the Gibeonites in his zeal for the children of Israel and Judah. And when he was converted, he retained not only the recollection of Stephen's death, but of the multiplied murders which he had ordered or encouraged, when, during the wild anarchy of Caligula's reign, he sought and obtained authority from the chief priests to bind and slay, following the Nazarenes to strange cities and compelling them to blaspheme Christ. His resolution and strength of purpose were the traits of his youth, his manhood, and his age. Thus, in later days, when the real work of Paul was understood and acknowledged, and the old jealousies had become extinct, the Christian commentator interpreted the blessing of Jacob, and discovered in his prophecy the career of the greatest among the sons of Benjamin, — " Benjamin shall devour in the morning as a ravenous wolf, and in the evening give nurture."

When St. Paul wrote his Epistle to the Romans, his missionary labors had extended in a circle, as he roughly names it, from Jerusalem to the eastern coast of the Adriatic, — this vast region having been untrodden by any Christian foot except his own, and those of his disciples. As yet, he had not visited Rome, nor did he visit it till he came thither as a prisoner. He remained at Rome for two years; the statement made at the conclusion of the Acts of the Apostles implying that his residence in the metropolis ceased at that time. The narrative of his labors after this period is wholly lost to us. He had intended a journey to Spain, and had resolved to take Rome on his way. It is reasonable to conclude that he carried out his purpose, and that the origins of churches in the far west of the ancient world were the preaching of this unwearied Apostle. There are legends of his having visited Gaul and Britain. That his writings were known in these western churches is plain from Irenæus; that his authority as a teacher of the Gospel was recognized in those regions, even before it was accepted in the eastern world, is plain from the quotations which the early Fathers of the west make from his writings, — from the store which they set by his robust and practical doctrine.

In point of fact, St. Paul possessed, together with the spirit of a missionary, much of the shrewdness of a statesman. But he was no *doctrinaire*. He was the founder of churches, not the framer of constitutions. He had none of that pedantry which insists on a uniform method of ecclesiastical government, and disdains any diplomatic intercourse between diverse forms of church administration. He knew that religious, just like civil, communities can, if they are left to themselves, discover and adapt to their own ends the machinery of their own organization. Hence, even in the pastoral epistles, — where we should naturally expect some distinct theory of church government, — his advice bears rather on the qualifications of those whom the churches should select as their officers, than on the administration or government of the Church. Deacons there must be, — for the essence of the Christian life in the early ages of the Church was mutual succor. Elders there might be, — for the habits of Judaism naturally influenced the Christian converts. Or there might be some special overseer, or overseers, who made themselves responsible for the good government of the Saints. Or there might be no officers whatsoever, beyond some temporary chairman appointed to keep order, — as was the characteristic of the Corinthian church, and, apparently, that of Justin's place of worship at Nablous. But no one can cite the Apostle as an authority on the creation of a caste of ecclesiastics, — as the founder, or even the adviser of a hierarchy.

The activity of the Apostle's mind, the energy of his spiritual nature, continued to the last days of his life; and, unfortunately, so did the bitterness of his enemies.

It is manifest that the Second Epistle to Timothy was written just before his second trial and condemnation; when, in the general desertion of his friends, he was expecting death; and when he almost dreaded that his beloved disciple would join the timid or the malcontent. But the words of the epistle are as full of religious confidence as any which he ever penned or dictated before, when his career was in mid-course. He is still the preacher, the apostle, the teacher of the Gentiles. There are sayings which may be trusted, even in the darkness of unbelief and worldliness; and these sayings are to be continued through a long and unbroken succession of teachers. There is no sign in the last words of the Apostle, that old age, imprisonment, ingratitude, sickness, had worked any weakness in his will, or diminished, in any single particular, that which had been the absorbing interest of his life. He has enemies as well as false friends, — Phygellus and Hermogenes, Hymenæus and Philetus, Alexander the coppersmith. And he has friends — Luke and Onesiphorus — besides those who were faithful to him at Rome, and in whom antiquaries have discovered a Roman bishop, a Roman senator, and a British princess. He has his word for his enemies, his expressions of loving regard for his friends. With such men as Paul, there is no cessation in the fervency with which they carry out the purpose of their life. They relinquish their hold on the work before them, only when they die. The veteran falls on the field in full panoply. The helmsman is torn from the rudder while his grasp is as vigorous as ever.

It is a matter for profound regret, that the world has had to undergo the irreparable loss of the letters which the Apostle wrote during the last years of his life, and of the narrative in which it is probable that Luke recounted the events of his western journeys, of his second captivity, and of his death. The impression is irresistible that the Acts of the Apostles is a series of mutilated fragments, — the remains of a far larger history, which conclude abruptly, but which originally contained a complete narrative of Paul's life. Were this narrative preserved, we should learn what was the activity of those five or six years which elapsed between the residence in the hired house at Rome and the chain of which Onesiphorus was not, though so many others were, ashamed. We might, perhaps, hear also how it was that all in Asia, who had owed so much to the Apostle, were turned away from him; and what were the machinations by which Phygellus and Hermogenes were constituted the leaders of this schism. That it was the old rancor admits of little doubt. These intruders must have brought forward the old charges, — that he had advised a compromise with idolatry, that he had taught everywhere against the people, and the Law, and the Temple. The malice of polemical rancor knows no bounds, is unsleeping, implacable, insatiable. Paul had offended the conservatism of the Jewish Christians, and their vengeance kept no truce.

More than once in 'his writings, Paul has described the labors and troubles of his apostolate, and always with exceeding clearness and concentration. For example, he recounts the characteristic traits of his ministry in a passage of great beauty and eloquence, when writing his last existing epistle to the Corinthians. He begins by avowing his anxiety to avoid offence. We know that he accommodated himself to all, Jew or Gentile, when no real question of conscience was involved; that he discouraged sectarian narrowness, and dissuaded his followers from those theological cavils which he rightly named doubtful disputings. This lenity of opinion was of course misrepresented, and Paul was charged with the vice of a perverted casuistry, — of having advised to do evil that good might come of it. But the motive which he had in practising this wise complaisance, was that of preserving the office of the evangelist from ridicule, of disarming dislike to the strange doctrine which he preached, — that, namely, of salvation by reason of the resurrection of a crucified prophet, — by careful and studied courtesy. He knew very well that earnestness and conviction seldom fail to win men over, if they are coupled with a genial consideration for the feelings of others; with the charity which suffers long and is gentle; with the love which he had previously described in so exalted and so impassioned a strain.

As he defers so much to the habits and feelings of men, so he is unsparing of himself, as becomes the minister of God. The most obvious and recurrent of his experiences are those pains and penalties which he undergoes in order to commend the Gospel which he preaches, — the endurance, the heavy cares, the straits, the hair-breadth escapes, the personal violence, the imprisonments, the restlessness, toil, sleeplessness, privations which he has to bear on behalf of his convictions. But there are also exacted from him a blameless life, a copious knowledge, extreme patience, gentleness, enthusiasm, unsuspected and disinterested devotion, truthfulness of spirit, the power which God gives the pious, a scrupulous and perpetual fairness, the armor of righteousness, as he calls it, on either side. And all this is to be maintained against discredit and calumny, or, perhaps harder still, amidst good repute and fair report. Nor, is it to be wondered at, that this apostolic character is in appearance made up of contradictions, is interpreted variously. Paul himself understood it to be so, and states the different picture which it presents to those who can understand it, and those who look on it as Festus did.

A life of this kind seems a daily death, while it gains perpetual vitality: one of ceaseless grief, and yet of constant consolation; of deep poverty, but copious in its power of enriching others; as utterly destitute, and yet grasping at and containing a wealth which transcends all worldly possessions. For, in fact, if tried by any human standard, these endless toils, and ceaseless dangers would warrant men in those contemptuous jibes which were commonly cast on the early Christians. But they balanced against misery and contempt that certainty with which their enthusiasm supplied them, of an assured victory, an everlasting triumph over their enemies, and the enemies of their Master. The glory to come is infinitely greater than the present distress; the toil of the race, the abstinence and hardship which constitute the training for this supreme struggle, is as nothing when compared with the prize which the righteous Judge is certain to bestow. So enraptured were these men by the prospect, that they scorned the world and its treasures; so assured were they of the future, that they took no care for the present. They were even so entranced with the blessedness of the time to come, of the day which they believed to be at hand, that they did not care to pray for vengeance on their foes. They do not seem to have thought of that alienable privilege of wretchedness, — the invocation of the wrath of God on the persecutor and wrong-doer. The Gospel is more concerned with the unspeakable comfort and consolation of trust in God, and in his Christ, than with the misery of those who forget the one and repudiate the other; is more conversant with mercy than with judgment.

The life of Paul was one of enthusiasm, but of enthusiasm coupled with a sober judgment, and lofty morality. With him faith was the guide of action, action was the manifestation of faith. To such a nature nothing is impossible. It can, of a truth, turn the world upside-down — reconstruct it. There is no state of society, no general habit of thought which can come in contact with it, and yet remain unaffected by its power. Give it power of speech; and let human nature be ever so cold or sluggish, it will stir it up to warmth and energy. It is an error to imagine that mankind is less impressible in our own age than it has been in bygone times — to believe that enthusiasm is a mere historical force — to think that it is impracticable, in these later days, and, in the greatness of modern society, to move nations by a vast and wide-spread sympathy. The hour for such an upheaval is always at hand: it is only the man that is wanting. There was never an age in which men's hearts so much failed them for fear, as that in which Paul began his missionary labors; no state of society which was less likely to be roused to religious zeal, less apt to fervently accept a spiritual creed. A period of great social suffering is no way favorable to a religious impulse, but is more likely to advise that license of despair which gives the gloomy counsel, "Let us eat and drink, for to-morrow we die." At that mournful epoch, one man laid deeply the foundations of a new faith, certainly through half, and probably through the greatest part of the vast Roman empire. To repeat the same events, it is only necessary that the same characters should reappear — with the same purpose, the same zeal, the same perseverance, the same judgment, the same tenderness and courage. But a great missionary is, perhaps, even rarer than a great general, for his genius is higher, his task more difficult.

There always will be those who seek to conquer or enlist the sympathies of men. If they whose culture is high, and whose motives are pure, disclaim all enthusiasm, and, in their attempts to assist the progress of mankind, shun warmth, fervor, sympathy as irrational and deceptive impulses, and substitute for the awakening of man's moral sense the hard logic of a bare moral system, they will never wield the deliverer's rod, will never be able to rescue a nation from the bondage of a merely material life, and renew the image of God in the soul of man. The religious sense is no invention of human policy, though it may be made its tool. It is the necessary outcome of two facts. Man is, collectively, far from having reached the virtue which some have arrived at — still farther removed from that which all might achieve. The only means by which the growth of this perfection can be assisted, is the disinterested self-denial of those who set to the work of saving and serving their fellows. But the willingness to serve man in this manner comes from the conviction that such beneficence is the work of God, and the will of God.

It is a mournful sight — a sad presage, when the natural leader of men refuses his office, and flies to that Epicurean ease which, in the early ages of Christianity, in the flourishing times of Judaism, in the best days of practical Stoicism, and even during the last struggles of a reformed Paganism, was abhorred as the worst treason against human duties and human hopes. But it is a more mournful spectacle, a sadder presage, when they who can guide and reform a world by speech and action, bow down to and worship successful force.

Such a degradation of genius and power is the last

consequence of neglecting these public duties which men owe to men, and in the disinterested satisfaction of which the great Apostle not only saw that he was a follower of Christ, but avowed that he was filling up that which is left of Christ's sufferings. They who will not lead when they can, must in the end honor those who usurp their office, will extol the charlatan, will walk contentedly in the triumphal procession of those who win the foremost place by chicanery, fraud, or violence, and will even shout a pæan over the humiliation of mankind. It may be that they will, like the four hundred who stood before Ahab, promise their hero victory, and assure him that God is on his side, while no Micaiah is left to foretell the inevitable doom of license and injustice. Humanity is never so degraded as when its highest powers are worshipping its lowest forces, when genius utters an encomium on wickedness in high places.

To the early Christians, and notably to the apostle Paul, power used for merely selfish and sensual ends was Antichrist. The mission of Christ, according to these votaries, was the recovery of the human race, by the agency of moral forces, disinterested labor, fervid self-sacrifice. They believed that Christ deliberately relinquished power which made Him higher than all created beings, in order to restore mankind to the image of God, and that during His life on earth He could have returned to that power had he chosen to leave the regeneration of man imperfect, since it was possible to effect that regeneration in no other way but by self-abnegation. They had not yet attempted to define the process by which this enormous boon was conferred on mankind through the life and death of Christ, but they were assured that the boon had been given, and that it was given only by reason of that voluntary sacrifice.

The spirit of Antichrist is precisely the reverse. It uses power for selfish ends, and it must degrade mankind in proportion to its success. It was the policy of the Greek tyrant, says Aristotle, to keep his people impoverished, mean-spirited, suspicious of one another, and this has been the policy of every oppressor ever since. All virtue, courage, truth, are his enemies; all baseness, meanness, falsehood are his allies. And just as they who work according to the pattern of Christ's life are the perpetual representatives of His mission, so they who follow the sordid ends of a cold selfishness are incarnations of Antichrist, while they who extol such a theory of human life and action are the preachers and apostles of this devilish revelation. In the days of Paul, and to the author of the Apocalypse, Antichrist was incarnate in the cruel and frivolous sensuality of Nero. The same power has been recognized in every personage who has constrained mankind to assert that he is the agent by which the mystery of iniquity works; for human nature has produced her monsters and portents, and has been amazed or distressed at their doings.

The ancient world busied and tortured itself with the origin of evil up to the time when the question was finally settled by the dogma of original sin, by which is meant the transmitted vice with which an act of disobedience infected all the reputed descendants of a reputed ancestor. Between the Gnostic who made evil a god, and the Pelagian who asserted that it was subjective and acquired; a host of thinkers occupied themselves with this mysterious and inexplicable fact, some tending to dualism, some to that Nihilism which makes all acts, in so far as they bear on the agent only, indifferent in their effects; few recognizing the truth, that the victory of man's moral nature lies in the fulness with which man refers all the facts of his own being, and all the principles of his own action, to the behests of that Divine Law whose stringency and completeness are demonstrated by overwhelming experience.

Infinitely more startling, however, than the question of the origin and purpose of evil, is the truth referred to above, — that the moral progress of mankind can be effected only by the suffering of man. The hopes of humanity do not lie in the fulness with which science discovers and employs the forces of nature. On the contrary, there is no danger which is more imminent than the appropriation of these powers by the coarsest despotism which can enslave and corrupt its subjects. It does not consist in what is called culture, because art and poetry are easily made the slaves of that wealth which is willing to have its existence certified, and its power acknowledged by the homage of cultivated parasites. It is not learning which can save man; for, at the best, learning only influences a few, and is very apt, in those who possess it, to degenerate into self-sufficiency and ease. Least of all, do the hopes of man lie in the aggregation of wealth; for experience tells us that wealth is not only apt to be arrogant and domineering, but that it tends to the formation of a coarse and harsh oligarchy, which is degraded by low tastes, and is prone to ferocious fears, and that it is perhaps better to discourage the growth of opulence than to admire and welcome it. Nor, finally, do the hopes of humanity reside in the adoption of any form of polity. It may be that one form of administration is better than another, because it offers least resistance to the influence which ought to leaven society, gives a freer course to those forces which can chasten and exalt mankind. Despotism degrades us, but it does not follow that liberty purifies us. The atmosphere is cleared of its accumulated poisons by some furious storm, which does in the end bring health to the many, but bestows its benefits amidst the waste and ruin of those whom it smites. And so the moral purification of society is effected by the suffering of those whom the cleansing storm catches in its course; the victory of the most righteous cause demands the suffering and death of some among those who enter into the battle. When the stronghold of truth and virtue is to be built, the foundations are laid in the first-born, and the youngest perishes before the walls are finished. Everywhere we have to witness the reign of the same mysterious law. There is no joy which is not bought with sorrow, no happiness which is not secured by pain. The Syrian is before, and the Philistine is behind, and men must perish in arresting the march of each, before it is possible that the day should come in which His government and His peace shall increase, and have no end.

It has been observed that the Jewish race has furnished splendid examples of dominant energy over almost every subject upon which human power has been able to exercise itself, — in other words, that it has exhibited abundant and marvellous examples of concentration and force. Perhaps the vigor which it really possesses has been exaggerated. But, it is certain that the world is indebted to the Jew for two great principles. Israel has taught the unity of God, and, therewith, has affirmed the reality of religion, and the obligation of man to society. Other races have inculcated the necessity of loyalty to a form of government. The Athenian and the Roman did so. But loyalty to a government inevitably degenerates into fetich worship, if it is made to constitute political virtue. The Jew was saved from this risk by the fact that his loyalty was not wasted on an institution, but concentrated on his race. His loyalty, too, was not aggressive but defensive. Only once in the long annals of this people was Judaism a military power. This transient splendor is even now remembered in the East, — where historical memory is ordinarily only of yesterday.

But the Jew has suffered a perennial martyrdom for

his monotheism, while he has been leavening civilization with his belief. For the sake of this tenet, he has been an alien among nations, has been persecuted, scorned, trampled on. But he has not been crushed. His tenacious vitality is a standing proof that it is impossible to annihilate a germ of true life. He has given to mankind a great doctrine. His race supplied humanity with one — and that, a perfect Teacher, a perfect Example, the chief Saviour of mankind, the Master of all them who attempt the same office. His race gave the world the great exemplar of the missionary — the wise, loving, fervent, resolute man of Tarsus, the Apostle of the world. Pity that the veil is still on their hearts, as it was when Paul wrote and predicted that it should be taken away. That it has not been removed, is the fault of those who have never acknowledged what mankind owes to the testimony of Israel, and, therefore, have never echoed that desire of the heart and prayer which he who suffered so much for his own nation constantly entertained and uttered, when he thought upon the deeds God had done for Israel, and the service which Israel has done for humanity and Christendom.

## CHAPTER VIII.

"TO us," says St. Paul, "whatever may be believed to exist elsewhere and by others, there is one God, the Father, the source of all existence, the object of our being; and there is one Lord Jesus Christ, by whose agency all things exist, and by whom we are what we are." Throughout his epistles this contrast is perpetually stated. God is our Father, Christ is our Lord. The Lordship which Christ exercises is frequently designated. The disciples of Christ, the recipients of His Gospel, are His servants or (the word bore a far more gentle meaning to the ancient world) His slaves. He has purchased them, and they are His; He has renewed or regenerated them, and they are thereupon a new creation. He is their future Judge, for He is to come from heaven again in order to execute His last office in the great scheme of redemption. He is to gather His own together, in order that they may receive those indescribable joys which will reward their patience. And, meanwhile, He is related to them in the closest and most personal manner. Every phrase which can denote the nearest and most indissoluble connection of which we can have experience, is adapted to indicate the relation of Christ to His people. The favorite analogy which St. Paul uses, is that of life and intelligence in union with the corporeity of man. Christ is to His Church what the life, soul, intellect, spirit, are to the human organism.

Except during the instant ecstasy on the road to Damascus, it does not appear that Paul ever claims to have seen Christ. He had not sat at His feet, and he had not heard that voice to which even the soldiers who were sent to take Him were constrained to listen, and listen wonderingly, when they said on their return after a fruitless errand that "never man spake like this Man." The Twelve had enjoyed the benefit of His instruction for a lengthened period. He had expounded to them the depths of the Divine Law, and had revealed to them the mysteries of the kingdom of heaven. He and His had lived together, as a little community, in terms of the closest intimacy, with a common purse, sharing plain lodging and humble fare. Christ had taught the Twelve continuously. The recorded sayings of the wise Master do not represent in quantity more than one day's discourses of those three momentous years, are but the scantiest fragment of the childhood, youth, manhood, of the great Nazarene. The author of the fourth gospel, with a pardonable exaggeration, says that the doings of Jesus could fill all the books that the world might contain. We possess but a slender portion of those parables by which He illustrated His teaching, of those discourses in which He expounded the new commandment; of that grave irony with which He exposed the pretensions of self-seeking teachers; of those indignant reproaches with which He drove hypocritical Pharisee, time-serving Herodian, well-born or wealthy Sadducee, to insatiable wrath. These things, forsooth, were not done in a corner. The light was set on a hill. They came to Paul, as they come to us, from the narrative of eye-witnesses, from the memory of listeners. He had heard of them, no doubt, to a far larger extent than later generations have, when he was in Damascus, in Arabia, but most fully during the fifteen days of his visit to Peter. It may be that a summary of what he heard and told his own disciples is, as antiquity believed, contained in the gospel of Luke. It is not a little remarkable, however, that he does not allude in his epistles to the discourses, miracles, commandments of Christ, but only to the supreme facts of his life and death. Whatever he may have known of those events which are narrated in the gospels, he does not make them the basis of his teaching.

It would be, however, a total misconception to believe that, in Paul's eyes, Christ, the Son of David, the Prophet of Galilee, the rejected of His people, the Saviour of mankind was, in any sense whatever, an abstraction. On the contrary, He is always a vivid, manifest, real personality — the very intensity of individual being. Many of the expressions used of Christ were, of course, familiar to Jewish ears as formularies in Rabbinical theology. Such were "the Word of God," "the Son of God," "the power and the wisdom of God." The personification of those exalted qualities was natural enough to the mind of antiquity. But the Christ of Paul was no incarnation of a Divine attribute; nor, conversely, was it the apotheosis of a Jewish Augustus, in whom might be supposed to reside the loftiest manifestations which the world had ever seen of moral goodness and intellectual power. Paul always preached Christ crucified. It was not easy to treat a crucified person as a glorified, deified being, merely from the fact that he was a teacher of the highest righteousness, and had been slain by those whom he came to instruct and benefit. That event is and has been too common. If men worshipped all the teachers whom they have sacrificed to their jealousy, their suspicion, their weariness, the gods of the human race would be as numerous as those of the Egyptian Olympus.

Towards the Christ whom he preached Paul entertained the most ardent affection. The love of Christ for man is reciprocated intensely by the love of this man towards Christ. It is the one great and abiding consolation in all the labors of his energetic life. He was not without other joys. Sorely tried and harassed as he was, by secret and open enemies, — by his craving after sympathy, by his enforced distrust of men, by his unsatisfied claim for fidelity, — he gained, as such ardent natures do, many devoted friends. He had warm attachments, and no man, however enthusiastic, disinterested, persevering, wise, he may be, can conciliate men's affections, unless he be genial and affectionate himself. But there was one friend who was closer than any other could be, who never failed him, who watched and strengthened him in his labors. And hence he can boldly ask, after enumerating every influence which can hinder human weakness from the consciousness of the Divine presence — whether trouble, penury, persecution, hunger, want, danger, or the prospect of death — can separate him from the love of Christ, can confidently, nay, triumphantly, assert that in the face of all these hindrances, he is overwhelmingly victorious by the love of Him, and that no created force or power can seclude him from this perpetual warranty of his hopes. The other apostles speak almost faintly of the personality of Christ when they are compared with the last of the chosen, the Benjamin of the new Israel Hence Paul is the permanent teacher of that school of Christians, which has dwelt with such tenderness on the humanity of Christ, which worships Him as God because it loves Him as man, which delights itself in any association which it can frame in order to designate the inclusion of every affection of which the human heart is capable in the love of Jesus. Paul is the apostle of the Quietists, of the Passionists, of those who would seclude themselves from every part of the business of life, in order that they may occupy their hearts with the absorbing contemplation of that glorified, but veritable humanity. So comprehensive was the nature of Paul's faith, that he — the most active and cool mind which Christianity has ever enlisted in its service — is, from this tenderest part of his character, the perpetual example of those women, and those womanly hearted men, who have suffered themselves to dwell with such loyal intensity on the merits of their Lord, who have clung to him (the simile is Paul's own) with much the same trusting attachment that a pure-hearted and earnest wife does to the husband of her love, and pride, and happiness. With such natures faith supersedes a creed, for there is no power by which the emotions of the heart — its trust, which is the faith of the New Testament — can be translated into a set, dogmatic avowal, which is too frequently the faith or the creed of later Christianity.

And yet St. Paul has also become the Apostle of dogmatic Christianity throughout ecclesiastical history. It is from his writings, almost exclusively, that controversialists and polemics have forged their weapons. A text or two in his epistles has been made the basis of some definition or article of faith which has agitated or divided Christianity from time to time. The Gnostics acknowledged no authority except his catholic epistles, with the Gospel which he was supposed to have dictated or revised; while the earliest Christian Fathers, who contended with these sectaries, drew their replies from these very writings. When men entered into controversy about the nature of Christ, both Arian and Athanasian appealed to the Pauline epistles in support of their rival theories. The grim logomachies of Sabellius and Eutyches and Nestorius were defended and impugned from the same authority. Again, the world of Christendom was threatened with disruption in the days of Pelagius; and the irrepressible question as to the harmony of man's free will, with the divine scheme of redemption, was made a forbidden topic for many a century by reason of the energy of Augustine, and by virtue of a quotation or two from St. Paul's writings. Slowly, it is true, and indirectly, the Christian world slid back into a theory akin to that of Pelagius; and Luther, who well knew that the best way to depose the Pope was to prove him heretical, insisted on the doctrine that man is justified by faith, — understanding by faith the acknowledgment of certain abstract propositions on the nature of good, of Christ, and of man.

The Pauline epistles were ransacked, and his words subjected to an elaborate exegesis, in order to prove that the Divine economy of Christianity commanded the universal establishment of an episcopal form of church government. Nay, some of the more eager and imaginative of these controversialists have discovered the authority for a liturgy, and that ritualism which deals in costume, in the parchments and cloak which were left at Troas. No words ever written have been studied more carefully and more persistently than those of St. Paul, none have been quoted more confidently on behalf of foregone and repugnant conclusions. And yet there is no writer in the latter part of the New Testament more free from formal definitions than St. Paul is, none the articles of whose creed are plainer and fewer. With how strange an irony is he — who discouraged the Roman converts, in admitting men to church membership, from entering on doubtful disputations — made the chief authority for the attack and defence of theological subtleties.

The fact is, no large-hearted man is ever intolerant of opinion. He may be persuaded that unless he comprehends and affirms his creed as emphatically as he holds his faith, he is in peril. But, in dealing with others, he is certain to be considerate. There are times in which creeds lose much of their hold on men's minds; but faith, real trust in God, manifested by patience, and demonstrated by earnest and self-denying love to man, is stronger than at other periods of ecclesiastical history, when controversy has been sharp and definitions have been more exact. The gospel which Paul preached is singularly free from anathemas, even when the preacher is strongly provoked. He does not fly to that armory of polemical strife, whence some men have scattered imprecations on every thought and action which seems likely to challenge authority, or threaten usurpation. He would rather win than terrify. Even when he is constrained to insist on curing a grave scandal by sharp discipline, he is careful to excuse the act on the plea of its absolute necessity, and to limit its stringency as narrowly as possible. He knew that the best way to obviate quarrels was to recognize differences. He was well aware that men may work for a common purpose, even though their several methods of procedure may be so various as to seem incongruous, and that, provided the means be just and honorable, identity of end is a sufficient bond of unity. Experience proves that the higher is the object which men propose to themselves, the easier is it for them to invite the co-operation of different forces. The wisdom of the statesman consists in effecting a harmony of interests, that of a great religious reformer in enlisting all action on behalf of one grand purpose. Both wreck their reputation when they ally themselves to party cries, and narrow rules.

No writer in the New Testament, however, has written so much as St. Paul; and none has written nearly so much about the nature of Christ. It occurred to him — in pursuance of his charge over the churches which he had planted — to communicate by letter to his disciples or followers, on topics which, though they seemed temporary or incidental, have a perpetual interest because they perpetually recur. In these communications he had to deal broadly with the Christian character and the Christian system, as became, to use an analogy, the great statesman of the infant Church. Had he been a personage of ordinary temper and character, he would have had a policy, as partisans always have. But a great statesman has no policy; he accepts a few leading principles; his wisdom being to show how these principles apply to the various occasions of human life. And, similarly, the leading rules of St. Paul's gospel were a few inductions, the application of which is universal. But the acuteness and wisdom of the teacher are found in the aptitude with which he points out the universal character of the position which he affirms. In St. Paul's teaching, this is the redemption of man by the sacrifice of Christ. But the four facts contained in this formula are of enormous extent, and are exhibited under a multitude of phases, — redemption, the nature of man, sacrifice, the nature of Christ. Can any conceptions be more vast? can any interest be more absorbing? And need we wonder that, in explaining these conceptions, distinct as they are from each other, it is impossible to gather any clear notion of the mechanism by which the harmony between these facts and operations is effected, except by estimating them from every point of view which can possibly come within our ken? The Pauline interpretation is multiform; but, under no circumstances is it presented as a harsh, dry, monotonous analysis, in which the fire, spirit, life, of the Christian polity has totally evaporated. Paul has, perforce, been made the authority for speculative opinions; the warm-hearted, impetuous, earnest, resolute, loving man has been treated as though he were a cold doctor of arid logomachies, a chief of the schoolmen, the convener and presiding genius of an assembly or a synod. If the Apostle were estimated by the use which men have made of his writings, we might say that no man has ever inflicted so much evil on mankind. But, in fact, if men had been content to judge him by what he says and means, and not by what they wish to prove, Christianity might be understood in all its tenderness, generosity, attractiveness, and power.

It is said that the earliest Christian sectaries, — those Gnostics, who, not having developed the theogony of Valentinus, merely busied themselves with the place which Christ occupied among the emanations from the Supreme Being,—retained or reconstructed those gospels only which narrate the facts of the Saviour's childhood. The object of these persons was to find authority for the theory which they entertained about the nature of Christ. For a different reason, there is hardly any part of the gospel narrative which awakes our sympathies so profoundly as the story of the Child-Christ. The gentle mother, the journey to Bethlehem, the birth in the stable, the cradling in a manger, the visit of the Magi, the flight into Egypt, the escape from Herod, the return to Nazareth, the obedience to Mary and Joseph, the visit to Jerusalem, the scene with the doctors in the Temple, are of the deepest interest, are the vehicle of a thousand tender associations, justify that reverence for childhood which is the most marked characteristic of Christian society. In no part of His life is Christ more human than in His childhood, in no part is the feeling of affection towards Him more keenly felt than in the recurrence of the season which reminds us of His birth and growing up. Christ has granted the Shechinah to childhood, has invested it with the white robe of His holiness. To this St. Paul bears witness. They who care little for the circuit of the Christian year, its times and seasons, its reminders and its memories, are drawn perforce to the children's festival, the time of Christmas, the record of the birth of Jesus.

The fullest statements as to the mission and work of Christ are found in the shorter epistles. Thus, in that to the Ephesians, we are told that the mystery of Christ was not known to mankind in former generations as it is now revealed to His apostles and teachers by the Spirit; that by the Gospel preached to them the nations should be reckoned as heirs, incorporated, and made partners of the promise contained in Christ. And then St. Paul goes on to speak of the undiscovered riches of Christ, of the work of creation being done through Christ, of the wisdom of God dwelling in Christ, of God as the Father of Christ, of Christ's indwelling in His people, of the glory which comes from the presence of Christ in His Church. Several of these expressions are indeed familiar phrases of Jewish theology, and would be perfectly intelligible to those who are acquainted with the language of the Jewish doctors; but together they form a weight of significant epithets, each of which illustrates some relation in which the Founder of Christianity is supposed to stand to His people, and all by reason of the relation in which Christ Himself stands to God.

The Epistle to the Colossians contains even fuller statements on this subject. The Colossians do not seem to have been the converts of St. Paul, if we take the words, "those who have not seen my face in the flesh," as applying to the persons who are to receive the letter. But here Paul speaks of God as One "who has saved us from the control of darkness, and transferred us to the kingdom of the Son of His love, in whom, and by whose blood, we get redemption — namely, the remission of sins; who is the image of the invisible God, the first-born of every creation, since in Him are all things created — things in heaven and earth, things visible and invisible — be they thrones or lordships, governments or powers; all of them have their creation by Him and for Him; He is before every thing, and all things exist in Him; and He is the Head of the body of the Church; He is the beginning, the First-born from the dead, that He may be chief in all things, because all the fulness" (a word which afterwards was used in a strange significance) "was content to dwell in Him, and by it to conciliate every thing to Himself, who brought about peace by the blood of His cross, by Himself, to whatever is on earth and in heaven. And you," he adds, " who were once alienated, and foes to Him in mind by wicked deeds, He hath now conciliated in the body of His flesh, by His death, so as to bring you before Him holy, spotless, and irreproachable, provided ye remain firmly founded and settled in your trust, and are not distracted from the hope of the Gospel which you have received — a Gospel which is proclaimed in every creation under heaven, and of which I, Paul, am a servant."

Much, again, of this ascription of attributes to the person of Christ, is identical with that which the Hebrew teachers recognized in the Word. But all that portion of the Apostle's exposition which transfers the power of the Word to the work of human redemption, and which makes the agency of that redemption to consist in the death of Christ, is distinctively Christian, and is characteristic of that Gospel which Paul had preached throughout his life.

A little further on in the same epistle, St. Paul

returns again to the declaration of the effects which were secured by the sacrifice of Christ. He is warning these Colossians against the figments of a vain and treacherous philosophy, — against the traditions of human science, — against the materialism of physical laws. To these unsatisfying pretensions he opposes Christ. "He is the incarnate habitation of the fulness of Divinity, and ye are filled by Him, derivatively. He is the head of all authority and rule; He has given you a spiritual circumcision, — that of Christ, — by stripping off the body of fleshly sin. You are buried with Him in the baptism, and by His means ye are awakened up through trust in the work of God which raised Him from the dead. Once ye were dead in sins, which are the uncircumcision of your flesh, and now, having made you the gift of pardon from your sins, God is raising you to life in Him." He hath blotted out that which was written against us, which stood in our way — the letter of the law — has taken it out of our path, has nailed it to the cross of His Son, has stripped of their authority other masters and other rulers, and has publicly exhibited them "when (as a Roman general did the captured kings and vanquished commanders in the procession of victory) He celebrates His triumph over them in the victory of the cross." Here, again, in a passage of dithyrambic exultation, the Apostle starts from the same topic — the fact that Christ represents the fullest incarnation of God which the theosophy of his age allowed, and thence argues to the prodigious effects which the sacrifice of so glorious a personage must have worked for the regeneration and exaltation of humanity, for its freedom from sin, for its reconciliation with God, for its introduction to a new, a final, a holy covenant.

It is impossible to compare these passages from the two epistles — written, it would appear, at the same time, and that late in St. Paul's life — with those which are to be found in such writings as the epistles to the Thessalonians, without discovering a great development in what we may call Christology. The epistles to the Thessalonians are the earliest parts of the New Testament. St. Paul had not yet been driven into an open rupture with Judaism. He still commends, among Gentiles, the imitation of the Jewish churches. The expectation of a speedy appearance of Christ was at its height, and men were looking forward, with feverish anxiety, to that coming in the clouds of heaven which had been predicted and promised. It is true that the Apostle invokes, as is his wont, the grace and peace of God and Christ on his converts, at the commencement of the first epistle, and utters the same blessing at the conclusion of each. But there is little or no trace of that mystical force which is ascribed to the death of Christ in the passages just commented on. We read of the hope of Christ, of the imitation of Him, of His endurance, of His death at the hands of His people, of His resurrection and its pledge, of His presence, of His Gospel, of the commands which He communicated, of the salvation effected by Him, of His speedy advent. It may be that the larger theory of His constructive office, in the regeneration of Humanity, was present to the Apostle's mind, but it is not expressed. There were, indeed, abundant reasons why that which was not revealed in the earlier, should be insisted on in the later epistle. As a religion, Christianity was incomplete, until it not only guided the life, but satisfied the needs of the soul, in its search after the means of union with God. We do not know, and never shall know, what were the struggles of men after a theology in the early days of Christendom. We cannot see the thick of the fight, but we know something about the forces which stood in most marked antagonism to each other, and yet with some similarity of equipment. The Christology of St. Paul is before us, and so is the theosophy of the Gnostics.

The purpose of the Epistle to the Romans is to show, though in a less marked manner than is done in the letter to the Galatians, that the Jewish ritual and ordinances are superseded by the revelation of Christianity. Hence the Apostle insists on the effects which have been induced by the sacrifice of Christ, in the reconciliation of man to God, and on the guarantee which the resurrection of Christ affords that this reconciliation is complete. Here, then, Christ is the perfect man, who stands in contrast to Adam; the First-born among many brethren; the Advocate of man in the presence of God; the Lord of dead and living; the Judge of men; the Minister of circumcision, whose mission it was to confirm the promise made to the

Fathers; the descendant of David according to the flesh, but the Son of God in power; by whom we are heirs of God, fellow-heirs with Christ; who, if we suffer with Him, may be glorified with Him in the end. He is exalted and glorified, because He has been humbled, betrayed, put to death; He reigns over all, because he has undergone, for man's sake, the lot of a servant. He is the perfect Type of humanity, in whom converges every grace, power, gift, function, which may be needed for the grand purpose of His coming, — that of recovering the race of man, of aiding the suffering and groaning creation in gaining that which it expects so earnestly, — the redemption of the body, the adoption into sonship, which even the first-fruits of the Spirit need.

In the First Epistle to the Corinthians, there is a passage which is full of beauty, tenderness, and hope, and has thereupon been selected as a most consolatory exhortation to those who are saddened by the bereavement of their dearest and best beloved. In the chapter which is read at the Anglican burial service, occurs a remarkable statement as to the place of Christ in the Divine economy. Beginning from the position laid down in the Epistle to the Romans, that death is the lot of the sons of Adam, life the gift of Christ's resurrection, the Apostle proceeds to say that this re-grant of life is exhibited in a definite order, — that the firstfruit of the great harvest is Christ; next, those who, at the sudden presence of Christ, are His. And then, St. Paul continues, "the end will come. Christ will then deliver up the kingdom to God and the Father, in order that He may bring to an end all rule, authority, and power. Christ must reign till He hath put all enemies under His feet; the last enemy who is to be brought to an end being death. God," says the Apostle, quoting the words of the Psalmist, when he speaks of the power conferred on man, "has put all things under His feet." "But," he adds, "the words, 'He hath put all things under him,' imply that the Being who has granted this authority is external and superior to such a dispensation; and that, therefore, when this subjugation is finally accomplished, the Son Himself must be subject to the God from whom this authority is derived, that God may be supreme in every thing." It is impossible to explain away these unambiguous words, which distinctly express the Apostle's conviction that the present relation of Christ to the Father, and to the creation which He has saved, are determined by the cessation of the visible creation, by the second coming of Christ. This event, as we have already seen, was perpetually expected by the believers in the Apostolic age, and is nowhere declared to be more immediate than in this very passage. "I tell you," he says, "a mystery. We shall not all die, but we shall all be transformed." The existing generation is to see the greater advent, and, with it, the reabsorption of all imparted power into the unity of God. In the Pauline Christology, the perfection of Christ's Being is achieved by the death on the cross. "He puts on the figure of a slave, exists in the likeness of man and in the fashion of a man, humbles Himself, subjects Himself to death, the death of the cross; and is therefore highly exalted by God, is gifted with a name above every name, is the object of reverence to every thing in heaven, earth, and hell, and is confessed to be Lord by every tongue, to the glory of God the Father." The completion of His office is contained in His second coming, in His judgment, and in the final and eternal reconciliation of man to God. Then His work is done, — His mission is a glorious memory, — He is again the perfection of humanity, the first-born of all creation, the first-born among many brethren. Such a Christology differs largely from that of the Nicene doctors. It is bounded by the period which lies between the death of Christ, or rather His resurrection, and that consummation of all things which the Apostle thought so near.

But, though the Christology of Paul contained none of the exact definitions which the conflicts of later theology developed, nothing, on the other hand, which we can conceive, is so intense to the Apostle as the personality of Him whom he saw on the road to Damascus, and saw but once. None even of those who had passed the three years in His company, had so vivid, so permanent an apprehension of Christ as Paul had. The Master, Saviour, Redeemer, Advocate, Judge, is present to him in every act, in every relation of life. Christ, a real, living Person, is the beginning and end of his thoughts, is ever in his heart, always on his lips. He never loses sight of the vision. It carries him — how, he knows not — to heaven, and fills his mind with Divine voices, with words which, like the name of the Almighty, were incommunicable. In all his bodily weakness, in all the trials of his life, he is triumphant, a conqueror through Him who strengthened him. He is never alone, he can never be separated from the love of Christ. Christ has literally come to him, and taken up his abode with him. He has the mind of Christ, bears the marks of Christ on his body, fills up what is left of His afflictions, knows and exults over the deep, the unsearchable riches of Him whose servant, minister, apostle he is. The fourth gospel tells us of one whom Jesus loved. The Pauline epistles depict us a man who loved Jesus, with a perfect, all-absorbing, unremitting devotion. Other men have served Him, worshipped Him. Paul dedicated his whole nature to the Person whom he once persecuted, but now loved with every power of a large heart, a vigorous will, and an imaginative mind. However long we may search into the history of religious emotions, we shall find no parallel to this man's concentrated love for Christ. He combines what is seen or told to us in the characters of Peter, Mary Magdalene, John — ardent zeal, loving adoration, rapt contemplation. To such a person, the definition of that which is beloved would be unnatural and even odious. Who attempts to analyze his own heart, when it is occupied by one engrossing affection?

In degree, this feeling towards Christ was shared by the early Christians. The celebrated letter of Pliny to Trajan is evidence of its prevalence in Bithynia; the

## FADING OF MEMORIES OF CHRIST. 307

contemptuous sneers of Lucian are proof that it lasted in Syria and Greece. Gradually, however, as the personal memories of Christ faded away, and the survivors of the Apostolic age became fewer and fewer — as the expectation of His coming grew more distant by delay, and men even murmured at the slackness of His promise — as the watching for His appearance was superseded by the dream of Chiliasm — as the thousand years of the Petrine Epistle, and of the Apocalyptic vision, were developed into the belief in a visible reign of the glorified Son over an impregnable Paradise on earth, into which the faithful should be gathered, — Christ ceased to be a person, a man, and became a nature, an hypostasis, a debate, a disputation. The love of Christ was ultimately strangled by the growth of opinion. The faith of the Apostolic age — originally trust in a living, present, energetic power, which was able to save to the uttermost all who came to God through Him, as the author of the Epistle to the Hebrews declares — became the acceptance of a series of abstract propositions, not one of which touched the heart, or strengthened the will. But Christianity is always compelled to seek for its sanctions in something more impulsive than a series of definitions; perpetually revives itself by tearing to pieces, or breaking through the cobwebs of a subtle logic; and always puts before the believer's mind a personal Christ, a perfect Man, a Being to love, to live for, to labor for, to die for, to hope in. The humanity of Christ makes martyrs; disputes about the nature of His divinity have bred schoolmen and inquisitors. The teaching of Christianity always encounters the typical Jew and the typical Greek;—the one, being occupied by the dream of an exact system, finds impassioned faith a stumbling-block, a wild enthusiasm; the other, wrapt up in the invulnerable armor of his own intelligence, moralizes on the weakness of humanity, its liability to impulse, its uncritical acquiescence in sentiment and emotion. But, when once the religious sense is thoroughly aroused, these critics cavil in vain. The love for the perfect man, Christ Jesus—whose wisdom, beneficence, self-sacrifice, are so old, and yet so new; so wonderful, and yet so familiar; so wide in their effects, and yet so intensely personal in their appeal to individual sympathy—again occupies the heart of man, and gains its fervid allegiance. In brief, whenever Christianity is reconstructed, and the mind of Christ reigns in man, man reverts to the pattern of the Apostolic age, exhibits an intense affection for the humanity of Christ, and inaugurates a fresh epoch of charity towards his fellows. But, as soon as dogmatism reasserts itself, Christ is lost in a maze of definitions, and the preacher of the Gospel is tempted to become a persecutor and injurious.

The reader will not, of course, conclude that this attempt at expounding the Pauline Christology intends to indicate a judgment on any theological hypothesis as to the Nature of Christ. The utmost inference which it is intended to make is, that the popular belief in that which since the days of the Nicene Fathers has been accounted orthodox, finds no positive proof in the Pauline epistles, but rather, to judge from the important passage already quoted from the First Epistle to the Corinthians, is repugnant to this Apostle's conception of Christ's place in the Divine economy. It is possible that, had Paul been questioned as to the Nature of Christ, he would have answered according to the Nicene symbol, and that he might not have considered the phraseology of this creed a mass of those dialectical subtleties which he advises the Roman Christians to avoid. It is idle to inquire what would have been the attitude of the Apostle towards the heresiarchs of the third and fourth centuries, had their opinions been matured in the earliest age of Christianity, just as it is superfluous to ask what he would have recommended as a permanent form of church government, had he been appealed to by the first advocates of the Roman primacy, or by the opponents of ecclesiastical centralization.

Nor can it be denied that the author of the Epistle to the Hebrews, — who was certainly not St. Paul, whoever else he may have been, — makes far more positive declarations as to the Nature of Christ than Paul does. The first chapter of this epistle indicates a development in the history of Christology which goes beyond the Pauline utterances. It is true that, in the course of the argument, the humanity of the Saviour is made the basis of the parallel between Him and the chief of a superseded ceremonial; the eternal priesthood having been, in the language of the writer, conferred on Christ by the initiative of God. In other particulars, the epistle ascribes to Christ those qualities and attributes which the philosophers of the Alexandrian Jewry assigned to the Messiah of their hope. But the fullest witness to the Nicene doctrine is given by the author of the Apocalypse and of the fourth gospel. It was not, then, without reason that the emperor Julian was, as we are told, accustomed to say, that the Divinity of Christ was no tenet of the three Evangelists, or of Paul; but of John, — the John, who is the reputed author of the fourth gospel and the Apocalypse; for the epistles ascribed to this apostle do not go beyond the Pauline doctrine.

It is possible that the doctrine of the Nicene Fathers is nothing more than a necessary inference from the position which the earliest teachers of Christianity assigned to the great Founder of their faith. The mission of Christ was to save a world, and this function could not be fulfilled by any but one person. In view of this great office, it was natural, perhaps necessary, to accumulate on His person the attributes of the Almighty. As men came more and more to feel and believe that the salvation of each man was a mystery of miraculous power, they were more and more led to see that He who was gifted with this exalted mediation was in the counsels of the Father from the beginning, and that He shared for ever in the majesty and power of the Eternal. To lower His Nature was to disparage His work. To exalt it was to confess the unworthiness of man, and the mighty mercy of God. The harmony of the human and the Divine nature occupied, as is well known, the keenest intelligence of the Eastern world, then the centre of dialectical skill and philosophical speculation. The result is to be found in those creeds which were gradually elaborated during the fourth and fifth centuries, and notably by the termination of the last great theological controversy — that in which the teaching of Pelagius was formally condemned, and the Nature of Christ was formally and precisely defined. It is probable that soon after this, the last of the creeds — that, namely, which has been ascribed to Athanasius — was constructed.

The death and resurrection of Christ were the special facts on which St. Paul insisted. The former was not of course disputed, though, after a time, a strange sect pretended that a phantom was crucified, the true Christ having been mysteriously conveyed away. But the resurrection was no novel utterance from the mouth of Paul, at least to the Jews, — who generally accepted the doctrine of a corporeal resurrection. It was a characteristic tenet of the Pharisees; and the story of St. Paul having created a diversion in his own favor, by affirming that he was charged with maintaining the resurrection of the dead, is completely in accordance with what we know of the dissensions which prevailed on this topic among the Jews. The rationalists denied and ridiculed, the mystics affirmed the doctrine. On the other hand, the heathen world thought, with Festus, that a man who held the resurrection of the dead to be a possibility was a madman. The mass of the people believed in a world of spirits, — as men have almost invariably believed. Much of the familiar theology of the ancient world was based on spirit-worship. The Penates of the Roman household appear to have represented the deceased ancestors of the family. The early civilization of Rome gathered from the mysterious Etruscan race — who were, probably, a fragment of that great family which throve in ancient Egypt, and still exists in Eastern Asia — the characteristic tenet of reverence for the spirits of departed relatives. But this worship had become an archaism in the Christian era. The gentry of the Roman empire accepted that notion of a comfortless immortality which is stated in the Odyssey in its naked gloominess, and which is pictured in the phrase, "Let us eat and drink, for to-morrow we die." The lowest condition of life was better than the best hopes of the dead. So Achilles, the type of Greek heroism, is made to think. The last representative of Etruscan nobility, Mæcenas — the friend and minister of Augustus; the patron of art, learning, poetry — shuddered at the change from life to death, and welcomed any suffering if he were only left with the boon of existence. This dread is not fear of annihilation, of absorption into a universal essence. It is a belief that sensation survives death, and that the departed soul exchanges for the gladness, the light, the warmth, the energy of corporeal existence, a sad, dark, cold, motiveless being, in which the memories of departed

## HIS IDEAS OF RESURRECTION. 313

and irrecoverable enjoyments remain, to curse rather than to console. This exchange of death for life — from the point of view taken by the Epicurean who believed in the soul's immortality — has never been described with such precision as by Shakspeare, in the words put into the mouth of Claudio, —

> "Ay, but to die, and go we know not where ;
> To lie in cold obstruction and to rot ;
> This sensible warm motion to become
> A kneaded clod ; and the delighted spirit
> To bathe in fiery floods, or to reside
> In thrilling regions of thick-ribbed ice ;
> To be imprisoned in the viewless winds,
> And blown with restless violence round about
> The pendent world ; or to be worse than worst
> Of those, that lawless and incertain thought
> Imagine howling : 'tis too horrible !
> The weariest and most loathed worldly life
> That age, ache, penury, and imprisonment
> Can lay on nature, is a paradise
> To what we fear of death."

The resurrection of Christ was, according to St. Paul, the earnest of a general resurrection. Whether he held that they who had failed to reach the Gospel of the Divine mercy, would partake of the resurrection which Christ had secured for them who were His at His coming is not clear. In the Acts of the Apostles, he is represented as holding the view of a universal resurrection in his address to Felix, in which just and unjust shall appear before the Judge. But, in the epistles, the hopes of the resurrection are generally limited to them who believe, though he speaks in the

Second Epistle to the Corinthians, of all appearing before the judgment-seat of Christ, each to receive good or evil according to what he hath done in the body. But, as has been observed before, the theocracy of St. Paul does not concern itself so much with those who are rejected as unworthy of salvation, or with the destiny of those who refuse to accept the Gospel, as it does with the hopes and the blessings of those who receive and keep it. It is enough that a glorious immortality is promised to them who love Christ. There was no interest in curiously investigating the case of the wicked and unbelieving.

To this resurrection of the just, Paul clings with intense earnestness and confidence. Take it away, and all the purpose of his life is gone, every sacrifice which he has made is valueless, the redemption of man has not been achieved, they who have fallen asleep in Christ are perished. They who have lived in this hope are the most pitiable of all men; the only alternative in this blank despair is a life of epicurean enjoyment. And this expectation of a bright future, an eternal existence of rest and joy, is heightened by the conviction that he will live with the object of his unwearied love, the glorified man Christ Jesus. In some undefined place, in the third heaven, at the right hand of God, in some house not made with hands, but eternal in the heavens, He, the Lord Christ is; and there His disciples, His new creation, will meet Him and dwell with Him, what time this earthly habitation — this mere tent of passing life — is dissolved or destroyed. It is in the air, the heavens,— the symbols of light and brightness, and purity. But these places are a figure, as the resurrection is a mystery, the representative of an unexpounded future, of a new Jerusalem, the eternal home of the true and just. As yet, however, though we cannot see Him with mortal eyes, this Jesus, the Saviour and the Friend, is present everywhere. They put Him on; He dwells with them. Hereafter the union will be closer, the presence perpetual, the vision one of inexpressible glory.

The Apostle anticipates the retort of those who object to him, and who may raise the question, — How are the dead raised, and in what body do they come? In the visible world there are diversities of existence, and the analogy holds in its invisible or transcendental counterpart. And then he compares the resurrection to the growth of the plant from the seed, in language well known to every one, the figure being worked out with great poetical beauty. Such comparisons between physical development and growth, and the resurrection of the body, were instituted by the Jewish doctors. Thus the Gemara contains a conversation between Gamaliel and Cæsar — by whom is probably meant Augustus — in which the great Rabbi is represented as victoriously refuting the emperor's scepticism, and proving that the resurrection of the body, wonderful though it be, is paralleled by the perpetual occurrence of other and greater wonders in the ordinary process of physical generation.

To accept the doctrine of the resurrection, and to

extend it to the race of man, or at best to the faithful, was a difficult problem to the Gentile mind. That audience at Athens which listened with attention to the Apostle while he discoursed of the spiritual Nature of the Almighty, the unity of the human race, the providence of God, the search which man must needs make after Him, the coming judgment, and the person of the Judge, were startled into contempt when they heard him speak of the resurrection of the dead. But the doctrine, once accepted, was full of profound consolations. They who believed this tenet were afterwards afraid of nothing. Assured of a real, a conscious eternity of unimaginable blessedness, they could endure any calamity with confidence. The restitution was to be complete, perpetual. The loss, suffering, scorn which could be inflicted on them by any human power was transient, trifling. They who believe that a happy immortality is the reward of this life and labor are invincible. And thus, as by anticipation, the Apostle speaks of those who have been admitted into the commonwealth of Christendom as already dead. His words appear to have been misinterpreted by some who heard them, and who, like Hymenæus and Philetus, alleged that thereupon the resurrection had happened already. But to the mass of them who believed, death was an exchange from a life of sorrow, persecution, weakness, into a perfect and glorious eternity, as soon as ever the second coming of Christ took place — an event which was daily expected. Then, immediately on the sound of the trumpet which should summon them to accompany Him who would meet them in the air, the kingdoms of the world, the cruel empire of Antichrist, would be shattered, and every thing would be made subject to God and His Christ.

To this belief in a risen Christ, who has all that profound sympathy with human nature which makes Him so winning — all that gentleness which invests the Saviour with such ineffable grace — all that holiness which at once attracts the soul, and yet constrains it to be ever watchful, lest some contamination should hinder intercourse with Him — Paul links his conception of a church, his rule of Christian life. From Christ came all gifts. In Him is the unity of the brotherhood. In Him begins the life of the believer. In Him the believer rests. For Him the believer labors. In Him he gets his strength. By him he has abundant confidence in the mercy and love of God.

The derivation of Christian duties from a trust in Christ is a matter of frequent exhortation in the Pauline epistles. Take that, for example, in the letter to the Ephesians. "I who am a prisoner in the Lord, exhort you to walk worthily of the vocation to which you have been called. Show all conciliation, and gentleness, and patience, considerate love for each other, making it your business to maintain oneness of spirit, in the bond of peace. There is one body, one spirit, just as you have one hope in the fact of your calling; there is one Lord, one trust, one baptism, one God and Father of all, who is over all things, who permeates all things, and is in all of you. Each one of us has His grace conferred on him according to gifts of Christ. This is what the text means:— 'Having ascended to the height, He led captivity captive and gave gifts to men.' The expression 'ascended' implies that He previously descended to the lowest region of earth. And He that ascended is the very Person who has ascended above the whole heavens, that He may occupy all things. And this Person has of his gifts made some apostles, some preachers, some evangelists, some shepherds and teachers, in order to effect the perfection of the saints, for the work of service, for the building up the body of Christ, — to continue till we all converge in the unity of our trust, and of our acquaintance with the Son of God, into a perfected manhood, to the measure of that growth which contains Christ. Be not, therefore, any longer foolish children, tossed about and twisted round by every blast of dogma, by the tricks of men, who, for sinister ends, would cunningly entrap you in error; but, on the contrary, uttering the truth in love, let us grow in every thing up to Him who is the head, the Christ, from whom the whole body is fitted and brought together in every joint of its perfection, and, according to the vigor which belongs to every member, who effects the growth of the body for its own construction in love."

This passage is only one among many in which the Apostle — comparing the union of Christian men to the highest living organism — intends to imply that Christ is to the Church what life and intelligence are to the physical nature of mankind, — the source of its vitality and enlightenment. Nothing can be more simple than the elements of the creed with which this analogy is consistent. To know that Christ lived and taught, died and rose again, in order to redeem man from bondage, reconcile him to God, save him, was the knowledge needed for that primitive faith. To know this, and know it thoroughly, was to trust in Him and the Father, and, thereupon, to obtain the benefits of Christ's coming. Then comes the perpetual indwelling of Christ, the transformation of man's moral nature, and the code of duties, which, flowing naturally from the conditions of a Christian polity, have a permanent sanction, by being fulfilled in the highest Exemplar of human life, the life of Christ; and by becoming, as they are fulfilled by the disciple, the pledge and requisite of His indwelling.

It cannot be said that this perpetual reference of the Christian life to the assistance of a glorified Person, who sustains, exalts, and perfects it, is accompanied by any concession to laxity of practice or conduct. On the contrary, the rule of the Pauline morality is as high as can be conceived. He utterly broke with the ceremonial law, his indifference to Judaism growing into complete antipathy to it as he had greater experience of its narrowness, its pedantry, its inconsistency with Christian liberty. He is manifestly careless about observances which were exacted rigorously in his own time from the Jewish Christians. For example, he speaks of keeping the Sabbath as a matter of indifference, in the Galatians as even a mark of feeble compliance with what he calls the "beggarly elements." He assigns no overwhelming importance to those rites which are peculiarly Christian — the Sacraments of the Gospel — for he expressly declares that he did not himself baptize, except on rare occasions, and he makes only one marked reference to the Lord's Supper; when, indeed, he strongly condemns the practice of those who perverted it into a scene of selfish jollity, of grossly unbecoming levity. He is practically silent on church government. He speaks almost contemptuously of the Twelve, and of their pretensions to authority. So little was he characterized by exactitude of phrase, and precision of definition, that those heretics of the first ages, against whose tenets much of the early controversial theology of the Christian fathers is directed, a knowledged his authority, and quoted from his epistles in confirmation of their theories.

On the other hand, St. Paul is, after the Master, the moralist of the Gospel. His directions as to conduct are numerous, precise, exhaustive. Besides those which address themselves to the individual, and which exact from him obedience to a pure and searching code of conduct, he gives directions as to the behavior of men as members of churches, as holding intercourse with the world around them, as united in the great brotherhood of Christianity. He lays down rules for families, — on the relations of husband and wife, parent and child, master and servant, — all these rules being genial and rational. He commends neither asceticism, first preached by the Buddhists, and afterwards affirmed by

Manichean perversity; nor monachism, which is a form of apathetic communism. His Christian is a man in the world, who must, perhaps, considering the purpose of his life, and the peculiar trials of his calling, abstain from what is in itself lawful and expedient, in order that he may be disentangled from the temporary risks which his profession ran. But, on the whole, the Pauline morality is personal and domestic. The advice which he gives to the Corinthians, that, under existing emergencies, a single life is the safest, is professedly an opinion. In the Epistle to Timothy, he expressly speaks of compulsory celibacy as a doctrine of devils. This plain-spoken sentiment may be a contemptuous allusion to the Ebionite Christians, who had given him so much trouble, but the experience of society is not adverse to the judgment of St. Paul. He would have people work for their living, inculcating the duty of industry in terms as plain as those which are used by the Political Economist. His language about those who lazily depend on chance or charity for the wants of their family or their dependants is even stronger, for he speaks of such as denying the faith or trust they should have in God, and as lower in tone than the unbeliever. That he was no advocate of niggardliness towards such as need help, is proved by his continual advice to those who were able to assist poverty or distress from their abundance; for he knew that poverty will always exist, and that the habit of judicious almsgiving is a good means of moral culture; but he was slow to receive assistance himself, and it is hardly possible to fail of seeing a covert sarcasm in the solitary injunction which he confesses to having received from the Apostolic College, that he and his associates should remember the poor, by which is meant the community at Jerusalem. He did remember them, and owed his imprisonment at Cæsarea and Rome to his efforts on their behalf. However ascetic Christianity may have become in the second and third centuries of our era, there is no warranty for such a theory of religion in the Pauline teaching of the first.

It is unfair to the great moralist and statesman (if we may employ the latter phrase) of the infant Church, not to distinguish him from those who succeeded to his mission. Christianity was charged — has been charged continually — with making men austere, reserved, unpatriotic, dreamy. There is no warranty for this reproach in the teaching of Paul, whose estimate of the claims which even the corrupt society of the time in which he lived, and in particular that of Corinth, is just and forcible. In a true spirit of toleration, he would not have his converts avoid the society of idolaters, though he would — as every respectable heathen would have advised — recommend them to abstain from intercourse with profligate or immoral persons. He does not advise married persons, one of whom may be brought under the influence of the Gospel, while the other clung to heathenism, to use the freedom of divorce which the Roman law gave, — and this for domestic as well as for religious reasons. Even his advice of patience to slaves is part of the theory which he held,—that Christianity can accommodate itself to any condition of society, provided men are obedient to the Divine law, are scrupulous in the fulfilment of all duties.

They who charge the Christianity of the New Testament with timidity and want of spirit, should remember what the social state was in which it began its work. The world never saw before or since so relentless, so wide, so jealous, so immoral a despotism,—has never seen one which was so strong in sheer force. Now, there are two ways in which a reformation of morals and opinion can be attempted. The one is resistance—which is rarely efficacious, and in this case would have been madness; the other is endurance, —which generally succeeds, and which would have succeeded far more completely in the history of Christianity, had not the Christians of the fourth century clutched at power as soon as they were able to grasp it. The Roman empire became Christian by the patience of the first three centuries; but Christianity failed to regenerate society, because it readily became the tool of the later empire—became an establishment instead of a gospel, a logomachy instead of a rule of life. The dower which Constantine gave the Church was, as Dante says, the parent of vast mischief, and more than counterbalanced the splendor of the imperial conversion. Let any one compare for himself the theoretical teaching of Paul with the practical bearing of all that he affirms, and he will have no difficulty in determining what would have been the history of the world if those who came after the Jew of Tarsus had been representatives of his spirit, as well as successors to his office.

## CHAPTER IX.

THE soul of man longs for illumination and pardon. It is ignorant, and led astray by evil impulses. It is conscious of transgression, whether the law which it has violated be natural — or, to speak in the spirit of modern philosophy, one which society has elaborated and enforced for its own preservation; or conventional — by which must be understood some rule of municipal custom; or divine — that is, has been propounded by an authority which claims to be instructed by God. The construction of human society renders it necessary that interruptions of its peace, or invasions of that security which all political institutions profess to warrant, should be repressed and punished. Punishments inflicted by human law are sometimes treated as vindictive, sometimes as corrective, according as it seems necessary to avenge a wrong, or to prevent the recurrence of an injury; to compensate the sufferer, or to protect the general order of society by deterrents which intending criminals can appreciate and dread. A later theory of punishment, which has been developed from humanitarian Christianity, and from it alone, proposes to effect the reformation of the offender. It is possible that the acceptance of this humane theory of punishment may be assisted by the fact, that the judgment of law is fallible, both in its decision of the act and in its interpretation of the motive, and that, therefore, the case of the criminal is and should be open to favorable consideration. But this is not the original theory of social defence. Men must accept the risk which the administration of law by a fallible judge involves, since they obtain the advantages of its administration, for the latter are immeasurably greater than the former. If a legislature seeks to reform its criminals, it does so because it has been interpenetrated by that instinct of the religious sense which makes the salvation of a human soul at once a duty and a merit. In this country such an opinion is strongly entertained. But there have not been wanting jurists and moralists who, looking at society from the stand-point of utility, have entertained a harsher theory of punishment, — have conceived that crime is best checked by relying on the deterrent force of punishment only, is even stimulated by the machinery of a reformatory in which criminals are to repent and amend.

It is to be observed that law ignores many offences against morality, and frequently punishes acts which are no violation of morality whatever. A man may lead a life which is profligate and scandalous, may set an evil example, may mislead or debauch others. But, however mischievous his course of action may be, society may not visit him with any penalties of law, — partly because it has seen good reason to limit the operation of criminal justice; partly because the evil which the culprit does is legally imponderable or vague in its effects; sometimes because the check which law could impose might induce other practices quite as mischievous, or even more dangerous in their effects, but less open to detection or reprobation. For it must not be forgotten that custom has a wider range of corrective action than law has, and that its preventive power is even more efficacious than that of judicial punishment. And, on the other hand, both law and custom visit with penalty and rebuke practices which are not in themselves immoral. The laws of nearly every country inflict disabilities, and prohibit acts which are in themselves just and natural. Thus, for instance, they have disabled persons who entertain particular beliefs, or are unable to entertain other beliefs, — sometimes treating certain opinions as the highest crimes. They who challenge the value or advantage of established institutions, whether political or ecclesiastical, have been visited with nearly equal rigor; have been condemned, proscribed, banished, though their opinions have been simply speculative. Over and over again it has happened that the fathers have slain, and the sons have canonized the prophets. Christianity has lasted for nearly nineteen centuries, and Christian men have not yet accepted the command laid down by the great Master of their religion, — " Let wheat and tares grow together till the harvest."

It is inevitable that man should recognize among the attributes of God the functions of a judge. He does so from the analogy of civil society. The office of the judge is the most beneficent and the most sacred of human institutions. Reverence for law is the first condition of civilization; the administration of law is the most permanent and useful service which a citizen obtains from the State; obedience to law is the first civil duty, and the judge is the impersonation of these benefits. This is the power to which the Apostle commands subjection — ascribing its authority, even when wielded by the heathen, to the direct ordination of God. But human law is confessedly imperfect, — cannot right all wrongs — cannot punish all injuries. Hence they whom law does not reach, and they whom law does not aid, will inevitably be cited to appear before the Judge of all, in order that the question may be tried, and right may be done. So the religious sense, whenever it intrenches itself in moral obligations, always affirms. Recompense, restitution, are assured in that judgment; patience, hope, faith, are developed from a confidence that it will be pronounced. The Divine tribunal is a permanent court of appeal from human error and human partiality. It is set up in the mythology of Greece and Rome, in Eastern nations, in the polytheism of Egypt, in every creed which is spiritual. In the Mosaic theology the Judge chastises the offender with temporal suffering, rewards or recompenses the injured person with temporal blessing — the appeal being immediate, the providence secular, since the ancient Israelite is always represented as living under the direct government of Jehovah. The people were in view of the Shekinah, and the doctrine of hereafter remained undeveloped in the majesty of His presence.

They who cherish the thought that God is a judge between man and man, cannot but confess that their own acts are open to His interpretation, and within the scope of His judgment. Sometimes, indeed, persons have believed that they run no risk of His anger, — that they are elect, impeccable, assured of His perpetual favor; that in their case at least, judgment is foregone. But the conscience of most men is proof against this egotism. They are not arrogant enough to claim perfection, but, on the contrary, are alive to faults in themselves — to infirmity of purpose, negligence in practice, readiness in yielding to temptation, forgetfulness of duty, unfair or ungenerous dealing towards others. They know that such acts and feelings, if unchecked, are the beginning of those offences which even human law reaches; and if they know so much, how much more must He know, whose equity as a judge is the consequent of His perfect wisdom, transcendent knowledge, universal providence.

The range of the Divine judgment, therefore, must be vastly wider than that of human law. Man can deal only with that which is actual, but the prescience of the Almighty detects the offence in its beginnings, when it is only potential, when the germ of the evil is commencing its growth. Man can deal only with some offences — those, namely, which inflict a definite and intelligible injury on individuals or on the security of society; but God judges that which offends His holiness, or does damage to the *civitas Dei*. Man adjudicates on intentions when they are developed into action; the Divine sight takes cognizance of thoughts, from which actions may spring. The fallibility of man constrains him to treat doubtful cases with leniency, unless justice is to become unduly severe and intolerably capricious; but in the light of God's countenance there is nothing doubtful, in the clearness of His judgment nothing fallible. It is no wonder then, that when this conception of the great Judge occupies the religious sense, no sacrifice is too costly to deprecate the anger which He may be supposed to feel at the offence which He sees so plainly and so unerringly,—the extent and meaning of which He recognizes with far greater distinctness than the tenderest and most susceptible conscience can conceive it. To acknowledge the judgment of God is, by inevitable sequence, to confess and know that a clear, vigilant, penetrating eye is always fixed on the innermost nature of each man, and that as this vision sees every thing, so it forgets nothing. The scriptures of the Old Testament, and particularly the Psalms, constantly affirm the unwearied and watchful scrutiny of the Divine presence. The language of the New is not less precise as to the universality of the same Providence.

The conception would be intolerable, were it not that so sensitive a religious instinct invariably assigns to the Almighty a beneficent regard for His creatures, a willingness to accept repentance, a readiness to bestow strength and deliverance,—the qualities of forbearance, long-suffering, patience, compassion. He is the Father, who not only supplies the wants, but bears with the petulance and disobedience of His children. His wrath is roused against those only who deny Him his due honor, who say He is not, who go astray after other gods, who repudiate His authority, as well as disregard His injunctions. But to those who acknowledge Him, He is always placable. He always invites them to repent, He always accepts their penitence, He always grants them forgiveness. It is every thing to know Him, for when He is known, the awful features of the great Judge become a vision of ineffable tenderness and pity, of sympathy for weak and struggling humanity, of Fatherly love for wayward childhood, of watchfulness over feeble steps, of attention to the utterance of wants and desires, of solicitude, bounty, gentleness. He is the wise and tender Father, who shows compassion to all His children.

One thing, however, He exacts, — as He is merciful, so man must be merciful. He will not forgive the unforgiving. The surest sign of impenitence is a hard, imperious, unpitying temper. It is as though He could not but exact on behalf of those who are wronged, whatever is their abstract right; but as though with this, He would give nothing but that bare right to him who mercilessly rejects the suit of another. Man can forgive the offence which has been committed against himself. For thus far, at least, he still retains that image of God in which he was created. But if he insists on his literal due from his neighbor, he cannot expect consideration from another, and least of all from Him who knows how imperfect has been the obedience of His creatures, and how unwarrantable it is for man to be implacable, when he most needs such forgiveness himself. To be unmerciful and unforgiving is to deny the Fatherhood of God, and to look on Him only as a Judge. " To him," says the Apostle James, — speaking in the spirit of the Hebrew prophet, and as the servant of Christ, — " who does no mercy shall be pitiless judgment given ; mercy has higher claims than judgment."

It is inevitable, in so far as a belief in God and in His Providence exists, that religion should develop, to a greater or less extent, such conceptions of the relation in which man stands to the Maker, the Judge, the Father, as have been stated above. The Law must be stricter and more rigorous than that which human society can enact, the Lawgiver must take clearer cognizance of facts and motives than human legislation can achieve or attempt. The justice of the All-wise will be tempered with mercy. On the other hand, as no injury can, except by a figure of speech, be put on the Almighty, but only on those who are equally the objects of His Providence and Love, the mercy which He shows can be anticipated by forgiveness, granted on the part of those who are wronged, and can only be obtained on the condition that the penitent is willing to accord the pardon which he begs for. And, in a more or less perfect form, these religious tenets characterize all theological systems which have ever contained a just conception of the Deity. The forgiveness of injuries is no peculiar maxim of Christian ethics. It is Jewish, Zoroastrian, Pythagorean, Platonic, Stoic. So is the great defensive rule of social morality — that of doing as we would be done by. It is not without reason that the Psalmist — having averred that the fool hath said in his heart, There is no God — portrays the converse of that picture which a lively conscience of God's presence exhibits, narrates the deeds of those who deny His Providence and Justice, and accounts for that social panic, that fear where no fear is, which follows on the extinction of the religious sense — the absence of God's fear before men's eyes.

The Epistle to the Romans contains the Pauline doctrine of sin. The passage just referred to, or rather two passages grouped together from the Psalms — the fourteenth and the fifty-third — are cited in order to prove the universality of sin. The narrative of the fall of Adam is made the basis of a similar generalization. Death was the penalty annexed to the offence committed in the garden, death has been the lot of humanity ever since, and, therefore, the sin of the first progenitor of mankind was propagated through his offspring. This position, on which St. Paul insists more than once, was derived from the teaching of the Rabbis. The facts of the Mosaic cosmogony were admitted, and the explanation was obvious and convenient. It is to be observed, however, that the derived sin of Adam's descendants was inferred from the mortality of man's body, — the dogma of transmitted guilt was a gloss.

That the Apostle fully believed in the sufficiency of his explanation as to the origin of moral evil will be readily allowed. That he quoted the passages from the Septuagint — in which David is celebrating some victory over his foreign and domestic enemies, and contrasting their evil doings with the character of the generation of the righteous, — as though it were a theological declaration about the universal depravity of mankind, and that he made the quotation in perfect good faith need not be doubted. The allegorical interpretation of Scripture was so customary among the Jews of the Pauline era, and was adopted so naturally by Christian teachers, that we need not be surprised at the citation of this passage, in which a slight analogy is taken to be a conclusive proof. A glance, indeed, will show that David did not mean to affirm, in the passages quoted, the universal depravity of man's nature, still less to apply these words to those who are under the Law, as the Apostle implies that he does. It is possible that he was thinking of his rebellious son and the associates of his revolt; but, it is far more likely that, when he speaks of the bones of them that besieged Zion, he had before him Chemosh, or Milcom, or Moloch, — the abomination of the nations round about; whose worship the Israelite contemptuously, perhaps justly, called fornication; and who had been eating up Israel as though they were eating bread.

And, similarly, it may be proved that the varieties of the human race cannot be referred to a common origin; that the history of humanity is not retrogression from a pure exemplar, but progress from comparative or actual barbarism; that the primeval Adam, at least of many races, was no dweller in a Paradise, who talked with God, and had the gift, or, at least, the prospect of immortal life, but a savage who slowly elaborated the arts of domestic life, who maintained a warfare against wild beasts, and who lived at so remote a period, that many species of animals had disappeared since he first walked on the earth. If such a theory can be maintained, there is no escape from one of two alternatives. Either the man and woman of the Mosaic account are the progenitors of one family of mankind, and, therefore, have transmitted their sin and their hope to those only who have sprung from them; or the story of Adam and Eve is one of those allegories in which men have always delighted, and by which they have wished to express the conviction, that the facts of later social life represent a decline from primeval purity,—just as the Greeks consoled themselves in the depravity and violence of their own epoch with the dream of a golden age, with a Hyperborean felicity, with the islands of the blest, with the garden of golden fruit, and similar schemes of an imagination which protests against the evil which it sees, but cannot or will not cure. Under neither explanation, however, can the narrative of the garden be an exposition of the origin of evil.

The historical origin of sin, vice, infirmity of purpose, selfishness, sensuality, is not so important a matter for consideration as the fact that these things are. The discovery and application of remedies for those evils is a problem, pending the solution of which all creation groans and travails in pain. Every religion which contains in itself a spark of the Divine fire professes to have discovered a more or less effectual remedy for such mischiefs. Every religion which has actually found out some aid towards the moral progress of mankind has done its part in the general scheme of social regeneration. It is matter of very little consequence whether this or that teacher has accurately traced out the sources of the disorder which he has learnt to rectify. It is enough to cast out devils in the name of Christ. In the treatment of disease, — moral no less than physical, — it is important to know the cause of the sickness only when the cause and effect exist and cease to exist simultaneously. When the infection has been taken, it is of very little importance to the patient or the physician to be able to identify the origin of the malady. In such a crisis, the first thing which has to be considered is the treatment. Nay, when the symptoms are grave, and the situation is urgent, it is worse than a waste of labor to speculate on the source of the complaint — to wrangle over theories, and to abstain from prompt and decisive action.

St. Paul thinks that he has the Spirit of God. He says so modestly, and if ever man could say it, he says so truly. If life and labor such as his were, — if intense activity, and equally intense love, such as constituted his very nature, — were delusions, he might well call himself of all men most miserable; we might despair of the human race, and assert that the heaviest curse which has fallen on mankind is that gift — suicidal, as we should then justly call it — of a disinterested and self-sacrificing sense of duty. If it be the case that they who have diligently set themselves to profit by the order of society and the convictions of others, in order to gather together the means of rank, wealth, pleasure, ease, are the equals or superiors of those who have slighted such advantages, in order that they may effect a permanent improvement in the lot of their fellow-men, — if a refined and temperate selfishness, a shrewd, cold prudence, is as good an end of human life as a lofty perseverance after great and generous objects, no delusion can be more gross than Christianity. But, it must be added, that the awakening from this delusion would arrest civilization, and rapidly drive men back to savagery. For a time, indeed, power might ally itself with intelligence, and might oppress mankind. But very speedily every man's hand would be against his fellow-man, and the sneer of the sophist would become the law of nature. Justice would be the interest of the strongest, and internecine war the unchanging lot of humanity.

There is an inveterate difficulty in believing that the Apostle is the mouth-piece of a positive revelation. If there is reason to know that he misquotes, or misunderstands the authority to which he appeals, or that the historical statement to which he refers, in order to substantiate his generalization, is no fact at all, but an apologue or a parable, we may, we ought to decline acceptance of the proof. His conclusions may be true, though his premises may be irrelevant or false. When a conclusion is certified by experience, formal and precise proof is not always necessary in order to secure conviction, just as it is not always possible. Such a condition is frequent in moral science, — all but universal in the case of religious conviction. And so it does not follow that the Pauline conclusion is false because the Apostle's premises are irrelevant. The words of the Psalmist may not mean that human nature is universally corrupt, — the derivation of sin from the taint of Adam's transgression may be a paradox, as it certainly seems to be at variance with what we believe of the Divine justice; but man's nature may yet be universally corrupt, — man may be naturally inclined to evil, — we may have no truth in us, and deceive ourselves if we say that we have no sin; we may still need a Teacher, a Saviour, a Redeemer. St. John is as powerful a witness to the sinfulness of man as St. Paul is, though he does not ascribe this infirmity to the hereditary taint of descent from a disobedient ancestor.

It matters nothing whether man has sprung from a savage ancestry, the mental powers of which were hardly higher than those of the other animals with whom the primeval barbarian herded, or whether he is the defaced copy of a Divine Exemplar. The fact of interest is that he is now liable to impulses which, if unrestrained, would make instant havoc of society, and which are therefore partly coerced by law, partly by custom, partly, and most of all, by the religious sense. Take away the influence which the latter exercises,— and it appears that no substitute can be found for it,— and it seems inevitable, either that social forces, which are nearly equal in strength, will engage in the fiercest struggle for supremacy, or that power will create a rigorous and jealous despotism, under which the ruler and his instruments need only to be active and cunning, and the people will be permanently sunk in ignorance and degradation.

Philosophers and publicists have frequently busied themselves with the project of constructing a common life for voluntary associations; but they have never been able to discover any thing which shall be strong enough to make these associations cohere together. There are no secular Cœnobites. Religious associations, on the other hand, have existed in plenty, and have had a very tenacious vitality. The apostolic college at Jerusalem is the earliest Christian exemplar. The French missionaries found monasteries in abundance through central Asia, among the Buddhists. In the United States there are several communities of Cœnobites. So vast is that country, and so little is any attrition of sects felt in the rural districts of the Union, that these social experiments have a fairer chance of success and endurance in America than they would have elsewhere. But every one of these communistic schemes is founded on a religious basis—

even when, as is charged against some of them, the practice of the community is licentious. A religion may consist of little more than dogma, or it may ignore dogmas and court asceticism, or it may be neither dogmatic nor ascetic, but demand an active charity and a pure heart. Each of these religions has its schedule of offences. In the first the sin is called heresy; in the second it is called worldliness; in the third it is a breach of the inner law, which God has ordained and conscience sanctioned. In each case it is supposed that the commission of the sin secludes the man who commits it from his Maker, leaves him to the anger of the Judge, excludes him from the love of the Father, cuts him off from illumination and pardon.

An offence against religion is called a sin. The word commonly used for this state is one which expresses an error, mistake, misconception, less culpable than deliberate or wanton wickedness, but blameworthy because care and forethought would have prevented its occurrence. The sinner is one who has missed his way, whose path has been dark, and who has therefore strayed from it. The word suggests excuse, pardon, reconciliation; is contrasted with another state in which the light is deliberately put out; in which the offence is wilful, daring, insolent; in which the man is lawless or unjust. Thus, the synoptic gospels affirm that there is a sin against the Holy Ghost, — against that Power which enlightens, strengthens, teaches men. The author of the Epistle to the Hebrews contemplates the case of those who have been enlightened and have repudiated the gift, in language containing the strongest phrases of nascent Gnosticism, the phraseology of the Alexandrian Theosophists. The beloved disciple declares that there is a sin unto death. Paul speaks of the rejected, those who fail on being tested; or, as our version gives it, though with a force which familiarity has weakened, the cast-away, — the vessels which the potter has framed and found to be unsound or unserviceable. But, generally, the language of the New Testament is merciful towards sin, excluding no one from penitence and pardon. "This is good and approved before God our Saviour, who wills that all men should be saved and arrive at an insight into the truth," says the Apostle in the first letter to Timothy. The charity of Christ is universal, the love of God is unbounded, the door to repentance is open, and the Gospel of the New Covenant is as merciful as the teaching of the Prophets.

As religion leans to the contemplative, the ascetic, or the practical consequence of illumination or regeneration, so it stigmatizes as sin a departure from the rule of the life which it has inculcated. It has happened that the first of these forms of religious opinion has exercised so energetic an influence, that conformity to written creeds is treated as the highest duty, divergence from them as the most grievous sin. The Roman Church, for example, has multiplied the "articles of faith," and has uttered its anathema against those who decline to accept any of its dogmas. It is probable that the terrors of this denunciation have been weakened, but there are millions of professed Christians to whose conscience doctrinal heresy is the highest crime that can be committed against the Majesty of God. Perhaps there has been no country where this dread of unbelief has been more general than in Spain. Here the suspicion of heresy was more feared than the reputation of any moral depravity. So there are parts of Italy, where people have united the profession of brigandage with the most scrupulous and sincere orthodoxy. It is obvious that the most lively horror at the imputation of unsound opinion on theological topics is quite compatible with the utter absence of all the other elements of the religious life, and that the strictest, the most heartfelt profession of a creed is no guarantee of a single Christian virtue.

To any one who considers how different are the capacities of men for comprehending facts and reasoning out conclusions, how difficult it must be to form any comprehension whatever of those remote and exalted conceptions which theology attempts to define and limit, — how much less responsible, on the plainest principles of justice, a man must be for an error of judgment or opinion, than he is for an offence against virtue or morality, — it must seem strange that false opinion has been treated as sin. Hitherto, indeed, old and new forms of religious organization have been at one on this point, and have held the non-acceptance of a tenet as a criminal act, as one which should be visited with social or even legal penalties.

They have even asserted, perhaps in justification of

their practice, that theological error is the consequence of moral guilt. But men have constantly lived in accordance with the highest and purest moral virtue, while they have been sceptical or heterodox on speculative questions. And conversely, men whose orthodoxy has been unimpeached have often set an evil example of conduct, have allowed their lives to belie their profession, have even attempted a compromise, under the terms of which strictness of conformity is made to compensate for laxity of practice. Such persons have frequently been treated with the greatest leniency by those who agree with them in opinion. But if theological error were the cause of vice, it ought to follow that the possession of theological truth must be a guarantee of holiness.

There are opinions, positively entertained, which are immoral in their tendency. Any opinion, for example, which separates a man from those relations to God, which are at once the pledge of his trust in God, and which exact a constant watchfulness over life or action; any tenet which would induce a man to substitute any other agency than his own conscience, or his own duty, in the satisfaction of a moral obligation, — is in itself immoral. The guide may be a Pharisee, and the blind may lead the blind; the ceremonial need not purify the heart, but may leave the man a whited sepulchre.

There is, however, a serious danger involved in the doctrine that the acceptance of certain definitions and tenets is the necessary foundation of the Christian character. What if overmastering doubts, honest disabilities of judgment, make men decline to admit certain statements, or formulas, or presumed facts? What if such doubts and difficulties are met by stern declarations and angry anathemas? Is it not possible to conceive that men may be alienated from a beneficent religion by the harshness of its advocates? Has it not, unhappily, been the case that Christianity has been rendered distasteful to many by the intemperate severity of those who pretend to expound it?

The time must come in which the teaching of Christianity — if it is to retain its hold on the hearts of men — must ignore differences of opinion, or, in other words, must accept the fact that while men agree closely on the ground of common duty and common action, and are willing, nay anxious, to make duty more stringent and action more heroic, they cannot all be made to think alike. When this teaching is current, the reunion of Christianity becomes possible, because the teacher has reverted to the examples which the Founder of the faith has given. To have the mind of Christ, it is not necessary to busy one's self with abstract and dark speculations; but it is necessary for each to do the work which God has given him to do, and thereafter commit one's self to Him who judges righteously. To forget the mind of Christ, and abandon the continuity of that great office which His life, and the life of those who conformed to Him, began, in the vain struggle after effecting a uniformity of opinion, is to nail Him anew to His cross, and then to cast lots for His garment.

The faith which removes mountains is not that which creates stumbling-blocks, but it is the zeal which is unsparing of itself, and gentle to others, the love which Paul commends as the greatest and most enduring of the Christian graces.

That morbid asceticism which believed that motiveless and inactive self-torture was the highest form of the religious life, which made austerity a virtue, and the enjoyment of God's blessings a sin, has probably passed away for ever. This extravagant theory of perfection was imported into Christianity, it would seem, from Buddhism, through the imitation of those devotees who, before the Christian era, congregated in the deserts of Lower Egypt. It is difficult for us to conceive the process by which men, who voluntarily lived a brutish life in caves, or passed their existence on lofty pillars, or went through sharp and meaningless penances, came to imagine that their practice was the truest service that could be rendered to God, and that they were the peculiar favorites of Heaven.

This strange opinion, derived, it is believed, from the practice of rival devotees in the Brahman and Buddhist creeds, once completely permeated Christianity. It formed the leading characteristic of many religious orders. It still lingers among the more rigid sectaries of the Roman Church, its Carthusians and Trappists. It has peculiar attractions to those who have lived a while in reckless pleasure. It is really akin to that Manichæan doctrine, which, holding that matter is evil, has divided creation between a beneficent God and a malignant demon, and assigned the largest and most important share to the latter.

In a modified form, it has developed that unhealthy anxiety about personal salvation which has tormented so many good men,— has cast a blight on their lives, has benumbed their energies, has crippled their usefulness. There is no sadder sight than that of a tender and loving nature, which, giving itself up to this dread of God, thereby dishonors His love, and doubts His mercy; which creates for itself a valley of the shadow of death, a vale of misery; which brings the terrors of Sinai into the region of the Gospel. But Christianity has no claim on society — does no service to mankind, if it is to be considered only as the machinery for saving the individual soul, least of all if that soul is only to be saved by an agony of dread. Christ did not live to save men but man. They who are Christ's have the same purpose before them, and any anxiety about their personal safety is superfluous and debasing.

Christianity demands that man should do good to man for God's sake, and for no other object besides. The opportunities are multiform; the claim on the individual is perpetual. To such an extent only as is needed for the satisfaction of this great function, does religious duty assume the ascetic spirit. It is possible, when men resolve on such an employment of their powers, that they have to forego not only the regular reward of their labors, but the legitimate enjoyments of life. Christ, who expressly repudiated the ascetic life in its mildest form, — drawing a contrast between

His own practice and that of the Baptist,— contemplates the case of the man who sacrifices domestic happiness to a high sense of public duty. St. Paul takes credit for the self-denial with which he adopted celibacy, or at least suspended that companionship which he considered honorable and pure. He even urges, in his anxiety to detach his followers from the temporary dangers of their calling, and to accustom them to the contemplation of Christ's immediate advent to judgment, that they should be celibates also. James, the head of the communist church at Jerusalem, inveighs against the rich, only as forgetful of duty and sunk in sensuality. Now, it is undoubtedly the office of Christian men to avoid temptation, and to keep their passions, appetites, impulses, in check. The favorite metaphor of St. Paul is that of the palæstra. He "keeps under" his body, — the word being equivalent to that which Horace employs when he speaks of Sybaris as bruised by the exercise of the gymnasium. The Christian, to use a modern phrase, is always in training—is under a permanent regimen and diet.

The world owes every thing to voluntary labor. The energy which pursues knowledge for no material profit, and which eagerly imparts it; the true pleasure which is felt at conferring lasting and general benefits; the temper which gains the highest satisfaction by knowing that the cause of humanity, civilization, progress, has made a firm advance by reason of some act which has strengthened and assisted them; the addition to the knowledge which lightens the sorrows of mankind, and extends the blessings of an all-wise Providence to the largest possible number of His creatures, and therefore to brutes; the self-devotion which visits the sick, aids the poor, builds and sustains school, hospital, and a pure Church; the courage and gentleness which check oppression and disarm anger; the tenderness which tames savage nations, and reclaims desperate, but not impenitent vice, speaking peace and pardon to them who are fallen, but not incurable; the love which wins the young, and thereby confers the most exquisite pleasure on those who gain the confidence and receive the caresses of childhood, — are examples of the Christian temper, imitations of Him who bade little children run to His arms, and who, on the eve of His Passion, with the sad presentiment of His own destiny, and the sadder sense of the ruin which brooded over the beloved city, would still have gathered her people to Him, as a hen gathereth her chickens under her wings.

The greatest victory, however, which the spirit of Christianity achieves is obtained when it permeates the mind of the statesman. In the days when the Gospel was first preached there was no opportunity for sketching the career of such a man, and the Scriptures of the Gospel do not portray undeveloped characters. But the statesman of the divine commonwealth is contained, by implication, in those descriptions of Christian worthiness which Paul loves to draw. To win assent by patient and persistent vindication of the truth, to wait for neither honor nor reward, to use power wisely, never desiring it and never wasting it, to bear misconstruction patiently, and to learn vigilance and forbearance from the bitterness of hostile criticism, to outlive calumny by perfect simplicity and candor, to administer affairs justly, and to cherish every force by which social morality and mutual good-will may be strengthened and made permanent, to make no compromise between ambition and honor, to be unmoved and just amid the din of rival sects and clashing interests, to defer not for an instant to the selfish clamor of a factious mob, whether the mob be one of grandees or peasants, of partisans or opponents, to withstand the subtlest of all temptations, the gratification of a sordid patriotism, the flattery of a selfish nationality, to be prudent, incorruptible, alert, — these are some of the qualities of a Christian statesman. A few men have been such examples, and they have been the apostles of a Divine wisdom, have left ineffaceable traces on the history of mankind, have brought back on the scarred and distorted visage of humanity some features to the likeness of God. Man can give them no reward for their benefits; the recompense of their labor is laid up in the treasury of God. Man could not stimulate them to such efforts and such sacrifices as they make. It is the Spirit of God which dwells within them, and by which they follow the great Captain of man's salvation, like Him being made perfect by suffering.

The man who counselled the avoidance of doubtful questions in the reception of members into the Christian brotherhood, and who spoke contemptuously of all ascetics, whether they were the emissaries who unsettled the Galatians, or the punctilious forerunners of Gnostic idealism, was not likely to have taken part in those theories which have made conformity in religious opinion the most essential feature in the Christian character, or to have discovered any special sanctity in unmeaning austerities. According to the simple creed of the Apostolic age, there is one God. This is the contribution of pure Judaism to the Christian Church. There is one Christ, Jesus of Nazareth. This Man died and rose again. He is the Power of God, the Word of God, the Redeemer of mankind, the present Saviour, the perfect Example, the future Judge. In Him, through Him, for Him we live, work, suffer, hope. This, St. Paul could say, is my gospel, and from this teaching I derive my religion. There are other forms in which the Gospel is preached, but if they preach the Spirit of Christ, I am indifferent to variations in the manner, and heed not hostility to myself. "Some, indeed," says he in one of his last letters, "preach Christ enviously and contentiously, some generously. They who do it contentiously, have no pure purpose, for they think that they will make my chains gall me the more. They who do it lovingly, know that I live in prison to defend the Gospel. But what of this? In every way — be it with a sinister or an honest purpose — Christ is announced, and this is and shall be matter of congratulation to me." What a comment on the rivalry of sects! How naturally does the writer go on to warn his beloved Philippians against cavilling and logomachies — the perennial curse of Christendom.

The danger of doctrinal sin is made of little account in the Pauline religion. There are traces, indeed, of the idea, that misapprehension as to theological tenets is an offence, or, at least, a danger. There were men, according to the second pastoral epistle, who entertained views about the resurrection, which contravened the habitual teaching of the Apostle. There were men whom the Apostle anathematized in his wrath, because they renewed the yoke of Judaism, and frightened the Gentiles into the acceptance of superfluous observances. There were conceited visionaries, who prided themselves on a special illumination, on a knowledge which puffed them up, who were given over to the deadly delusion of spiritual pride, the heretical men who were to be twice warned and then avoided. But, of the later doctrine which harsh creeds have engendered — that the non-acceptance of ecclesiastical definitions is a sin against God, a wicked error, an act of treason against the Divine majesty — there is no trace. The common sense and sagacity of the Apostle would have scouted the idea of those jurists, who, having recognized the conception of conspiracy, rebellion, treason against the human ruler, have applied it to those who will not, or cannot, accept the precedents of successful polemics. Men have asserted, that the result of an attempt to define the transcendental mysteries of Divine Providence ought to be as plain to ordinary minds as those human laws are which may be unjust, but are certainly intelligible, and they have added to this fallacy another which is still more gross. They have affected to consider that a misapprehension of the Divine nature is the same sort of offence as that which seeks to overthrow the authority of a secular ruler, who is a man as much as the malcontents are; and that hesitation as to allowing some of the attributes which they assign to an omnipotent God is identical with the crime of seeking to destroy a government by violence or fraud, of subverting a power which cannot exist and continue without weapons of defence. Alas, to be ignorant of His beneficence and justice, to live without knowledge of Him, is no matter for anger, but occasion for pity, — for that compassion which the strong should feel towards those who are weak; the wise for those who are ignorant; the rich for those who are poor; the child whose father and mother love him, and whose home is cheerful and happy, for the fatherless, the orphan, the destitute, the homeless; the man of strong, clear, active mind, for the hypochondriac who suffers under baseless illusions. But sometimes the armor of confident assertion is the cloak of doubt. Shall we admire or pity the audacity which utters the famous paradox of Tertullian, — "Credo quia impossibile est"?

For the sin of the ascetic, Paul mentions to dismiss it with disdain. It was no part of this Apostle's theory that his converts should go out of the world, — that they should be sour, mortified, recluse. The advice which he gives, and of which so much has been made, as to marriage, is given for temporary and special reasons. Elsewhere, he commends the connubial state, and reckons among the signs of the latter times, — of the days of wandering spirits, and the teachings of devils, — the repudiation of marriage and those alimentary restrictions which ascetics have always insisted on. There is, it may be, some benefit in the subjection of the body to discipline; but piety, religion, is of universal benefit, for it conveys with itself the promises of the present and of the future life.

It remains, then, that the sin which the Apostle denounced, and against which he uttered his warnings, was that against the Moral Law, — such sin as the Jewish prophets condemned, and made the object of God's wrath, — and, in particular, the sins of sensuality and greed, the sins of a reprobate intellect. The details of such a depravity are described in the first chapter of the Epistle to the Romans, where, in accordance with the teaching of the Hebrew jurists, the tendency to these offences is connected with ignorance of the Being and Providence of God, — with the absence of the religious sense, — with the folly, as David says, which denies God in the heart. So, again, it is the flesh against the spirit, — the animal impulse of man contravening and degrading the diviner element, — which leads to the sin which dishonors man. In one remarkable passage, the Apostle compares the logical act of appetite with the logical act of the nobler nature of the spirit, and notes their antagonism, — his contrast being probably suggested by the familiar language of Aryan dualism. Sin, then, is partly the consequence of unworthy conceptions of God, partly a yielding to the temptation which is perpetually recurring in the body of this death, in the facile obedience to an imperious law which campaigns against the law of my intellect (the origin, according to Aristotle, of all law), and which takes me captive to itself,—to the law of sin which exists in my body, and in its passions.

This contest between appetite and reason, between the flesh and the spirit, is elaborated in the Epistle to the Galatians. "Walk by the spirit, and you will not satisfy the desire of the flesh. The flesh has its impulses which would subdue the spirit,—the spirit those which would subdue the flesh. These contravene one another, and so you do what you do not wish to do. If ye are led by the spirit, you are not subject to a law;" or, as is explained a little afterwards, when the Apostle has sketched the vices and virtues of those contrasted forces, "there is no law against those who practise the latter." Law, be it ceremonial or municipal, is directed against those who break it, and has no practical existence to them who are exempted from obedience to a ceremonial code, or whose conduct is such that they do not incur the penalties of municipal legislation.

Whenever the Apostle utters his warning against sin, and enumerates its various phases, he invariably reckons unchastity as the greatest or most prominent of vices. The extraordinary impurity of social life among Romans, Greeks, Syrians,—the shamelessness with which licentiousness was practised and avowed,—may have induced the Apostle to lay great stress on the necessity for purity among his converts. In the Epistle to the Corinthians he speaks of incontinence as specially degrading. In that to the Thessalonians he urges the necessity of keeping the body pure, in contrast to Gentile practice. But, apart from the immediate effect of this particular vice, the Apostle knew what were the associations of ancient prostitution. The practice was part of the system of nature-worship. Antioch, where St. Paul resided so long, was notorious for its dissoluteness, for the openness with which wantons were recognized and patronized. In Corinth, Paphos, and a hundred other cities, prostitution was considered, not merely — as some of our publicists have reckoned it — a social necessity, but a *culte*, an act of worship. The earlier Scriptures of the Old Testament allude to the women who lived near the precinct of some idol shrine. The story of Israel and Moab bears testimony to the close connection between licentiousness and idolatry. For this reason, fornication is commonly used in the Old Testament as a synonyme for idolatry, and sometimes in the New, as for example in the Revelation. As the Jewish creed grew more strictly monotheistic, it proscribed with peculiar energy any practice which was associated with that nature-worship which it detested and despised.

To the moralist, sin is vice,—which, as far as its influence extends, wrecks society. Violence, fraud, rapine, endanger the institution of property; licentiousness insults the sacredness of home, the dignity of woman, the instincts of paternal fondness and care. It is not because the effects of unchastity are less mischievous than those of lawlessness, that criminal law does not take cognizance of, or punish the former, but because the machinery of repression or punishment is less easy. No civilized community neglects, however free it leaves the Press, to punish those who sell indecent or immoral books, pictures, and the like. Nor, were it possible or convenient to check the vice to which these publications pander, in the interest of society, is there any doubt that a legislature might and would use the forces at its control in order to purify, as it does to protect society.

The effect of sin on the individual is, that it deadens the religious sense. It perverts the sight of God, inducing the man to frame such notions of the Deity as characterized the nature-worship of Greek, Roman, and Syrian. God, argues the Apostle, had made Himself known, — the invisible verity being made intelligible by the analogy of the visible creation ; as, for example, the eternal power and divine majesty of the Almighty. But, though the heathen world knew God, its inhabitants "gave Him not the glory and praise that was His due, but argued themselves into folly, so that they were darkened in a senseless heart. Calling themselves wise they became stolid, and transferred the glory of the unchangeable God to some image of changeable man, or to that of bird, beast, or reptile." Hence, he goes on to infer, their vices, — on which he dwells with vehement disgust, concluding with a description of the depravity into which the heathen had fallen, and the satisfaction which they felt in their depravity.

The sight of God which sin perverts, the revelation of God's justice which is made in the Gospel, and which leads to an ever-increasing trust in God, — that process from faith to faith, according to the Hebrew, a formula of growing intensity, — is no mere knowledge. Men may be acquainted with every thing which has been alleged, proved, accepted, on behalf of a doctrinal system, and may acquiesce in every tenet which theologians have affirmed, — may be of unimpeached orthodoxy, — may dread heresy as though it were some dangerous or deadly contagion, — and still be far removed from the apostolic sight of God, from the manifestation, the revelation, which Paul thought the choicest gift of the Gospel which he preached. Nay, a precise orthodoxy may be coupled with those very vices which are denounced in the Epistles to the Romans and the Galatians. The history of Christianity can supply abundant illustrations of the fact, that no religious system, however positive may be its tenets, is any guarantee against that laxity of practice which the Apostle speaks of as the proof of a reprobate mind, or as the logic of the appetite, or as the works of the flesh. Faith, as commonly understood, is neither the life of Christ nor the sight of God. And, conversely, if the sight of God and the life of Christ are the highest hopes and the best pattern which can be before the mind of man, it is possible that heresy, free-thought, resolute inquiry into the ground of our belief, may be no bar to the imitation of the latter, and the possession of the former. The sight of God is not, in the economy of Christ's teaching, reserved for the learned theologian, but for the pure in heart. In this particular, the Apostle's doctrine does not swerve from that of the Master. Man may become the temple of God, but the building must be cleansed for the Divine indwelling.

In the system of St. Paul, the process of illumination and reconciliation, of forgiveness and hope, is simple. To trust in Christ, to believe in the mercy of God, is sufficient for pardon, is a pledge of grace given, of mercy vouchsafed. The symbol of this trust is baptism into the name of Christ. The warranty of the hopes which baptism affirms is the Passion of Jesus. The gospel of the Apostle contains, as has been said, a few facts, and one simple act of initiation. Nothing can be more brief than this gospel of doctrine, for it ascribes the salvation, the regeneration, the reconciliation of man to the sublime self-sacrifice of the risen Christ. It is stated in its most succinct form to the Philippian gaoler, — "Trust in the Lord Jesus Christ, and thou shalt be safe." In the symbolism of the Alexandrian gloss on the Jewish covenant, as expounded in the Epistle to the Hebrews; before Christ came there was a vail shutting men out from the Shekinah. The proof that God was there was afforded by the occasional entrance of a Jewish priest. He came and the vail was for ever taken away. Every one has a right to enter now. Salvation is no longer the heritage of a race, it is the right of all the families of the earth. Eagerly accepting the universality of the Saviour's mission, the apostles, who treated Christianity in a catholic spirit, were satisfied of the fact that He has invited all men to the mercy of God, and that the Covenant of Abraham is extended to the whole human race.

But when the convert is admitted to the Gospel, the work of grace commences. The change of conversion is vast, — it is no less than a new creation, a new birth. But it would be rash, irrational, ruinous to suppose that the great work is achieved in the instant of confession and in the avowal of allegiance. The growth of the spiritual man, like that of the natural man, is from babyhood to manhood. The work of the Spirit is solid and gradual. Men are builded up, increase, grow to a full stature. The life of the Christian man needs care and watchfulness, self-denial and self-control. The religious change is one of slow accession, of anxious and continual watchfulness. It could not be effected but by the aid of the Divine Spirit, — by the presence of Christ, — by the perpetual practice of Christian duty, — by the concurrence of the will of man, and the help of God. "It is not," says the Apostle, "in my presence only, but in my absence still more, that I insist on the rule that you should accomplish your own safety with fear and with anxiety; for it is God whose energy effects this in us, that we should will, and we should show our energy in the direction which pleases Him." St. Paul uses the same emphatic word — a word for which philosophy is indebted to Aristotle —

to show that the will of God and the will of man are simultaneously operative in the Christian soul. Man is no inert matter, but without God the man can do nothing.

Each man is aided in this great work of regeneration and reconciliation by the Spirit of God, and is thereby renewed in the likeness of the Great Father. But surrounding, combining, pervading, knitting and binding together them who are engaged in the labor of the spiritual life, is the glorified Christ. He begins the redemption of the individual, by constituting these units into a Church. Man cannot live in a religious solitude, any more than he can dwell apart from the social life in which he moves. Christianity is a fellowship, a company, a community. In this association, no man can say to his neighbor, I have no need of thee. The aggregate of Christian men is a building, in which the individuals are the separate stones, a body of which they are the separate members. Christ is the life which pervades them, by which they are mutually sensitive, by which they exist, move, grow. "We have," says St. Paul, "our commonwealth in the heavens. From this we are expecting our Lord Jesus Christ, who will transfigure the body of our humiliation so that it shall take the shape of the body of His glory, in accordance with the living energy by which He can marshal all things under Himself.". Then the illumination is completed, the pardon is sure, the victory is won, the sight of God is everlastingly obtained, and the mission of Christ is ended.

## DUTY TO WORK FOR HUMANITY. 361

That the great scheme of human redemption and moral progress should fail for want of advocates who can win assent, and gather forces for the battle against selfishness and sin, is not to be believed. To entertain this doubt, to sit with folded arms while the course of humanity goes backward, to be dismayed at the present, to despair of the future, is the highest offence which a clear conception of truth can commit against duty. " Woe to me," said Paul, " if I preach not the Gospel; to do it is no cause for boasting; I must needs do it." To decline the work is to sin against God's Spirit, to refuse Him who speaks, to enter into the peril of that sin which is, above all, inexcusable. And, on the other hand, it is certain that they who, for no other purpose than that of doing justly, and curing the hardships and sorrows of life, seek the good of man, will find that they are, though perhaps unconsciously, the truest teachers of the Gospel of mercy and grace, " though Abraham be ignorant of them, and Israel acknowledge them not."

## CHAPTER X.

THEY who have busied themselves with the chronology of the New Testament, generally set a period of about thirty-three years between the time at which the "young man Saul," eager to vindicate the Law, set out for Damascus, and that at which, in his last imprisonment, " Paul the aged " declared that " he had fought a good fight, had finished his course, and was now ready to be offered." This interval had been spent in founding and in confirming churches. The Acts of the Apostles give us an account of some among Paul's many labors. His own Epistles supply us with a little further information. But the narrative in the historical work is imperfect, even where it professes to state the facts, and is silent as to the last years of Paul's life. The letters which the Apostle wrote, were, we must believe, very numerous. His care of all the churches certainly led to frequent communications with them, so that, even at a comparatively early period in his career, his letters were reckoned to be weighty and vigorous. But only a small number of these can have been preserved. His labors were incessant, and he was always seeking to occupy new ground. But we hear about none of his doings from the time in which he rented a house at Rome, — six years before the commonly received date of his martyrdom, — to the final consummation of his career, when he stood, almost friendless, before the judgment-seat of Nero, and was looking forward to his rest and his reward.

During this vigorous life he had preached the Gospel over the Western world, avoiding only those districts where other men had laid the foundation, and renewing by letter, when absent, the teaching which he had given by word of mouth. Some of these congregations must have kept archives, and a few of these archives were preserved till such time as the Jewish reaction abated, and the surviving writings of Paul were sought after, especially by the Latin Christians, in order to develop a systematic theology. It was for this object especially that the Epistles of Paul were collected, studied, and expounded. But nothing was less before the eyes of Paul than the foundation of a school. His aim was to establish a divine commonwealth, which, dwelling within the organization of the Roman empire, should leaven, purify, and finally reform society. The universal acknowledgment of Christ is a part of the recompense of His suffering. He is to have the homage of every knee and every tongue. Such a result, however, is impossible, unless the Gospel of Christ is capable of reaching every heart, and instructing every mind. Now, nothing is more certain to hinder this universality, than a hard and dry system of definitions and restrictions. Hence the Apostle warns men against these refinements. "Do what you do without them," he says in his last public epistle — that to the Philippians. "Have peace among one another," he enjoins in his earliest epistle — that to the Thessalonians, whom he speaks of as an example to all the believers in Macedonia and Achaia.

It is plain that justice is the foundation of civil society, and that the essence of secular justice is to grant each man full freedom to labor, and to secure each man that he should enjoy the fruits of his labor, subject only to the condition that the exercise of his faculties shall not inflict wrong on others. Nor is it less plain, that the organization of civil society is perpetually exposed to attack on that side which forms the most vital part of its existence, and that it can only by perpetual effort ward off force and fraud, the success of which is fatal to its being. Government exists to do justice, though the decline and fall of nations have been due to the fact that the power of government has not only not been employed for the primary object of its existence, but has perpetually aided rapine and oppression. The Platonic Socrates is made to show that any theory of government which warps justice, even in appearance, to the sustentation of particular interests, contains that which is in the end certain to effect the dissolution of civil society.

The profound sympathy of Paul, which made him suffer with any distress, and be indignant at any offence which his disciples endured, suggested a striking and exact illustration of that distributive justice which constitutes the key-stone of civilization. He bids men treat each other as members of the same physical organization, urging that injury done to one part induces suffering and disease on the whole. Such a theory of civil government corresponds with that of those economists who allege that, from a material point of view, society is best off, not when the largest amount of wealth is collected, but when the largest amount of persons live in affluence or comfort by means of labor naturally or spontaneously distributed. In the social and economical state alike, the spontaneous distribution of these benefits, which industry and order collect, is of more profound significance than the circumstances which attend on their production or collection. In the physical body, nature effects this distribution; health being the state in which such an equipoise is indicated or affected, disease an abnormal growth or a local repletion. In the Pauline hypothesis of a perfect society, the rectification of a wrong is not due to the clamor or plaint of that which is immediately distressed, but to the sympathy felt by the whole of society towards the suffering or the injured part. From St. Paul's point of view, a social evil sends a pang through the whole body, urging it to take note of the disease and to discover the remedy. That the remedy can be found, and the disease subdued, he did not for an instant doubt. To ignore the disease, or to deny the remedy, is to acquiesce in the wreck of humanity.

Conceive, if you can, a public conscience so keen and tender as to be instantly alive to the moral evils which corrupt, enfeeble, blemish those powers whose uninterrupted action designates the vigor of true and unbroken progress, and so wise as to instantly busy itself with their cure. Imagine men, comprehending that the corrective forces of public morality are not, except indirectly, concerned with the reformation of offenders, but principally with the purification of mankind itself from some taint which it has ignorantly, wilfully, or carelessly contracted. Picture a society busily engaged in finding out the means by which poverty, ignorance, vice, selfishness, can be chastised or healed, not because the victims of those morbid growths are afflicted, but because society itself is degraded and dishonored by the presence of such calamities, and is therefore restless till it cures or alleviates them. Whenever man begins to purify the society in which he lives, under the stimulant of these feelings, and from these motives, he begins to construct the divine commonwealth, the perfect man, as Paul conceived and expounded it. Well would it have been if the reformation of man had but been continued in this spirit. The utmost that men have done as yet, is to concede a right, perhaps no more than the right, of complaint to the sufferer. But they will find no remedy for the diseases and depravity of social life, till they recognize that the worst part of the case is the influence of these malignant growths upon the health of humanity itself, and perhaps on its very life.

It is not, therefore, utopian to project a social system which shall be formed and governed upon the principle that vice and misery must be obviated in the interests of society itself. Nor is it visionary to conceive a force which shall so permeate the common life of men as to sustain such a policy when it has once been adopted, and, therefore, form an obstacle to the beginning of that which demoralizes and degrades all in the depravity of a part. We may imagine, with perfect reasonableness, a community where wrong is unknown, and, therefore, from which misery is banished. No excellence, either of the State or of the individual, is impracticable simply because it has hitherto been ideal, and has transcended experience. Paul, who avowed that man was depraved, contemplated his social perfectibility.

Now, whether it be that man has departed from the pure original in which he was once created — as is commonly conceived, — or, that he has, conversely, made some progress towards the perfection which may be developed in the future by the gradual growth of a wise morality, but that he has, historically, no higher origin than that of mere animal life, — it is clear, on either hypothesis, that society has hardly attempted to govern itself on the principle which has been adverted to, — that of righting wrong, and checking vice, in consideration of its own safety and health. It is also clear, that prodigious heroism is needed on the part of individuals who, foreseeing the only means by which society can be regenerated, seek to grapple with the evils whose ultimate consequence must be so disastrous. Such persons have been violently crushed, or mercilessly ridiculed at best, have provoked into active antipathy a host of interests, which can easily get credence for the fallacy that custom is nature, or that an habitual wrong becomes a prescriptive right. And, even if this angry panic of imperilled or alarmed self-interest be wanting, there is always the obstacle of inert apathy which calls enthusiasm a madness, and would rather indolently shut its eyes, than rouse itself to knowledge and incur the anxieties of resolution.

Paul was not wanting in courage. Testimony to his lofty and unshaken perseverance is to be gathered from the sufferings of his life. He is still unshaken as he contemplates the apparent failure which saddened his retrospect, when, deserted by his friends, he had the immediate prospect of a violent death. He had labored for more than thirty years, and all those in Asia — Asia, which had been the principal scene of his energies — were turned away from him, had left him alone. His career is an example of the trouble, the animosity, the disappointment which attend on those who strive to purify the world. The indomitable vitality of a true Christianity has rendered it impossible that the career of Paul should be a warning.

But Paul did not, and could not, attempt to grapple with society as a whole. As has been several times observed, he believed that the world was rapidly approaching its dissolution. There was some reason for this belief. Mankind has not even yet recovered from the desolation which was caused by the Roman Empire, and from the destruction of ancient civilization. That empire and that civilization perished by their own vices, by the persistent indifference of the Imperial government to all public duty. But, even if the Apostle had anticipated the duration of the world, he could not have directly attempted the task of a social reformation in the Roman Empire. The effort would have been a forlorn hope. There was risk enough in the indirect attempt, — risk which any but the boldest spirit would have hesitated to run. But to have openly defied the power of Roman conservatism, would have been to provoke instant destruction. And the sacrifice would have been as fruitless as that of Savonarola.

Hence Paul set himself to work to construct a society within a society, which should challenge as little attention as possible, beyond that which would be accorded to the blameless and virtuous lives of its members. Under circumstances which would not cause scandal or retort upon the Christian profession, he counsels his disciples to ask no questions for conscience' sake, to go into general society. With the same purpose he dissuades the believing wife from using the right of divorce against the unbelieving husband, because he anticipates that the latter will be won over to the Gospel by the pure and scrupulous life of his wife. The advice marks all the difference between a needless and offensive protest against the conduct of one's neighbor, and a rigid regimen of one's own life and action. If one's own reputation for consistency is challenged, the Apostle counsels no reticence, justifies no evasion, permits no cowardice. But it is neither good manners nor tact to blurt out one's own convictions in any company, or, under all circumstances, to perpetually protest against whatever one sees and hears. It was the vice of the Christianity which followed on the Apostolic Age, or, rather, on the age which followed the revival of Paul's teaching, for the professed Christian to court persecution by indiscreet and superfluous avowals. Hippolytus, in telling us, from the Christian side, what was the career of the worthless Callistus, — whom the Roman Church subsequently elected as its bishop, and has even canonized, — is evidence of the eagerness with which an adventurer affected martyrdom; and Lucian, from the heathen side, narrates, in the history of Peregrinus, how devotees, whose reputation was doubtful, wantonly affronted the habits of society in the third century after Christ. The man who intrudes such crude beliefs on his own age becomes the orthodox persecutor of a time when his beliefs are accepted. When Gibbon says that the virtues of a clergy are more dangerous to civil society than their vices are, he is thinking of those virtues of courage or rashness which simply aid the ambition, or affirm the egotism of those who exhibit them. It is not clear whether Paul knew the parable about the good seed and the tares, but it is clear that his advice is quite in accordance with the teaching of Christ. It is doubtful whether he had ever heard of those disciples who wished to call down fire from heaven, but it is certain that he was not of that spirit which Christ rebuked. It is manifest that he was all things to all men, if haply he might gain some, — that he was indifferent to those who preached Christ of contention, provided only that Christ was preached,— that he was thoroughly of the mind of Christ, who prayed that His disciples might — not be taken out of the world, but — be preserved from the evil of the world.

The Gospel which Paul preached was not intended to govern men, but to influence them. It was not intended to confer authority on its teachers, advocates, disciples, but to lay duties on them. "The Son of Man came not to be the object of service, but to serve, and to give His life as a ransom for many," is said by Christ when he was enforcing the great tenet of Christianity,— that personal power and influence are to be dedicated to public service. The object of the Christian life is to restore, to regenerate mankind; not to assure the individual of his personal salvation, in the first instance at least, but to assist in the reconstruction of society. The reward of this labor is an eternal identity in the midst of assured felicity, "a place in the kingdom of God," a share in that "which has been prepared by Christ" on behalf of them who wait for Him. And in order that as many persons as possible may be included within the number of those who have this great object before them, Paul was prepared to do away with every hindrance and obstacle in the way of union. What the difficulties were with which this plan was beset, has been repeatedly stated in these pages. They were not obviated during Paul's life; they recur in other forms after the obstacles which Paul sought to remove had become unimportant, when the Christian sects reproduced the temper, after abandoning the tenets, of conservative Judaism. The Church of Christ is not a society bound together by a written constitution, or by a set of formal rules, but by the work and the fruit of the Spirit.

Every epistle of Paul bears witness to his conviction, that the victory of Christianity is to be found in the holiness of its adherents. Having commented on the variety of powers and gifts, which the followers of the faith may possess and exercise, he lays down in the Epistle to the Romans a series of injunctions on the details of the Christian life. " Let your love be genuine. Loathe the evil, cling to the good. Into your mutual brotherhood carry the feelings of natural affection. Show that grace of courtesy which makes a man defer his own dignity to that of his fellow. Be diligent in the business on your hands, be eager in the spirit of your profession, serve the occasion which lies before you, feel joy in your hopes, constancy in your trials, confidence in your prayers. Be generous to the wants of those who hold your own belief, be eager to practise friendly intercourse with all, meet those who harm you with kind words, with blessing and not with cursing. Give the sympathy of cheerfulness and sorrow to those who need it. Have unanimity with one another, avoid haughtiness of spirit, condescend to be gentle with men of lowly station. Do not think of nothing but yourselves, do not retaliate evil. In your general intercourse with mankind, be anxious for a good reputation, and, if it be possible, for your part, be peaceable. Do not seek, my beloved, to exact satisfaction, but give place to anger, according to the scripture, 'Vengeance is mine, I will punish wrong, saith the Lord.' If thine enemy, then, hunger, feed him; if he thirst, give him drink, — for by doing so thou shalt heap coals of fire on his head. Let not evil-doing vanquish you, but overcome it by the good you do."

Such is a paraphrase of the conduct which Paul commends as the means by which the Gospel may be approved of, and its influence extended. It will be seen that these injunctions apply principally to the mutual intercourse of Christian men, and to their dealings with the world around them. They contain the quintessence of common sense. They are followed by a general rule of obedience to secular authority, and an acquiescence in the course of Providence, as indicated in the existing authority of the civil power. The arguments on which this acquiescence is based are these: — The Apostle urges that there is no reasonable ground on which Christian men can be apprehensive of that power which the magistrate wields. Law is for the wrong-doer, not for the just, whom Law virtually respects and defends. Next, the civil administration of affairs is part of the moral government of the world, and therefore resistance to authority is resistance to the implied Providence of God. Lastly, — and this is most to the purpose, — the order of the world is temporary, and will not long endure. "The night is far advanced, the day is near." In immediate proximity to that great change which will follow instantly on the appearance of Christ, it is idle to disturb one's self with the merely secular question of human government and law.

Had Paul anticipated the prolonged duration of the visible world, had he foreseen that the course of things would have remained unchanged for centuries after his own life and work were finished, he could not have varied the advice which he gives to the Christians whom he instructed. Had he contemplated a time in which absolutism would give way to popular government, and the Christian man would not only be invited, but would be bound to exercise his judgment on questions of public policy, and to take part in the administration of affairs, he would still have counselled obedience to law and authority, — even if the authority were selfish and the law unjust. Better have a bad administration than anarchy, better partial law than general confusion. But to suppose that he would have counselled indifference, or passive acquiescence in tyranny or wrong, is to misapprehend the whole tenor of his teaching. Christianity is a perpetual protest against evil, whether it be temporal or spiritual, whether it be that of ruler or subject, whether it be crime or sin. If it have the opportunity of using the force of civil authority conjointly with its moral influence to do what is just and right, it will not hesitate to employ such powers as Providence has bestowed on it. Men do not put off their civil duties to the generation in which they live, because they profess to believe in a religion which promises them certain future benefits.

They will still "walk in wisdom to those who live without their action, and will pay the price that it is worth for the use of the occasion which lies before them." It is true, that the best force which Christianity can exercise is to be found in the example of life which the Christian spirit affords. But the man who held that Christian men shall judge the world,— shall, in the language of the Rabbinical schools, judge angels, and much more what belongs to the interests of this life,— would certainly not have precluded Christianity from aiding natural morality and justice with all the forces at its disposal.

Besides, the mind of every Jew who cherished any recollection of his nation's glory, its prestige and its mission, was occupied with the memory of that ancient time, when the prophet stood before the king, and, if need be, rebuked him for falling away from the covenant of Israel, and the commandment of God. Paul never forgot the greatness of the race from which he sprung; never, even when he had been forcibly severed from both parts of it, — from the Jews of the old faith, for his unpardonable conversion; from the Jews of the Apostolic College, for his equally unpardonable indifference to ritual, — did his tenderness for the ancient people of God fail to break forth, did his pride of race forsake him. It is not without design that he lays so much emphasis on the prophetic office, implying by it the function of bearing testimony to the truth of God before an unbelieving and demoralized world; as the prophets of old did from the days of Samuel to those of Malachi.

The Jewish prophet is the representative of the principle, that the forces of government are, and should be subordinated to justice, mercy, and conscience; and that no office, however high, is, or ought to be out of the reach of reproof or correction. Armed with the Word of God, the prophet is — as we are told by Jeremiah — a defenced city, an iron pillar, and brazen walls against king, prince, priest, and people. A high office, but one full of danger to him who fills it; for Jeremiah, though constantly the counsellor of king and people, is frequently in great peril on account of his far-sighted candor, — most of all, at the hands of dishonest rivals, who prophesied smooth things, and deceived the people with the hopes of safety or impunity. It was in a spirit like that of a Hebrew prophet, — a Jeremiah, a Micah, or an Amos, — that Paul stood in the presence of Felix, and reasoned with him on justice, and self-restraint, and a future judgment, till the adventurer and man of pleasure trembled before his prisoner. In the same manner Paul argued with the younger Agrippa, though with less success, since he only extorted from the king an ironical compliment.

It must not, however, be forgotten, that the prophet of old addressed such a monarch, a prince, a priest, and a people, as — whatever were the short-comings in the practice of each — professed allegiance to the law of Moses. Even Israel had not really revolted from God; only from David and the worship at Jerusalem. The prophet of Israel does not reproach king and people for the dissent which reared the chapels in Dan and Bethel, but for the rebellion which led them to worship Baal and Ashtaroth in the place of the God of their fathers. Here, except during the dynasty of Ahab, there was, at least, a nominal acceptance of the national religion; and the prophet — though he incurred frequent risk for the boldness of his manner, and, occasionally, for the inferences which his denunciations suggested — had nothing to fear on account of the matter of his speech. Elijah, Micaiah, Elisha, are menaced or punished for their attitude to the king, not for their religion; and the false prophet, Zedekiah, who urged Ahab to his destruction, employed the common prelude to the prophetic utterance, — "As the Lord liveth." So, also, Jeremiah declares, — " Then the Lord said unto me, the prophets prophesy lies in My name; I sent them not, neither have I commanded them, neither spake unto them." This hypocrisy did not render these timeservers less bitter in their treatment of the true messenger, but it acknowledged that his mission, like theirs, was in the name of the God of Israel, and that he was justified in speaking openly before king and priest. Had the office of Paul fallen in times like those of the Hebrew prophet, he would have dealt as largely with the political circumstances of his day as his predecessors did, as boldly as he himself spake before Ananias and the Sanhedrim.

The teaching of St. Paul is as precise when he touches on the internal life of the Christian. Keenly alive to the reality of sin, occasionally using language about it which strongly savors of the dualism which was adopted by the stricter Gnostics; firmly holding that the beginning of deliverance is the purchase which Christ has made of the enslaved soul by the price of His Passion; the lesson which he reads his disciples is, in the highest degree, practical. He would have them look perpetually to the law of their mind, their conscience, the Spirit of Christ which inhabits them, and to gather a rule of life from its guidance. He is perfectly plain-spoken about the vices which he condemns, — the sensual and selfish practices which he saw everywhere about him, and of which he says, that they who permit the growth of these habits shall not inherit the kingdom of God. "The fruit of the Spirit is love, gladness, peace, forbearance, gentleness, kindliness, trust, good temper, self-control," he tells us in the Epistle to the Galatians. "Put on, then," (he says to the Colossians,) "as elect, holy, beloved of God, hearty compassion, gentleness, modesty, good temper, forbearance." He has advice to give to husband and wife, to parent and child, to master and servant, to men as members of churches, to individuals as engaged in the earnest struggle of the Christian life. "My exhortation, brethren, is," says he in the first of his epistles, "that you reprove the unruly, that you comfort the low-spirited, assist the weak, be forbearing to all. Take heed not to retaliate evil for evil, but always follow after what is good to each other and to all. Be always glad. Pray regularly. Give thanks on all occasions, for this is God's will in Christ Jesus on your account. Do not put out the light of the Spirit. Do not make scorn of teaching. Test every thing, and hold what is worthy. Abstain from any kind of evil." Similar lessons of moral virtue are given to the Ephesians, — if, as some have doubted, the letter which goes under this name was intended for the Church of Ephesus, — and are scattered up and down every epistle. A holy life, a blameless demeanor, a gentle temper, a winning manner, are the means by which Paul would have every man use the gift which is bestowed on him, and do his part in effecting the perfection of humanity.

Christianity recognized the corruption, imperfection, weakness of man's moral nature, and, withal, saw that this infirmity not only impaired the progress of the individual, but hindered the development of society. It discerned that the regeneration of man was to be effected by the sacrifice of man, and it discovered the original of this sacrifice in Jesus of Nazareth. These two facts constitute the basis of this religion. Furthermore, and by implication, Christianity affirmed the fundamental equality of all men, equality in the necessity of an atonement and a mediation, equality in the right to both. It acknowledged neither sacerdotal nor secular privilege, for its highest officer is a preacher or minister. As its advocacy is so lofty a self-abnegation, and as obedience to its tenets is so thoroughly spiritual; it was, and ever is, absolutely separated from that nature-worship, which destroyed the civilization it attempted to influence, and which, under one form or other of materialism, has survived its earliest manifestations. As it was intensely sympathetic, it was driven into antagonism towards that Gnostic particularism which offered its devotee perfection, by the contemplation of a wisdom which might be achieved by culture and knowledge, but which never sought to regenerate or benefit the world.

It is by means like these which have been recounted, that Paul contemplated a general leavening of society by the genius of Christianity. He knew — who had better personal experience of the fact? — that a resolute and wise spirit is certain to attract attention and win allegiance. For there is at least this consolation to those who, being credited with disinterestedness, seek to impress their opinions upon their fellow-men, that even though a very moderate amount of freedom may be given to those who strive to reform society, the effect of every lofty purpose is rendered more intense and lasting by reason of its exceeding rarity. Even those who are sunk in sloth, sensuality, and selfishness, are attracted by the energy which disdains their pleasures and purposes, and shapes out for itself some novel, but beneficent end. The only real resistance which earnestness and activity meet, is that of being confronted with an antagonist resolution, which is equally persevering and determined. A strong will can be withstood only by collision with another will, whose weapons have been tempered by the same, or by an equally skilful armorer. To such an energy as that of Paul there was no antagonism, either in the sluggishness and ignorance of popular idolatry, or in the subtle but nerveless refinements of ancient philosophy. His tenets interpreted, methodized, and modified, permeated ancient civilization rapidly. But, unhappily, the master-builder had no true successor. His mantle fell on no one. No Elisha obtained a double share of the Christian prophet's spirit.

No successor of St. Paul, no disciple, no companion is known to us as having labored like him, or as having written like him. With the exception of Luke, none of his associates in the ministry have even been canonized. There are other compositions of the Apostolic Age, which have never, or only temporarily, been admitted into the Scriptures of the New Covenant. There are others which may have been written by those who had heard the apostolic teachings. But they are wholly inferior to those relics which were collected and compiled into the volume of the New Testament. The schools of the prophets provided a succession of teachers from the days of Samuel to those of the restoration, and during six centuries the same teaching was proclaimed with unabated vigor and spirituality. But the Scriptures of the New Testament are concluded within a brief epoch, and are concluded abruptly. One successor of the Apostle — Clement of Rome — is a faint reflection from the man of Tarsus, speaks neither with his authority nor with his fulness and depth. It is not difficult, even if we look at the facts from no supernatural point of view, to discover why the Church, when it framed its canon, and when it had decisively admitted the authority of Paul, treated him as eminently inspired; for no teacher of Christianity ever possessed so great a genius, none was animated by so intense a religious sense, or enlightened by such profound sagacity, and endowed with such admirable tact.

It will be curious, perhaps instructive, to consider, in concluding this estimate of Paul and his times, what would have been the consequence had other men, equally gifted with the Pharisee of Tarsus, succeeded him in the conduct of the Church; and what would have been the attitude of such a man as he was, if he were to appear among us now, — if, according to the fancy which was prevalent among many theorists of his age, the spirit of Paul were to re-animate some human body, and to guide anew some human will.

The Christology of Paul might have been progressive. The epistles of Paul say nothing of the birth or childhood of Christ. They assign him no miraculous origin; they speak of Him as merely a descendant of the stock of David. The language of these writings implies that the perfection of Christ was finally effected at His death and resurrection, — that it was the recompense of His perfect self-sacrifice. The critical passage in the First Epistle to the Corinthians, from which it appears that the dignity of Christ was a development, and His office one which would ultimately be superseded by the Almighty Father, when its work was completed, indicates that Paul had by no means attempted that harmony between Tritheism and Monotheism, which tasked the energies of the Nicene Fathers, and which has finally been accepted by the general voice of Christendom. Minute and laborious search into the epistles proves nothing more than a general acquaintance, on the part of Paul, with the spirit of Christ's teaching, and gives no idea of his having been informed of those details which are found in all the gospels, and particularly in the last. He is thoroughly acquainted with the moral perfection of Jesus; he affirms the completeness with which the Lord satisfies the Messianic hope, and vindicates His claim to being the Founder of the Gospel, and of the kingdom of God. He asserts that Christ is not only the power of God, and the wisdom of God — *i.e.*, that He satisfies the conditions under which, according to Jewish teaching, God is manifest in the flesh, — but that He has become to us wisdom from God, justice, purification, redemption. He is the source of all hope and strength. But Paul never forgets that while there is one Lord Jesus Christ, there is one God.

Still, it does not follow that, as time passed on, and the intense belief in the humanity of Christ, and the nearness of His second coming grew fainter, Paul might not have developed more fully that theory of the nature of Christ which was first debated by the Gnostics, and ultimately settled by the Alexandrian theosophists. The Eastern mind was thoroughly impregnated with the idea of emanations from God. The Western was accustomed to apprehend the incarnation of God in man. The union of these two conceptions may have been the inevitable consequence of a religion which assigned the most exalted functions to its Founder and its Victim. As Paul lived, the breach between his teaching and Judaism became wider. Thus, had his spirit, his wisdom, his quick appreciation of what was necessary to the scheme of Christianity, been continued in his successors, it is possible that the monotheistic tenets which are comprised in his epistles might have been modified, or developed even into the Athanasian symbol.

But of this we may be sure. Paul would never have mistaken faith for belief — the trust in Christ and God for any mental assent to definitions of opinion and statements of fact. With him Christianity was intensely social and personal, and therefore never could have become dogmatic and logical. If he had admitted these formularies of belief, he would have treated them as matters of secondary importance, as positions which are inevitably and invariably obscure, as doubtful disputations, as attempts to know the mind of God, which is inscrutable, as imperilling that other knowledge which man may possess — that of the mind of Christ. He would have discouraged any investigation, the practical side of which is not manifest, whose solution is no aid to the Christian life. He would have been still more dissatisfied with these inquiries, if he found that they were rending the Church into fragments, — that they were exposing it to the derision of the heathen, — that they were preventing that quiet and steady leavening of society with a high sense of public and private duty, which it was the mission of the Church, in Paul's eyes, to achieve.

Again, a man whose theory of Christianity was so earnest and so practical would have discountenanced any persecution on the ground of mere opinion. It was not to be expected that a Jew would have had any respect for the caricatures of God which the heathen worshipped, or would fail to connect the depravity of the ancient world with that debased idea of the Divinity which was popularly entertained. The history of his own race, and the history of other races proved, or seemed to prove, that a false religion and a low morality are reciprocally cause and effect. Paul knew that the revolution of the Maccabees was a reaction, as well against the tendency to Greek idolatry, as it was against that impulse towards Syrian sensuality, which, as is plainly enough seen from the book of Sirach, infected Jewish manners. Still, Paul contents himself with strongly expressing his convictions on the connection between a false religion and general immorality. But he preaches no crusade against the former. He is no iconoclast. He does not counsel his disciples to affront the devotions which they witnessed, any more than he himself did those of Athens. No one would have condemned more strongly, more energetically, than he would have, the mad fury of Cyril, or have denounced more indignantly the murder of Hypatia. There were men in his day who erred concerning the faith, — who made shipwreck of it; and Paul, believing that physical suffering raises the moral, and purifies the spiritual sense, invokes, in the Hebrew phrase of deliverance to Satan, some physical evil on them, that they may be chastised into abandoning their profane avowals. But he never identified himself with Satan, or with Satan's function.

It is not to be supposed that Paul was indifferent to discipline. An ecclesiastical society can no more endure the presence of notorious offenders against the conditions of its moral being, than a civil society can neglect to chastise or coerce criminals. But Paul counsels the avoidance of such persons rather than their formal exclusion from the Church. Public notice must indeed be taken when the scandal is flagrant; but the penitent is to be restored upon submission. He could not have countenanced the proceedings of those who wished to brand the weakness or timidity of the lapsed after the Decian persecution, any more than he could have advised the rashness which provoked that onslaught. The discipline of an ecclesiastical organization, he would have argued, is a means to an end, — that end being the approval of the Gospel in the sight of men, and the conversion of those whom Christ came to save. To avoid the appearance of evil, to be scrupulously exact in the fulfilment of human duties, — which is as much the law of God as it is of man, — ought to be instinctive in every Christian community. Hence the avoidance of such persons as compromise the reputation of the Christian brotherhood is only an act of self-preservation. But discipline is much more easily effected by the gentle, sometimes silent, rebukes of wise men, or by just public opinion, than it is by law and verbal regulations. Paul trusted more to his own presence for the correction of faults in practice at Corinth, than he did to any code of statutes which he might draw up. He had to found a church,— not to compile a written constitution. The commission which he had received, his call to the apostolate, might be vouchsafed to other men, who might continue his work in his spirit.

He would have been totally indifferent to forms of ecclesiastical organization. Various forms of government may equally secure freedom and order both in Church and State. What is to be deprecated is that fanatical adherence to any form of government under which men seek to force their habits on the life of others. What is to be learnt from such a fanatical adherence, is that individuals are able to seek and find their own, not the general or public good, in every form of government. We can gather from the Second Epistle to the Corinthians, that there were men who, within that particularly democratic church, huckstered the word of God; for St. Paul's term, which we translate "corrupt," alludes as much to the petty manner in which the great office of man's redemption was treated, as to the adulteration with which these men had disguised its tenets. The reform of a church government may be necessary. Its institution may have been radically vicious, its conduct may have stereotyped the faults of its origin. But he is a very bad judge of human nature, and knows very scantily the history of the process by which human nature may be permanently bettered, who believes that changes in the form of an administration are organic, and therefore may be considered final. Least of all is this the case with a church, which, to be faithful to that by which it consists, must depend for its true vitality on moral — can hardly, except it be bent on suicide, trust to external — forces. In Church and State, that is the healthiest condition in which they, who having accepted or allowed a form of government, and who are clearly alive to their duties as members of a religious or civil polity, are indifferent to the details of the constitution under which they live.

It has been stated above, that Paul discerned in the low morality of the age through which he lived, and in the degrading conceptions which, as he saw everywhere, men entertained of God, a reciprocal connection. But unhappily, a neglect of public and private duty, an indifference to natural morality, and a habit of low and degrading vice, are not peculiar to heathendom. Such vices were witnessed during the prophetic age. There is, indeed, no reason to believe that Paul was imperfectly acquainted with those parts of the Hebrew Scriptures in which the deeds of a corrupt society in Judah and Israel are stigmatized and denounced. The transgressions of the two kingdoms were precisely those which have been committed in times of prosperity and wealth, and even in those of adversity and suffering, when men become effeminate and licentious, insolent and hard-hearted. That the rich should oppress the poor, that the strong should prey on the weak, that wealth and power should be employed for selfish and base ends, for low and coarse pleasures, are contingencies to be expected, for they have perpetually happened. But the corruption of society consists in the applause with which such malversations are witnessed, in the acquiescence or congratulation with which vice is recognized or commented on.

There are no grounds on which to infer that human nature has been materially changed since the day in which Amos testified against the depravity of the Israelite nobles, and Paul drew his inferences from the corruptions of the Roman world, though the Syrian kingdom and the military empire have passed away. Whatever may be the origin of those personal and selfish impulses which debase the man if they are unchecked and gratified, they are still the same as in the days of the Syrian prophet and the Christian Apostle, have the same consequences, need the same remedies. It cannot be denied that the world has made vast material, much moral, progress, but the work of maintaining the latter, not less than the former, has to be continually renewed in each generation of mankind. The labor of perpetuating the highest moral law, or, in the language of the New Testament, the kingdom of God and His Christ, is even more difficult than that of transmitting to posterity the conquest which man's intelligence has made over the material world; because the inductions of science, though arrived at with great difficulty and after long research, are communicated easily, since they can be easily verified; while the infusion of the divine law into the individual mind demands exactly as much pains now as it did when a pure morality and a spiritual religion first asserted themselves on behalf of civilization and progress.

Perhaps, if any well-informed person were asked, What are the chief difficulties which a preacher and apostle like Paul would meet with were a mission like his to recommence at the present day? he would answer that they would be found in the attitude in which religion and science stand to each other. He would say, that there has long been a breach between them, and that the breach is gradually widening, that their relations are ordinarily those of avowed hostility, — at best, of cold and hollow courtesy. He would point to the alienation of the inductive sciences from theology, to the scepticism with which even the philosophy of consciousness treats every thing which is suprasensuous. He would observe that there is an active and increasing school of thinkers who have assigned its distinct place in the history of human thought to the supernatural or religious movement; who assert that this phase of the human mind has now become an exploded fiction, and that it is destined never again to influence any high intelligence. He would add, that, to the foremost minds of the age, the reign of law had commenced; that this is the philosophy of the definite, while the philosophy of the infinite is transcendental and unreal. He would conclude that the deference which is still paid to religious belief is, on the part of those persons, transitional and politic; that it is partly due to the unwillingness with which such men would provoke interests which, however indefensible they are, are yet powerful, and partly to the fact that they consider it superfluous to attack that which will one day or other collapse by the gradual decay of its foundations.

Much of this is apparently true. But no man who has ever busied himself, though cursorally and superficially, with the facts of human life, can fail to see how far man is from having arrived at even a moderate standard of justice and goodness, even under the most favorable circumstances. Nor will he fail, also, of discovering that the prospect there is of elevating the moral nature of the individual, and of progressively purifying society, does not consist in the development of knowledge, or in the control which man has gained over the forces of the physical universe. He will see that it has been by the self-devotion of earnest and patient men that a generation has been purified, and that it is by the continuity of these moral forces that the work, once begun, can be maintained and extended. Now, it is not too much to say that no motive except the religious sense (by which is understood the practice of virtue and holiness, for the sake of a Being who is absolutely good and absolutely holy), has ever supplied the perseverance necessary for this labor of bettering mankind. Every religion must have its martyrs, the kind of martyrdom varying with the difficulties which have to be overcome. And there is too much reason to believe, that much of the hostility which exists between science and religion is not due to the fact that they are incompatible, but to the manner in which the professional advocates of the latter have met the inductions of the former.

In the hands, at least, of a man like Paul, the difficulty could not be capital. The difference between the secularism of the Mosaic system, and the spiritualism of the prophetic teaching, is far greater than that between the theology of Paul in his epistles, and such a harmony as he would try to effect between the deductions of modern science and the fundamental tenets of his gospel. He would have taken the fact of sin, of human depravity, of which there is too mournful and too general a proof, without troubling himself with its origin. He would have made no more stir about the cosmogony of Moses than Philo did, and would have recognized the hand of God in science as he did in natural morality, as he did in the order, as far as he understood it, of the physical universe. He would have experienced no difficulty in admitting the proofs which geology gives of the vast duration of the world. He would even have allowed, comparatively speaking, the eternity of matter, because he could have induced upon it the plastic power of a Divine intelligence, which creates by one method of law as much as by any other. He would have easily dispossessed his language of those phrases which imply a physical heaven; have discovered his new creation in conditions apart from locality; and perhaps have rejoiced in the prospect which science offers of the cognition of infinite space and endless worlds.

## HIS THEORY OF SALVATION

For, it must be repeated, the characteristics of the Pauline gospel are a few facts, none of which contradict human experience, and in many particulars obtain its support. He holds that man is, and has been, saved by suffering; and that the progress of humanity is due to the unbought and unpaid diligence of high and persistent well-doing. He affirms that the beginning, and well-nigh the whole of this work was done by One, in whom the power and the wisdom of God were immeasurably manifest; and that it is by the Spirit, and in the indwelling of this Personage, that the residue of man's appointed work is to be completed. How this work has been done, and must be done, is often expounded, and need not be repeated. How the agent is aided and consoled is equally affirmed. That the service done to man is paid by the perpetual consciousness of the benefactor, — or, in other words, that the life of such a person is not lost in death, — is a matter of natural belief, and of natural justice. The assistance which this belief gives towards the construction of society, and the aid which it affords to the regeneration of humanity, is of such profound significance, that its importance is well-nigh a test of its truth. And over all this system of lofty moral philosophy, and gentle catholic religion, is the wise, the loving, the beneficent Father, who claims the homage of His children's labor; who has given them for their guidance, their safety, their example, their hope, their stay, the object of their trust, His first-born Son, their Brother and their Lord, — to watch over their work, to aid His

Providence, to be with them always, even to the end. Such a gospel is intensely probable, prodigiously strong, profoundly consolatory. If it cannot be proved to demonstration, it is certain that, were it fully accepted, it would work without flaw or slip, and would realize the dream of the most sanguine optimist. If Christianity be not the light of the world, it is because the world is still lying in darkness.

Nor would such an apostle as Paul have had much more difficulty in dealing with that other hindrance to Christianity, which is derived from the impatient objection, that it fails to meet misery, suffering, injustice, wrong. The answer is instant, — It is no fault of the Christian spirit, it is the fault of those who will not accept and obey it. The gospel of Paul is not a communistic dream, but it is hard work and mercy; honest labor and patience. For no words can surpass in exhaustive force those in which he describes the spirit which should animate a Christian society, when — dealing with the extraordinary gifts which the Christians of Corinth had, or believed they had — he tells them and us what is the force and what is the working of love. It is sufficient to say, that the language rivals that of the great Master Himself. It is the loftiest poetry, the most exalted morality, the purest religion, the most consummate wisdom. It is no marvel that Paul, when he sums up, in superlative manner, his magnificent wishes for the grace and power of his Corinthian brethren, utters his thanks to God for so indescribable a gift as that which he prayed might be the character of all.

His heaviest task, beyond doubt, would not have lain in the objections which science and misery might make to the sufficiency of his teaching, and in the answer which he might give to their doubts or to their wants, but in the dull, heavy obstacle of that selfish, sensual, sordid, self-interest which is the Antichrist of the Pauline gospel. But who can trust himself to describe it, and why seek to picture that which is, and will be, the manifest, the perpetual enemy of mankind?

What, then, is the hope of the Divine commonwealth? It does not consist in a new revelation, for the moral progress of humanity is bound up with the principle which forms the foundation of Christ's death, of Paul's life, of the life of all who have done true service to mankind. It does not require the promulgation of a new code, for the tenets of Christian morality are rather exhaustive and exact than novel. That there is no foundation but Christ, — that is, that society is constructed on the basis of self-sacrifice, — was dimly, but certainly, seen by Plato, who commits the government of his ideal state to men whose life is to be one of unceasing toil and self-denial, endured from the profound conviction that they are developing their own highest nature, by spontaneous and diligent service to man. But in the Pauline teaching it is asserted, that to labor on this foundation is the duty and good of every man, — that each can and must contribute his share of work to the mighty edifice, and give such work as will stand the test of the severest trial to which work can be put. This gospel is as new as yesterday, because it is conterminous with the necessities of humanity,— because it can and should still exert its forces as long as "the perfect man" is inchoate and undeveloped.

To many men, indeed, Christ is not risen. He is still in the grave to them; still garrisoned by the soldiers who are set to watch the body; still a wasted energy — a dead power. For the significance of His resurrection is the commencement of His kingdom, — not only to each heart that believes in Him, and trusts in Him, and seeks communion with Him, and feels his presence; but to the race of man, which is still wrestling, in its long agony, with the forces which seek to debase, degrade, oppress, misuse it. When the preacher bids those who are smitten down by the coarse, hard hand of wrong and iniquity, to raise their eyes to Him who is lifted up — to open their ears to His Gospel, he often speaks to dim eyes and deaf ears, — to hearts hardened by misery, — to men who say or think, What is this Christianity which you preach to us? how does it deal with the toils of our life? how has it influenced those who profess to have governed human society by its precepts? He dwells, you tell us, in the midst of his worshippers. But His law is as far as ever from being the guide of life, — is still treated as Utopian, — is unfulfilled, unacknowledged. If he be the power of God, and the wisdom of God, how is it that the power is not exercised, the wisdom not obeyed? What a mockery, they say, is this world of Christendom! what a phrase! what a deception! It hardly protests against the evils it pretends to cure. To us, Christ is a history, a remote event, not a present and a living energy.

The Gospel of Christ, you would tell us, can answer every question which bears on the moral nature, the hopes, the fears of man, — can remedy every wrong, — can heal every wound, — can soothe every sorrow. How is it dealing with the problems of human life? To what extent does it confront that harsh and griping greed which accumulates its own pleasures on the misery of thousands, — which divides society into two camps, one of which is arrayed against the intolerable sorrow of its condition; the other is anxiously occupied in disarming the despair which it has created? How many, calling themselves by the name of that Master who, with such intense pungency of indignation, with such bitter irony, exposed and denounced the hard hypocrisy of His own age, follow His example in speaking after His Spirit to their own? Where is the champion of oppressed, of degraded humanity? Who seeks to lay bare the ulcers which fester in what men glibly call modern civilization, and, laying them bare, is prepared to discover and apply their cure? "The harvest is past, the summer is ended, and we are not saved." So said the wise prophet of a nation which was then about to enter into the valley of the shadow of death. Is Christendom to find no prophet; is there to be no physician for the sorrows of the people — no one to set forth Christ plainly as Paul set Him forth?

Thus, the chief difficulties which lie in the way of those who trust in the force of a revived and restored

Christianity do not arise in a discovery of the means by which the work should be set about, but in interpreting and combating the forces which will resist or withstand it. Debarred by the terms of its origin from any appeal to force; taught by the experience of centuries that its great obstacle has been that alliance with secular power which captivated and demoralized it in the fourth century, the divine commonwealth must not be led for an instant to desire a renewal of that ancient and disastrous association. The history of Christianity has been like that of Samson. It has been seduced by the charms of a Delilah,—has been shorn of its strength and beauty,—blinded, and set to work in the prison-house of political expediency. But though it ought to have no recognized understanding with secular government, it can exhibit no antagonism to the organization of civil authority. If it fulfils its mission wisely and efficiently, it will guide and purify the public conscience, and eventually supersede the functions of secular authority, by reducing it to a form and a routine. Appropriating all the forces of social life, and giving them one direction, while recognizing every variety of power and function, it can in this way only effect the fulfilment of the Apocalyptic vision, — " The kingdoms of the visible world are become the kingdoms of our Lord, and of His Christ, and He shall reign for ever and ever;" or as the prophet saw it in his ecstasy, — " Great is His government, and there is no boundary to his peace."

Such a reconstruction of Christianity, — such a renewal of the Pauline church, may have its origin in a fusion of sects, or it may commence in a movement external to them all. Men are weary of words, and turn away from the arid strife of polemical disputants. Traditions have ceased to hold a mastery over them. Day by day it becomes less easy to renew the ancient bitterness of controversy, and to array the facts of the Gospel against its spirit. There is less and less prospect of effecting a union of some of those who profess the name of Christ, against others. There is even less power of rousing passion against those who stand aloof from acknowledging the name of Christ at all, or from confessing His office. But however gentle our age may be towards opinion, it is not behind any in its admiration for the exact fulfilment of duty, and in the homage which it pays to self-devotion, kindliness and love. It neither inquires into the creed of misery, nor into that of charity. But it is conspicuous for its tenderness towards the former, and for the honor which it shows towards the latter. The world in which we live has, at least, understood the maxim of Christ, that "he who is not against us is on our part." Pity that the example is rare.

The greatest strength, however, which a New Reformation will require, lies in the need there is for a Religion. What is called civilization in our day, is, in many particulars, a failure. It has become a hot and bitter struggle for life, in which one may see, on the one hand, an ever-increasing wealth, surrounded by guarantees and securities of enjoyment,—securities which were accorded in no previous age of the world's history, — wealth which is too often, and with coarse ostentation, paraded with cynical insolence, worshipped with sordid adulation. And on the other hand, there is a vast and growing misery, for which ordinary palliatives are inoperative, — for which ordinary explanations are superficial and unsatisfactory, — for which no remedies are found, because few care to discover them, fewer still dare, on discovery, to announce them. Must we wait till men ask, and in terms of increasing menace? — What, then, if the only fruit of those labors to which we have given our lives is to increase our own misery, to tie us down more firmly to inevitable privation, and to swell the opulence which mocks our want? For us, and we are many, society needs reconstruction.

The attitude in which an earnest religion would stand to this morbid and dangerous condition, would not be that of stupid acquiescence in an inevitable destiny, but of an active and general determination to discover the remedy for that which dishonors and degrades mankind. The patience and content which are inculcated by the Christian temper are not indifference at the result, but the acceptance of a fact, for which there must be, and shall be a cure. Individuals may, as Paul says of himself, " learn to be content, whatever be the condition imposed on them." But the corporate action of Christian man is one which is the very reverse of this passive content. " The struggle," says Paul, using his favorite metaphor of the palæstra, " is not with flesh and blood, but with authorities and powers, with the world's rulers of this state of darkness which prevails in our generation, with the spiritual forces of wickedness in heavenly places." It is as though he had said, We have no quarrel with human government; we take up no arms to fight against civil authority. Our contest is with that godless and blind selfishness, which arrogates to itself the right of associating its aims with the destinies of man, and governing the course of society, which makes that light which is darkness, that sweet which is bitter; which affects to consider the rule of its own conduct as the rule of man's existence; which installs itself in the place of God, against which — the deadliest foe which humanity encounters — it is needful for Christendom to take the panoply of God, and to be steadfast in the work which it has to do.

# MESSRS. ROBERTS BROTHERS' PUBLICATIONS.

## THE INFINITE AND THE FINITE. By THE-
OPHILUS PARSONS, Author of "Deus Homo," &c. One neat 16mo volume. Cloth. Price $1.00.

"No one can know," says the author, "better than I do, how poor and dim a presentation of a great truth my words must give. But I write them in the hope that they may suggest to some minds what may expand in their minds into a truth, and, germinating there, grow and scatter seed-truth widely abroad. I am sure only of this: The latest revelation offers truths and principles which promise to give to man a knowledge of the laws of his being and of his relation to God, — of the relation of the Infinite to the Finite. . . . And therefore I believe that it will gradually, — it may be very slowly, so utterly does it oppose man's regenerate nature, — but it will surely, advance in its power and in its influence, until, in its own time, it becomes what the sun is in unclouded noon."

*From the Chicago Tribune.*

Few writers have obtained a more enviable reputation in this country than the author of this little book, and few are more justly entitled to consideration. His works upon jurisprudence are to be found in almost every public and private law library in the country; while his writings upon Christian philosophy and the science of religion are universally received as models of close and logical reasoning by those even who differ from him in the form of their religious belief. . . . Mr. Parsons has been pronounced to be "the most fascinating interpreter of the writings of Swedenborg," and the present volume will add to rather than detract from a reputation to which he is so justly entitled. The defects of the work are only such as necessarily attach to the subject itself. The finite cannot grasp the infinite, but the author has accomplished this: he leads the reader through new and pleasant paths of thought into the boundless immensity that surrounds us, where the mind, freed from the idea that the only source of spiritual truth is a revelation, the interpretation of which is limited to a prescribed class, feels and acknowledges the power of the infinite in newer, simpler, and not less holy truths.

*From the New York Evening Post.*

Professor Parsons, in his little work, does not undertake to controvert the huge volumes that have been written upon the philosophical problem of the Infinite and the Absolute: he merely attempts to show us how the problem has been treated by his master, Swedenborg. He has a profound veneration for the teachings of that illustrious seer, and his expositions of these teachings have the merit of unusual clearness and simplicity. . . . Whatever difficulties the reader encounters in his pages are difficulties inherent in the subjects themselves, and not in his methods of elucidation. Any one accustomed to think at all upon deep religious questions will be able to understand what he means, though he may not be disposed to accept his conclusions. And the inquirer who simply wishes to be informed of the general scope and purport of Swedenborg's remarkable disclosures will find few better helps than the small and unpretending volumes of Professor Parsons.

——◆——

*Sold everywhere. Mailed, postpaid, by the Publishers,*

ROBERTS BROTHERS, BOSTON.

# MESSRS. ROBERTS BROTHERS' PUBLICATIONS.

## RADICAL PROBLEMS. By Rev. C. A. BARTOL, D.D. One volume, 16mo. Cloth. Price $2.

CONTENTS. — Open Questions; Individualism; Transcendentalism; Radicalism; Theism; Naturalism; Materialism; Spiritualism; Faith; Law; Origin; Correlation; Character; Genius: Father Taylor; Experience; Hope; Ideality.

*From the Liberal Christian.*

What a wonderful, wonderful book is the "Radical Problems." We are not a third through it yet, and Heaven only knows where and how we shall find ourselves at the end of the journey. Already are we so shocked, stunned, bewildered, edified, delighted, — in short, thoroughly, thoroughly bewitched, — that we have no words to express ourselves. . . . That this book has a long life before it who can doubt, or that it will cause a grand commotion in the theological world? It will be impetuously attacked and vehemently defended, but will survive alike the onslaught of its assailants and the intemperate zeal of its defenders; and will be the fruitful source of many a brilliant essay and inspiring discourse and stimulating and suggestive club-talk, long, long after its gentle and gifted author has left us to receive a most cordial welcome by his brother thinkers in brighter spheres.

*From the Commonwealth.*

Spirituality, purity, gentleness, love, child-like simplicity, bless and sanctify him; but he is spirited as well as spiritual. In his gentleness there is a quick vivacity, and he sometimes exhibits a keen incisiveness as of whetted steel. His aim is not so much to solve as to suggest. He is no dogmatist, nor is he an expositor or judge. He finds open questions, and delights to leave them open questions still. Meantime he looks into them with the eyes of his inmost soul, discerns much, throws out a profusion of glancing and irradiating suggestions that open the questions farther instead of closing them, then retires to look elsewhere. . . . This man carries eternal summer in the eyes, and sees beds of violets in snowbanks. His own climate is his world, and he can make no excursions out of it. A pleasant world it is, with no deserts, jungles, reeking bogs, foul, ravening creatures, and poles heaped with ice. As some will see only with the physical eye, so he with the spiritual eye.

*From the Globe.*

It contains seventeen chapters, honestly representing the individual spiritual experience of the author, and at the same time indicating some of the intellectual tendencies of the time. It is "radical," not in the usual sense of the word, but in its true sense, that of attempting to pierce to the roots of things. Many of the opinions and ideas expressed in the book may be repudiated by the conservative reader, but its spirit and aim cannot fail to charm and invigorate him. Dr. Bartol, indeed, is one of those men who have religious genius as well as religious faith. . . . The book is a protest against popular theology, made from what the writer considers the standpoint of true and pure religion. We have considered it from a literary point of view, and, thus considered, its wealth of thought and imaginative illustration entitle it to a high rank among the publications of the year.

*Sold everywhere. Mailed, postpaid, by the Publishers,*

ROBERTS BROTHERS, BOSTON.

# MESSRS. ROBERTS BROTHERS' PUBLICATIONS.

## AD CLERUM: Advices to a Young Preacher. By JOSEPH PARKER, D.D., Author of "Ecce Deus." One volume, 16mo. Uniform with "Ecce Deus." Price $1.50.

*From the Lutheran Observer.*

We do not know how to begin or where to end our commendation of this book. . . . No one in the ministry, or looking forward to the pulpit, should fail to get it. He may have Porter, Vinet, Kidder, and Shedd, but he cannot afford to do without "Ad Clerum," which is complemental of all the rest.

*From Rev. Geo. W. Eaton, D.D., President of Hamilton Theological Seminary.*

I have perused it with delighted interest. Though not quite in sympathy with the flippancy and hyperbolical statements which occur here and there in the volume, its instructions are on the whole healthy, pertinent, and "put" in a form charming and impressive. I know of no work connected with homiletical literature which contains so much of valuable and timely instruction in a compass so small and compact.

## ROMAN IMPERIALISM, and other Lectures and Essays. By J. R. SEELEY, M.A., Author of "Ecce Homo." One volume, 16mo. Uniform with "Ecce Homo." Price $1.50.

*From the St. Louis Journal of Education.*

The author of "Ecce Homo" has been pronounced the typical writer of the present time. Those who have read his former work — and who has not? — will give this a cordial welcome. The Essays entitled "Liberal Education in Universities," "English in Schools," and "The Teaching of Politics," challenge the attention of educators; while "The Church as a Teacher of Morality" will excite some of the fierce criticism that followed the publication of "Ecce Homo."

*From the Pacific.*

The Essay in this volume on "English in Schools" we hope will receive attention from educators. It is shameful that so little *thorough* knowledge is imparted in our high schools, and even colleges, of our own tongue. Multitudes of young ladies, accomplished in many other respects, are wofully deficient in this; while graduates of colleges almost innumerable know more of the meaning, derivation, and power of Greek and Latin words and phrases than of their own native English.

*By Joel Benton.*

A new book from the pen of the author of "Ecce Homo" is not by any means a slight literary work. The memory of that exquisite picture set in the clearest crystal of polished thought — a perfection of art and logic — lingers as the faint, sweet aroma which recalls a wonderful but departed flower. In an age that seeks to analyze and reconstruct our dearest traditions, and re-base religion itself, it took, and still holds, a prominent place.

*Sold everywhere. Mailed, postpaid, by the Publishers,*

ROBERTS BROTHERS, BOSTON.

# MESSRS. ROBERTS BROTHERS' PUBLICATIONS.

## THE PRIMEVAL WORLD OF HEBREW TRADITION. By FREDERIC HENRY HEDGE, D.D., Author of "Reason in Religion." One volume, 16mo. Price $1.50.

*From the New York Tribune.*

Mr. Hedge may be called an eclectic: not as one who picks from different systems the detached bits that suit him, and then joins them skilfully together; but as one who, committing himself unreservedly to neither system, endeavors by independent and cultivated insight to get at the deepest truth contained in formulas, creeds, and institutions. His faith is wholly in reason: he will prove all things, and hold fast only what is good; but his crucibles are various in size and quality, his tests are of many kinds, and his reason combines the action of as many intellectual faculties as he can bring into play. His faith is planted in a firm but gracious Theism, moral like that of Moses, and loving like that of Christ. The belief in a divine origin, education, guidance, and discipline of the world, runs through his pages; and a conviction of the moral capabilities and of the spiritual destination of man shines in his argument and ennobles the conclusion. Those who do not agree with the book need not be offended by it; and they who do agree with it will be charmed by the beauty in which what they regard as truth is converted.

*From the London (Eng.) Enquirer.*

We have been unable to criticise because we find ourselves throughout in entire sympathy and agreement with the writer. We cordially commend Dr. Hedge's book as the best solution we have ever seen of the difficult problems connected with the primeval Scripture record, and as an admirable illustration of the spirit of reverent constructive criticism. Such a work as this is almost like a new revelation of the divine worth of the ancient Hebrew Traditions, and their permanent relation to the higher thought and progress of the world.

## AMERICAN RELIGION. By JOHN WEISS. One volume, 16mo. Cloth. Price $1.50.

*From the Philadelphia Press.*

Himself a clergyman, Mr. Weiss writes understandingly upon a very solemn theme. His closing chapter, entitled "The American Soldier," is one of the noblest and truest tributes to the patriots of 1861–65 ever put into print.

*From the Chicago Tribune.*

Mr. Weiss has presented to the public a scheme for an American religion which, it is almost needless to say, is a religion of the intellect adapted to the highest form of American culture, and not pervaded to any great degree with spirituality, as the term is understood among orthodox believers. . . . If Mr. Weiss had christened his scheme "American Morality," we would gladly have hailed his discovery. As it is, we cannot but commend its loftiness of purpose. It is a work full of noble thought, and, however much the reader may disagree with it from a religious point of view, there are very few who can fail to be struck with its purity of aim and its healthy moral tone; while the merely literary reader will derive equal gratification from the scholarly style and the richness of illustration and research it displays. The last chapter but one, "Constancy to an Ideal," is one of the finest and noblest essays ever written by an American, and deserves to be read and heeded by every American.

*Sold everywhere. Mailed, postpaid, by the Publishers,*

### ROBERTS BROTHERS, BOSTON.

**MESSRS. ROBERTS BROTHERS' PUBLICATIONS.**

# THE TO-MORROW OF DEATH;
### OR,
## THE FUTURE LIFE ACCORDING TO SCIENCE.

### By LOUIS FIGUIER.

TRANSLATED FROM THE FRENCH, BY S. R. CROCKER. 1 vol. 16mo. $1.75.

---

*From the Literary World.*

As its striking, if somewhat sensational title indicates, the book deals with the question of the future life, and purports to present "a complete theory of Nature, a true philosophy of the Universe." It is based on the ascertained facts of science which the author marshals in such a multitude, and with such skill, as must command the admiration of those who dismiss his theory with a sneer. We doubt if the marvels of astronomy have ever had so impressive a presentation in popular form as they have here. . . .

The opening chapters of the book treat of the three elements which compose man, — body, soul, and life. The first is not destroyed by death, but simply changes its form; the last is a force, like light and heat, — a mere state of bodies; the soul is indestructible and immortal. After death, according to M. Figuier, the soul becomes incarnated in a new body, and makes part of a new being next superior to man in the scale of living existences, — the superhuman. This being lives in the ether which surrounds the earth and the other planets, where, endowed with senses and faculties like ours, infinitely improved, and many others that we know nothing of, he leads a life whose spiritual delights it is impossible for us to imagine. . . .

Those who enjoy speculations about the future life will find in this book fresh and pleasant food for their imaginations; and, to those who delight in the revelations of science as to the mysteries that obscure the origin and the destiny of man, these pages offer a gallery of novel and really marvellous views. We may, perhaps, express our opinion of "The To-Morrow of Death" at once comprehensively and concisely, by saying that to every mind that welcomes light on these grave questions, from whatever quarter and in whatever shape it may come, regardless of precedents and authorities, this work will yield exquisite pleasure. It will shock some readers, and amaze many; but it will fascinate and impress all.

---

*Sold everywhere. Mailed, post-paid, by the Publishers,*

ROBERTS BROTHERS, BOSTON

*Messrs. Roberts Brothers' Publications.*

## THE GREAT RELIGIOUS BOOKS OF THE DAY.

# ECCE HOMO.
# ECCE DEUS.

Although it is now some years since the publication of "Ecce Homo" and "Ecce Deus," the sale of these extraordinary and remarkable books continues quite as large as ever. Some of the ablest and most cultivated minds in the world have been devoted to a critical analysis of them.

The foremost man in England, the Right Honorable W. E. Gladstone, has just published a book devoted entirely to a review of "Ecce Homo," in which he uses the following language: —

"To me it appears that each page of the book breathes out, as it proceeds, what we may call an air, which grows musical by degrees, and which, becoming more distinct even as it swells, takes form, as in due time we find, in the articulate conclusion, 'Surely, this is the Son of God; surely, this is the King of Heaven.'"

Of "Ecce Deus," which may be considered the complement of "Ecce Homo," there are almost as many admirers, the sale of both books being nearly alike.

Both volumes bound uniformly.   Sold separately.   Price of each, $1.50.

### Prof. Ingraham's Works.

**THE PRINCE OF THE HOUSE OF DAVID;** or, Three Years in the Holy City.

**THE PILLAR OF FIRE;** or, Israel in Bondage.

**THE THRONE OF DAVID;** from the Consecration cf the Shepherd of Bethlehem to the Rebellion of Prince Absalom.

The extraordinary interest evinced in these books, from the date of their publication to the present time, has in no wise abated. The demand for them is still as large as ever.

In three volumes, 12mo, cloth, gilt, with illustrations. Sold separately. Price of each, $2.00.

### The Heaven Series.

**HEAVEN OUR HOME.** We have no Saviour but Jesus, and no Home but Heaven.

**MEET FOR HEAVEN.** A State of Grace upon Earth the only Preparation for a State of Glory in Heaven.

**LIFE IN HEAVEN.** There Faith is changed into Sight, and Hope is passed into Blissful Fruition.

*From Rev. Samuel L. Tuttle, Assistant Secretary of the American Bible Society*

"I wish that every Christian person could have the perusal of these writings. I can never be sufficiently thankful to him who wrote them for the service that he has rendered to me and all others. They have given *form and substance to every thing revealed in the Scriptures respecting our heavenly home of love,* and they have done not a little to invest it with the most powerful attractions to my heart. Since I have enjoyed the privilege of following the thought of their author, I have felt that there was *a reality* in all these things which I have never felt before; and I find myself often thanking God for putting it into the heart of a poor worm of the dust to spread such glorious representations before our race, all of whom stand in need of such a rest."

In three volumes, 16mo. Sold separately. Price of each, $1 25.

Mailed, post-paid, to any address, on receipt of the price by the publishers

www.ingramcontent.com/pod-product-compliance
Lightning Source LLC
Chambersburg PA
CBHW022120290426
44112CB00008B/753